CRICUT:

Four Books in One:

The Step-By-Step Guide To Navigating Design Space & Cricut Software With Ease, with Over 33 Beautiful Holiday & Household Projects. + BONUS Monetizing Your Skills!

Kimberly Maker smith

© Copyright 2020 - All rights reserved.

THIS BOOK INCLUDES

BOOK 1: 12 (FIRST PAGE)
CRICUT FOR BEGINNERS

Step By Step Instructions, Beginner to Advanced Techniques, Design Space Tutorials, Professional Project Ideas & Selling Your Creations for Profit

BOOK 2: 112 (FIRST PAGE)
CRICUT DESIGN SPACE

Master the Software, Create Flawless Professional Designs in Minutes & Monetize Your Skills

BOOK 3: 220 (FIRST PAGE)
CRICUT PROJECT IDEAS

Over 33 Beautiful Holiday & Household Projects, Fully Illustrated with Step By Step Instructions and Tutorials for Design Studio & Cricut Techniques

BOOK 4: 342 (FIRST PAGE)
CRICUT ACCESSORIES, SOFTWARE, AND APP:

Maximize Your Cricut Machine Like A Pro & Turn Your Skills Into A Business

CRICUT FOR BEGINNERS

Step By Step Instructions, Beginner to Advanced Techniques, Design Space Tutorials, Professional Project Ideas & Selling Your Creations for Profit

Kimberly Maker smith

TABLE OF CONTENTS

Introduction

The Cricut system is a famous invention. It's helped scrapbookers and lots of individuals with their demands not just restricted in the scrapbook creating planet but also to other aspects. However, it's to mention that one sector helped us in the scrapbooking kingdom. From the fantastic old dark ages, even if you weren't proficient at carvings or in case you didn't understand how to compose, your favorite moment goes down the drain.

Those two would be the sole means of maintaining the memories back afterward. It might appear crude and ancient to us back then; it was that they needed. Now, we've got everything set up to preserve someone's memories, and we all to Father Technology.

When a scrapbooker decides to make a scrapbook, the layout is almost always a key consideration. Before picking a design can cause migraines of epic proportions but today is another story. According to a particular pattern or layout, the Cricut system to be mentioned is only accountable for cutting edge newspapers, vinyl, and cloth. The design or print can make or edited using a software application known as the Cricut Design Studio.

If you're searching for OK and straightforward - recognized designs that are already built-in, you proceed for capsules that are secondhand. There's no limit to everything you could think of using the layouts that already set up. The golden rule would be to allow your creativity to go crazy. It is a tool that any aspiring scrapbooker must possess. So far, is it? The prices generally start at $299 and will go up based on the version which you pick.

It might appear to be a substantial sum of money. However, the expense is well worth it. But if you wish to employ the additional effort to learn to locate a fantastic deal, you're more than welcome about this. The worldwide web is almost always a wonderful place to get some excellent bargains; you have to look. There is Amazon, eBay, so a lot more.

The Cricut machine has lots of uses besides being a cutter of layouts to get a scrapbook. The designs may use to make different things like greeting cards, wall decorations, and more. You simply have to believe creatively. There are no limitations, and when there are, they're only a figment of your imagination.

The Cricut Machine - A Short and Intimate Appearance

When you think about building a scrapbook, the first thing that comes into your head is what pictures to put. That is relatively simple as all you want to do would be to pick images that highlight a particular event or happening in your lifetime. After this complete, at this point, you should think of the layout of the scrapbook. Again, this can be quite simple as everything you have to do base your choice on whatever occasion has depicted in your pictures. Let us take, for instance, a wedding day.

Pick a design that will transfer that audience back in time and relive everything that transpired throughout your wedding day. Common sense is everything you may need here. How can you take action? Can you do it? No is the reply to those above queries. You do so through the usage of a Cricut machine.

How exactly, how does one cost? Every unit comes with an average cost of $299, with more excellent versions having more massive price tags. However, there are means by which you'll be able to find a less high price. In case you've got a pc with the internet, proceed to browse and hunt for great bargains and inexpensive cutting machines that are secondhand.

Recall, nevertheless, that carrying purchases through eBay can take dangers, so that you need to be sure you check out each of the vendor's profiles, which you may want to participate in. If you're the fantastic conventional shopper who'll never devote to internet purchasing, you could do this old - school and then buy from a mall through earnings or anything else similar.

The Cricut machine has additionally many applications that extend far beyond the domain of scrapbooking. Given the number of layouts in your cartridge or software application, you may always utilize them to make Cricut calendars, hangings such as partitions, and greeting cards for special events. Your creativity is the one thing that may limit your invention.

Marsha Brasher was crafting for several decades. She loves the challenge of producing cutting documents, and that she understands what is needed to make handmade crafts having the most complex of designs.

Cricut Suggestions - Tips That May Help You to Get Started

Capturing memories onto a virtual camera, even an HD camera, and a voice recorder make life much more purposeful. When there's a unique moment you would like to catch and be in a position to return to at any particular time, you can certainly do this so easily with the assistance of these instruments. However, pictures continue to be the favorite medium by the majority of people. If you wish to put together those images and compile them onto unique memorabilia, then you flip into scrapbooking.

Scrapbooking is a technique of preservation thoughts that's been in existence for quite some time, and it's evolved up to now better. With the creation of devices like the Cricut cutting edge machine, matters are made simpler. If you're Looking to Developing a scrapbook, this poor boy is the instrument for you. There Are Lots of good Cricut thoughts out there you can make the most of.

Scrapbooks are only some of the many Cricut thoughts on the market. If you understand how to optimize it, this instrument makes it possible for you to create things that go past scrapbooking, for example, calendars. If you buy a Cricut cartridge, then there is a slew of layouts uploaded in every and every one. All these pre-made themes may use for a whole lot of items like hangings for partitions, image frames, picture frames, and greeting cards for many seasons.

Your creativity will limit your advancement using a Cricut machine. Together with calendars, you can design every month to represent the weather, the disposition, and exceptional events connected with that. The Cricut machine will take care of this. But in case one cartridge doesn't have the layout that search, you may always go and purchase. It's that simple!

Cricut machines may be a little expensive, with all the cost starting at $299. That's pretty hefty for anybody to begin. Be a smart buyer. You may always turn into the World Wide Web to seek out incredible bargains on Cricut machines. Purchasing from eBay may also be a terrific move but can take several dangers if you experience eBay. In case you're quite worried about this, you always have the option to await a purchase to occur at one of the regional malls and buy out there since it will probably have a guarantee.

CHAPTER 1:

What Is A Cricut Machine?

Have another Cricut and don't perceive where to begin? Get creating with this posting of more than one hundred innovative and astounding simple DIY activities with a Cricut that is best for fledglings! Are you considering using Cricut to reduce the allocation of tasks that can be done by the machine? Or then again thinking what particular substances a Cricut can cut? With a Cricut, the potential outcomes are tremendous! To help energize you and supply you thinking about the numerous great Cricut ventures you can make, I've assembled a rundown of some beautiful undertakings underneath.

The Cricut machine is a fantastic creation. This poor boy can help you cut paper, cloth, and vinyl sheets to whatever pattern you would like. These actual production designs may be achieved via software tools like the Cricut layout studio or via capsules using pre-engineered structures assembled into them. Therefore, if you're an enthusiastic scrapbooker, this system is essential-have.

What Can I Make With This?

There are vast amounts of one-of-a-kind issues you can utilize a Cricut. While you know what type of task you want to perform, and at the same time considering what kind of decoration and supplies you need to use the machine, please take a look at the rest of the other projects and parts that Cricut has just started. Demand (and what are basically "decent possessions" that you can spend when you need them) Scrapbooking and Card Making

There are loads of scrapbooking thoughts and scrapbook designs you can discover for your Cricut!

Or once you don't want the opportunity to make cards yourself, here are some pointers and special effects for making cards quickly.

Weddings and Gatherings

Cricut machines are great for making custom stylistic themes for weddings and gatherings!

Occasions

Utilize your Cricut to make occasion stylistic layout for any event!

Home Stylistic theme. You can make loads of various undertakings to improve your home!

Everything from cushions and divider craftsmanship to big business thoughts!

Clothing and Extras

One of my preferred things to make with my Cricut is shirts, onesies, and tote sacks. You can put warmness switch vinyl on exceptionally much any material surface. However, you can likewise utilize a Cricut to make adornments, headbands, and then some!

Vinyl Decals and Stickers

Our assortment one intrigue is lessening vinyl decals and stickers, and you can do this with the Cricut Maker.

It can cut through any vinyl in no time easily — you should simply make your format in Cricut Design Space, teach the PC to begin cutting, at that point, weed and change the arrangement to your picked surface.

Texture Cuts

One of the essential selling elements of the Maker is the truth that it comes outfitted with the produce-new Turn Cutting edge.

On account of uncommon coasting and moving movement — by and large with the gigantic 4kg of power at the back of the Cricut Maker — this ability that the work area can lessen unmistakably any texture.

The truth is out. Denim? Check. Overwhelming canvas? Check. Silk? Check. Chiffon? Check. We've continually constrained using a particular texture shaper sooner than as the registering gadget lessening machines essentially weren't compelling to deal with more massive textures. We cherish the truth that the Maker is an across the board machine. It comes furnished with a texture-cutting mat so that you can lessen bunches of textures aside from the utilization of any support. Astonishing! Sewing Examples

Another key prepared of the Maker is the gigantic sewing test library that you'll get passage to when you've purchased the machine.

It comprises of earnestly many examples — comprehensive of some from Effortlessness and Riley Blake Designs — and capacity you can genuinely pick the model you like, and the Maker will remove it for you. No additional removing designs physically yourself (and not any more human blunder ruins)!

Additionally, secured is a launder-able texture pen that will call attention to the spot the example parts intend to stable together.

Balsa Wood Cuts

On account of the incredible 4kg of weight and the Blade Sharp edge (sold independently), the Cricut Maker can slice using substances up to 2.4 mm thick. That limit thick texture that had before been beyond reach with the Cricut and Outline machines are currently open to us. We can hardly wait to start cutting wooden with it!

Thick Cowhide Cuts

In a similar vein as factor #4, thick cowhide can cut with the Maker!

Natively constructed Cards

Paper crafters aren't forgotten about with the Maker either.

Paper and card cuts will be less complicated and snappier than at any other time because of the machine's vitality and exactness.

Your Scratchpad playing cards just went up a level.

Jigsaw Riddles

We comprehend that the Cricut Maker can cut through significantly thicker substances with the Blade Edge than any time in recent memory.

The central perspective we give it a shot? Making our special jigsaw confound. We'll save you, refreshed!

Christmas tree Adornments

The Revolving Cutting edge that vows to lessen through any texture is the ideal gadget for designing occasion improvements. Scour the sewing design library for Christmassy designs (we've purchased our eye on the gingerbread man adornment!), lessen out the example utilizing felt or whatever texture you want, and after that, sew it all in all independently.

Blankets

Cricut has collaborated with Riley Blake Designs to give various sewing designs in the sewing design library.

This capacity that you can utilize the Maker to remove your sewing correctly divides before sewing them aggregately independently.

Felt Dolls and Delicate Toys

One of the Effortlessness designs we have our eye on in the sewing design library is the 'felt doll and garments' example. We understand a couple of little women and young men who'd love a natively constructed dish to add to their accumulation. Just pick the bar, cut, and sew. Simple peasy!

Shirt Moves

You need to arrange the switch in Design Space, load the glow switch vinyl to the manufacturer (or flash it drastically on the HTV if you may feel timid); it recommends that the PC start cutting and ironing your switch the shirt. Or on the other hand, you should utilize the fresh out of the box new Cricut Easy Press to switch the vinyl — it's everything the solace of an iron meets the adequacy of a warmness press!

Texture Appliques

Additionally, available to get individually is the fortified texture sharp edge in lodging, which will allow you to lessen additional unpredictable material designs, similar to applique.

In contrast to the sharp rotating edge, the fortified texture edge requires reinforced sponsorship on the material to diminish adequately.

Calligraphy Signs

The Cricut Maker's significant selling element is its Versatile Apparatus Framework. It is the element that will verify that you keep up your Maker until the end of time. In reality, it's a gadget machine that never again exclusively suits every one of the instruments and sharp edges of the Explore family. However, it will fit as a fiddle with every future device and cutting edges made using Cricut.

The vitality of the Cricut Maker limit that you can cut thicker substances than sooner than that is appropriately perfect for intricate gems designs.

And keeping in mind that you aren't in any way, shape, or form to cut gold, silver, or jewel on there at whatever point soon, an excellent pair of cowhide rings are just inside reach.

Wedding Solicitations and Spare the Dates

As a whole, we know about how 'little' costs like welcomes and sexually transmitted diseases can add to the super price of a wedding.

As makers, we also know how to counterbalance a portion of those costs using making matters like ourselves.

The Cricut Maker is perfect for making staggering welcomes — presently, not exclusively, would you remove confusing paper designs, anyway that calligraphy pen will come in reachable once more.

Wedding Menus, Spot Cards, and Support Labels

You're nearly no longer compelled to creates before the wedding function — you can likewise utilize your Maker to adorn for the gigantic day itself. The sky is just the confinement directly here; however, in all actuality, make menus, region playing a card game, and lean toward labels. Attempt and ensure you utilize a practically identical arrangement for all your stationery to protect the subject upfront.

Shading Book

Do you know these 'careful shading' books that are extremely popular at present? And after that, the Maker's total direction is to make your own unique, unquestionably extraordinary, shading book utilizing the Fine-Point Pen device.

Liners

Another part we can hardly wait to make with our new Maker is liners.

The world you claim as far as substances go — whatever from cowhide to sew, to steel sheets and everything in the middle.

There are likewise some fabulous liner designs in the sewing library to investigate as well.

Texture Keyrings

Something different that got our attention in the sewing test library was, at one time, a couple of simple designs for fabric key-rings.

Once more, the Maker makes it advantageous — totally decrease out the example, and after that, sew it together.

Headbands and Hair Adornments

Presently, Cricut has propelled a registering gadget that is lessening through thick calfskin; we are fearless thought for mind-boggling, steampunk-motivated hair designs and even headbands.

Who realized the Maker ought to be so convenient for significant pattern articulations?

Cut-Out Christmas Tree

We know we know every individual needs a real Christmas tree eventually of the get-away season. In any case, just on the off chance that you don't have space for a transcending tree in your residence room or, God prohibits, you're hypersensitive to pine, you may support to make your tree. As the Cricut Maker successfully decreases thick substances like wood, we guess an interlocking wood tree is an incredible task to check with this year. No laser is required when the Maker is available to you, no matter what!

CHAPTER 2:

Model Overview

Cricut Explore One

Explore One is ideal for beginners and inexperienced users who want to get into die-cutting, craft cutting, and plotting. The machine is not advance like the other Explore models, and it is also the cheapest Cricut machine you can get.

Capability:

The machine is also highly capable, even if it's an old model. The system can also handle scoring and writing smoothly.

Materials:

Regardless of the simplicity and the inexpensive nature of the machine, it is still highly capable.

Cricut Explore Air

While this is quite similar to the Explore One model, it also comes with some additional features. The main difference between them is the presence of the inbuilt Bluetooth adapter. If you don't enjoy seeing cables and wires all around your workplace, especially with the danger of tripping over them, then this model solves that problem.

Capability

The Explore Air is also different from Explore One because it features a double carriage. It means that you can draw, write, or score while you cut because it has two clamps to hold both tools. It saves you money because you don't have to purchase a tool adapter.

Cutting Force

The system is more powerful than the older model when it comes to the cutting force. It features a Cut Smart technology made by Cricut, which enhances the blade control of the system and gives your creations a more professional look. It can cut anything that is as wide as 23.5 inches accurately and precisely.

It also has the Smart Set dial, which increases the control you have over your project's cutting.

The features of the Cricut Design Space are very similar. But, when using Explore Air, you get more freedom, and you are allowed to use .svg, .gif, and .dxf files in addition to the standard files allowed with the Explore One.

Sadly, Explore Air does not have either a knife or a rotary blade. Because of these two types of blades, the Explore Air recommends for more light crafts and scrapbooking. It does have an inbuilt cutter, though.

A brand new Explore Airbox comes with these tools:

A 25.4 x 10 x 9.2 inches Cricut Explore Sir machine with inbuilt Bluetooth technology

It has an inbuilt accessory adapter.

Inbuilt blade.

USB and power cord.

Metallic silver marker.

Iron-on sample.

Cardstock sample.

Over 100 images,

Over 50 ready-to-cut projects.

12" x 12" Standard Grip cutting mat.

Welcome guide.

Cricut Explore Air 2

It is the youngest sibling of the Cricut Explore line. It is the best of the machines in this line.

Explore Air 2 as efficiently as the other ones, but it does its work even better. It even has a better design, and it comes in different colors.

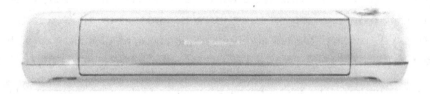

Cricut Maker

The newest Cricut die-cutting machine is the Cricut Maker. If you thought that the Explore Air 2 was a great model, then you should get ready to be blown away.

The Cricut Maker is a rare unit amongst other die-cutting machines. The rotary blade is already enough to attract experienced users.

For beginners, it provides an avenue for improvement and unlimited creativity.

The Cricut Maker, as an updated version of others, is mighty and flexible. It comes with a toolkit that includes a rotary blade, knife blade, deep cut blade, and fine point blade.

It also comes with a single and a double scoring wheel and a collection of pens. The pens include a fine point pen, a washable fabric pen, a calligraphy pen, and a scoring stylus.

The machine also improves its efficiency by adding some unique features. We have the adaptive tool system, which means that the device can automatically adjust the blade's angle and the edge's pressure depending on the material. It doesn't need the Smart dial feature because the Cricut Maker determines your cutting force for you, and its decisions are usually accurate. It has two clamps, one for the pen or scoring tool and the other for the cutting blade. This system is also unique because of its fast mode and precise mode. It works for any paper, cardstock, and vinyl.

Materials

As expected, the Cricut Maker will handle more and thicker materials than the Cricut Explore series machines. From light materials to basswood and leather, this machine will exceed your expectations.

Cricut Design Space also provides a lot of benefits for Cricut Maker users/. It allows .jpg, .gif, .png, .svg, .bmp and .dxf files.

The system also supports a wireless Bluetooth adapter. You can also enjoy the Sewing Pattern Library if you own a Cricut Maker. The library contains 50 ready-to-cut projects, and it is a result of a partnership between Cricut and Riley Blake Designs.

Another great benefit you get when using Cricut Maker with Design Space is to get Cricut Access free membership for a trial period.

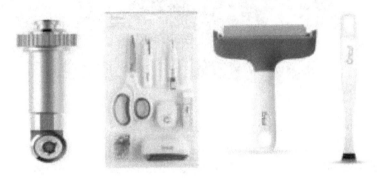

The only downsides to this model are that it is relatively slow when working with very thick materials, although that expects. It also produces a lot of noise because of the fast mode.

It is what comes in the new Cricut Maker box.

Which Cricut Model Should You Use?

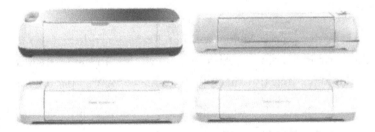

Although all Cricut models are great, the Cricut Maker or Explore Air models highly recommend, whether you're a beginner or an advanced user. These two machines are usually ideal for most people, no matter the type of craft you use.

For the person looking to go into serious crafting, woodworking, sewing, and quilting, then the Cricut Maker is highly recommended. It is highly professional, and it can work for any craft that you get. The system has a lot of benefits, especially on Design Space.

If you are a beginner who wants to start handmade, you should also buy Cricut Maker because it doesn't make sense to buy an old model and accumulate experience before purchasing a new model.

You might be planning on using your Cricut machine for business purposes. It will mean that you will be repeating the same action occasionally. For this use, you can use the Cricut Explore Air 2 because it has a fast mode and many other advantages.

Beginners, leisurely crafters, and those who have a tight budget will work better with the Cricut Explore One and Explore Air.

CHAPTER 3:

Tools And Accessories

Y ou can't possibly use a Cricut machine alone, but the type of accessories or tools you need depends on the kind of project you're using the device. If you're going into home décor, you'll need different mechanisms from those going into papercrafts.

Necessities

Irrespective of any project, some necessary accessories are essential. Some of these accessories come with Cricut, while some can purchase from Cricut.

Cutting Mats

Cutting mats come in three kinds, which are firm grip, standard grip, and light grip. You can also purchase any one of the sizes they come in, which is either the 12 inches by 24 inches or the 12 inches by 12 inches mat.

The firm grip mat is ideal when you're cutting stiffened fabric, glitter cardstock, chipboard, specialty cardstock, and other thick materials. We recommend the standard grip mat for thinner materials like embossed cardstock or ordinary cardstock, vinyl, pattern paper, or iron-on. For the lightest materials, the soft grip mat needs. Lightweight materials include light cardstock, office paper, vellum, or other materials.

A newly bought Cricut machine includes a cutting mat in the box, and so you don't have to buy a mat separately. After a while, the mat will lose its stickiness, and you can either apply glue to maintain it or buy a new one.

Also, when considering your project, you should get the right mat. If your mat is light grip and you try to cut a thick fabric, you might end up messing the entire project up because the material will keep on shifting from the mat.

Cutting Blades

Cutting Blades are the essential accessories needed when using Cricut. After all, you can't cut without a blade.

Cutting blades also come in three types. First, we have the standard edge that usually accompanies the Cricut machine. The knife is very sharp and robust, but you will need to change it when it becomes blunt after a while. So, you should have extra blades on hand just in case.

Next, we have the German carbide blade. You can easily purchase this from Cricut too. It's more potent than the standard blade, and it creates to cut through mid-weight materials. The knife also lasts for a longer time and doesn't easily break.

Lastly, designed for very thick materials, we have the deep cut blade. The deep cut blade means for cutting materials that go with the firm grip cutting mat. You can also use the knife to cut materials like stamp material, magnet, and other fabrics.

Spatula And Scraper

Not many people bother with purchasing a spatula and scraper when they want to use their Cricut machine. But these tools are useful when it comes to taking materials off the cutting mat.

You can use it for the spatula to remove the material from the mat without damaging the fabric. It provides accuracy. In the case of the scraper, you will need to maintain the mat by cleaning it. This tool is helpful with scraping off leftover materials on the mat and cleaning it. It keeps the machine durable, and it will last for a long time. When you want to start on a new project, you can quickly use the mat without cleaning it.

Apart from these essential tools, some devices are crucial for specific projects when working on those projects.

Vinyl or Iron-On

For example, when working on vinyl or iron-on projects, they both use the same tools because they are similar. Iron-on plans are pretty much heat transfer vinyl projects.

You can use vinyl to decorate tumblers, cups, or mugs; create decals for frames or walls and other projects. Iron-on is used to decorate fabric, like adding designs on t-shirts

Transfer Tape

Circuit also manufactures this tool, and it is entirely transparent. This way, when transferring or placing your vinyl project, you can see it easily and handle it more carefully.

Weeder

When carrying out a vinyl or iron-on project, a weeder is crucial because it can use to single out tiny pieces on your project like the pieces of vinyl that do not operate from the backing sheet.

Paper

Apart from vinyl projects, paper projects are probably the most popular projects that most crafters carry out. When using Cricut, most people start with paper projects because they are light and relatively more comfortable. You can use paper to create shapes, numbers, letters, cards, envelopes, banners, decorations, stickers, and more. For paper projects, there are two general tools that you will possibly need.

Pens

When using any of the Cricut Explore machines, you can quickly write out your designs. When you want to draw, Cricut provides some free fonts and some fonts that you can buy from Cricut Access. Also, if you have fonts on your computer, you can use that too.

You can buy different pens from Cricut that are compatible with any of the Explore machines. Their cells include calligraphy pens, fine tip pens, gold pens, metallic pens, and pens of a wide range of colors. Although you can use other pens, Cricut machines work best with Cricut pens. Cricut machines' great thing is that they provide two slots to simultaneously use the pen and the blade. It allows for quick designing and cutting instantaneously.

Scoring Tool

It is also called a scoring stylus, and it uses folding lines on boxes, envelopes, cards, or any other papers. In the same way, you can design or draw and cut simultaneously; you can also install the scoring tool in the machine when the blade already installs. It makes your designing process fast and easy.

Additional Tools

Apart from the standard design tools, you can also purchase some tools that make using the Cricut machine more convenient. Depending on the project you are using, these tools might be handy.

Tool Kit

Instead of purchasing your tools one-by-one, some people go for the economical option and buy a tool kit instead. A standard tool kit should include scissors, weeders, scrapers, spatulas, and tweezers. If you're going into iron-on or vinyl projects, then you should probably purchase this type of tool kit.

Some advanced tool kits add a paper trimmer and scoring stylus. This tool kit is excellent for those interested in paper projects.

Bluetooth Adapter

Cricut Explore One does not come with an inbuilt Bluetooth adapter. If you want to use this model, you can buy a Bluetooth adapter from Cricut. This way, you can easily use your Cricut wherever your computer, laptop, or iPad is.

CHAPTER 4:

Cricut Access

Sign in with your Cricut ID

Email / Cricut ID

Password

Enter your password

Forgot?

☑ Remember me

Don't have an account yet?

Create A Cricut ID

The simplest way to create a Cricut ID or account is to go to design.cricut.com, and you will see the option to create your Cricut ID (if you don't have an account yet). When you register, you will prompt to fill in your name, email (Cricut ID), country, and a unique password. You will need to accept the Terms of Use and to receive exclusive offers and inspiration.

If you genuinely want to make the most out of the Design Space application, you need the Cricut Access subscription. When setting the Cricut ID, you will choose your subscription plan, monthly, annual, or premium. After completing this step, you should select the "Maybe Later" option to benefit from the Cricut Access free trial.

When you are just starting with Cricut, perhaps you are only interested in the fonts, and you would like to have access to such fonts. If you are looking just for fonts, don't worry! Cricut has you covered with the select Fonts membership. You have a monthly option of $6.99 or the annual version of $4.99 per month and paid in a lump sum. This membership covers access to 400 unique fonts, but also the Priority Member Care line option.

If you want to have access to images, you won't settle for this subscription plan. In this case, you will choose the Standard Membership, which can be billed monthly at $9.99 or annually at $7.99 per month. This option will get you access to the 400 fonts and 30,000 premium Cricut images, including some beautiful designs unique to the brand. But wait, that's not all!

You will also get a 10% discount on ready-to-make projects, images, licensed fonts, or a 10% discount on product purchases from the Cricut Shop (machines, tools, materials, accessories, and many more). The Priority Member Care line option includes. Pretty neat, right?

There is a subscription plan that can offer even more than that. Sounds interesting? It is the Premium Membership, and it can only be bill annually. It has a monthly value of $9.99, and it already has the features included by the subscription plans, but also some extra features:

- Unlimited access to more than 400 unique fonts

- More than 30,000 premium Cricut images or designs

- Discounts on ready-to-make projects, ideas, or licensed fonts

- Discounts on purchases from the Cricut Shop, including materials, tools, accessories, machines, and more

- Discounts on designer images, fonts, or ready-to-make projects

- Priority Member Care line option

Bear in mind that you will need to invest more than the machine's value to determine what your Cricut machine can do for you. It is what these subscription plans. Besides feeling the need to access several designs, fonts, or images, you may need to purchase accessories, tools, or materials from the Cricut Shop. The benefits you get with a Cricut Access subscription can only be used in the Cricut Shop when purchasing different items from the store, and they can't use when purchasing from a retailer. These subscription plans do well to add loyal buyers to the Cricut Shop. Now that you have all the benefits and numbers of these subscription plans, which one best suit you? How much are you willing to spend monthly or annually to get the most out of Cricut? As you can see, there isn't that much difference between these subscription plans, and they are quite affordable; why not go Premium?

The subscription plan you choose should base on your needs and annual budget. If you are looking to work on many projects, the Premium membership is the best option for you.

CHAPTER 5:

Cartridges

C ricut the inks are mostly the center of any Cricut cutting machine positioned within the cutter printer to condition the style as the person wishes into a notepad.

A wide selection of cartridges is obtainable on the market worldwide; however, not all of these cartridges use all kinds of devices. For example, the Cricut cartridge harmonizes with Cricut devices. It's the primary key element through which artists and crafters may artistically produce different designs in beautiful colors and styles.

With all the printing technology modifications, a selection of cartridges will be released lately with increased packages to select from than the prior versions. The two standard types of printer cartridges out there are printer ink (utilized in the inkjet printer) and laser beam cartridges used in laser printers. In the situation of Cricut machines, they usually use inkjet printers just.

In the beginning, Cricut Ink Cartridges offer in white, but after some time, a couple of additional colors release. The improvement in printing technology, printer ink cartridges, and attempts to create to introduce various font types, colors, and designs for developing shapes.

The key to the Cricut machine's achievement is its unique and different cartridges that allow users to get inventive and cut in any font, design, style, and color.

Which Food Do Cricut Cartridges Are Offering?

You will find all sorts of Cricut cartridges that any person can use. These cartridges operate in numerous types and make to deal with several various things. They could additionally be straightforward to control in a Cricut unit. The characteristics included with these cartridges are remarkable and must utilize to generate a few right types that anybody can manage.

These Cricut cartridges make with the same bodily designs. It's all carried out to allow it to be more comfortable for an individual to load and eliminate a cartridge originating from a Cricut unit. The key element is keeping the magnetic functions that link the cartridge neat and very easy to handle. It's the cartridge that is going to continue working as well as it can.

A cartridge is going to feature two key points. For starters, it is going to feature a unique font. This font can connect with a specific theme and include both upper- and lower-case items, memorable characters, and numbers.

The cartridge will additionally include a series of graphics and shapes. These will be different from each cartridge. These should see creating good looks that cut correctly and evenly once the Cricut machine works effectively.

The themes which Cricut cartridges can come with are incredibly appealing. These cartridges can incorporate pieces that vary from conventional holiday themes to ones that deal with particular passions as flowers, other things, sports, and animals. The number of Cricut cartridges that anybody can discover is very significant. It will take some time to record all of the readily available choices. Each cartridge will also feature a pleasant keyboard layout that will go with the Cricut unit's computer keyboard. It utilizes to help with expressing info on how much the specific design type may be. It makes to keep products listed thoroughly and ensure that information produces to exactly where it won't be an excessive amount of inconvenience to handle.

A number of these specific cartridges will also include things that work with different colors in mind. These include designs in which the look can pair along with specific paper colors. A complete guide could use to propose that certain paper things that need to use cautiously. It could manage to keep everything looking as great as they can be.

You will find a couple of these cartridges which may work with unique designs useful for classroom needs. For instance, one alternative can use a style that enables a user to make all 50 states' cutouts. Types could also eliminate cursive letters, making it easier for pupils to discover how you can handle particular writing ways in cursive. The designs could be unique, but they must review carefully.

People should look into how Cricut cartridges can operate in numerous forms. These styles create some great looks designed to hold all sorts of capabilities functioning perfectly no matter what types of products one needs to handle.

Cricut Cartridges - Ideas And Choices

With regards to crafts and arts, you can never fail with Cricut Cartridges. Many aspiring artists influence by the various patterns and designs offered by Cricut's cartridges. Each day, many retailers can sell a couple of cartridges due to the increasing demand for these items regarding local area stores. With the line's undeniable interest, many merchants are also successful in reselling because of the brand. For all those who aren't into crafts and arts, you might not know a great deal about Cricut cartridges. Nevertheless, we assure you that understanding much more about these items can help you indulge in even more activities associated with papercrafts.

Cricut cartridges' very best aspect is that you won't ever appear to run out of ideas and choices. Whether you like fonts, shapes, or maybe cartoon characters, you will be ready to find a cartridge that will fit your preference. Nevertheless, when choosing a cartridge from Cricut, the first point you have to think about is just how much your budget will be. The variety of cartridges' prices can look close to a little under 50 bucks and may soar around 100 dollars.

If you're the person type who loves a lot of colors, you can stay with the fundamental shape cartridges and just make use of many-colored papers to do the cutouts of yours. If you prefer to utilize words, say for the scrapbook layouts of yours, you can also use the font cartridges. Additionally, there are those individuals who are an enormous fan of the qualified character series. You will be ready to work with cutouts of your favorite cartoon characters from Disney and other animated movies. For all those adults with kids at home, this would be a great opportunity to bond with your children and teach them tips on making their art pieces.

Using Cricut cartridges is additionally a learning experience all by itself. Whether you are in adolescence or about to reach the golden age, you will be able to enjoy all the designs that the ink cartridges and Cricut series can provide.

CHAPTER 6:

Materials That Can Be Worked On Using A Cricut Machine

Certain materials can cut on various Cricut machines, but it does vary from device to machine. The newer engines have more functionality with more materials.

No matter the machine, though, there are some materials you may have thought of, like those listed on the Cricut's website, while there are others you may not have considered. Just like you may not have thought of some out-of-the-box ideas for projects to do!

Main Materials

Cricut.com is a treasure-trove of information for both the new and experienced Cricut users.

One helpful feature is the list and store for materials. The items listed for sale on the website include:

• Cling for windows

• Washi sheets

• Vinyl

• Vellum

• Posterboard

• Iron-on materials

• Foils

• Leather-like materials

• Craft foam

• Papers, including cardstock

Within these categories, multiple items list. For example, under vinyl, items are included like basic vinyl, transfer vinyl, and adhesive vinyl. Ultimately, the Cricut website lists over 100 different materials that the machines can cut, many of which they sell on the site. It is very convenient if you want to guarantee the materials will work with the device, and you do not want to waste their time shopping around for things.

Other people prefer to try more out-of-the-box materials and projects to test their creative powers and those of their machines.

Alternative Materials

While vinyl and paper are the most popular materials to cut with your Cricut, that material is just the "tip of the iceberg," so to speak. There are so many other materials crafters have used successfully with their Cricut machines. Below is a list of some of the items to consider;

Balsa Wood

Balsa is a quick-growing, American tree. The thin wood it produces uses in model making or rafts. It is because it is very lightweight and slightly pliable.

Craft projects from balsa wood include favor tags for wedding or parties, rustic-looking placeholders for the table, or a natural-themed sign for a door or wall.

Duct Tape

The popularity of duct tape as a fashion or crafting item has blossomed over the past few decades, producing projects from wallets to prom dresses.

It is still a material that some Cricut DIY-ers underestimate. This material can be durable and fashionable. Projects made using Duct Tape include Bold and textured gift tags for packages or an art portfolio that showcases the artist's vibrancy and precision with the added touch of this material.

Fabric

Fabric is not an unusual material for some Cricut users. Still, because the variety of fabric available to choose from is complete, it needs to be mentioned again because some techniques and materials are a little more unusual. For example, cutting a lace-like pattern into fabrics can immediately add a color-palette of fancy lace to any project. It also makes it possible to have the same lace pattern on various complementary materials or colors.

Faux Leather and Leather

Cricut.com does not sell real leather. They offer a variety of different leather-like or "faux" leathers. "Faux" means "fake."

Depending on your preference, you can use either material. Despite what you choose, both are suitable materials to cut with the Cricut. Custom jewelry, like necklace pendants or earrings, are simple and stunning projects. These make beautiful and personal gifts or add the right touch to a particular outfit. Leather can also use for making fashionable bracelets or cuffs.

The bracelet is finely cut in cute leather or artificial leather and attached to an adjustable strap. You can also add a hair bow or bow to your clothes or handbag. For a hair bow, hot glue a hair clip to the back when the bow finish. Use hot glue or other adhesives to fix the bow to your clothes or wallet. You can make other hair accessories, such as flowers and different shapes. These can be attached to hair clips, like the bows, or linked to hard or stretchy headbands. Leather can also be used as an embellishment to pillows or other fabrics, like chair backs, or made into manly coasters.

Felt

Felt is another multi-functional material that You can use for a host of projects. Because this item is reasonably sturdy but has good flexibility, it is perfect for just about anything. Also, it comes in all different colors and is relatively inexpensive. Some unique projects that can make from felt including garlands of multi-layered flowers to hang over a window curtain or above a bed, a textured phrase attached to a pillow, an interactive tree-shaped advent calendar, banners, ornaments, and a cupcake or cake toppers.

Magnets

Magnets can use refrigerators, but Cricut can also help create novel and exciting ways to make magnets for all these different purposes. Be selective about the type of interest you choose to cut. Thick and solid magnets do not work well for these projects, but magnets' thinner sheets are suitable for fun crafts.

Some ideas that are outside the fridge-box include:

- Magnet to be attached to the dishwasher that indicates if the machine load with dirty or clean dishes

-Magnetic busy boards such as a mermaid scene with underwater characters or a race track with cars and spectators (do not forget a trophy for the first across the finish line!). Magnetic words to spell out messages on the side of the car or, yes, on the fridge, or school pride or mascots to attach to the vehicle.

Crafting Blanks

The objects you decorate using your Cricut can refer to as blanks. It can be absolutely any object, and it can be something you stick vinyl to, etch, paint, draw on, write on, or anything else you think. They called blanks because they provide a mostly blank surface to decorate, though they can also have colors or designs. Every project in this book will have a blank that goes along with it.

Some popular blanks are cups, mugs, wine or champagne glasses, travel mugs, tumblers, and other such drinking vessels. Craft stores will usually sell these, but you can find them at almost any store. They don't need to be considered a "craft" supply for you to use. Most stores have a selection of plain cups and mugs or travel mugs and tumblers with no designs. As long as you can imagine a Cricut project with it, it's fair game.

Drink wares aren't the only kitchen or dining-related blanks.

Get creative with plates, bowls, and serving utensils. Find blank placemats or coasters at most stores.

Decorate mason or other types of jars. Dry goods containers, measuring cups, food storage containers, pitchers, and jugs—anything you can put in your kitchen can serve as an excellent blank for your projects.

Clothing

Clothing is another popular choice for Cricut projects. T-shirts are easy to make with iron-on vinyl, and you can find cheap blanks at any store or a more extensive selection at craft stores. Craft stores will typically have a large selection of clothing blanks, such as T-shirts, long sleeve shirts, ball caps, plain white shoes, plain bags, and so on. Thrift stores or consignment shops can be an unusual option as well. You could find a shirt with an interesting pattern that you'd like to add an iron-on to something similar.

Glass

Glass is fun to work with and has many project options with your Cricut machine. Glass blocks can found at craft or hardware stores. Many stores that carry kitchenware will have bare glass cutting boards, or you can find them online. Craft stores and home goods stores could sell glass trinkets or décor that you can decorate. You can even buy full panes of glass at your local hardware store and have them cut it to your desired size.

There are plenty of blanks related to electronics, as well. Electronics stores, online stores, and some craft stores offer phone and tablet case blanks. They might be clear, white or black, or colored. Portable battery packs are another option as well. These blanks are often significantly cheaper than already decorated ones, or you can buy them in bulk for a lower price. Get your phone case for a lower price and customize it how you like.

Book covers

Book covers make great blanks, as well. Customize the outside of your sketchbook, notebook, or diary.

Fix the cover of an old book. Or, create a new book cover for the regular.

If you have old books that you aren't going to read, create a new fake cover for them and use them as décor.

CHAPTER 7:

How To Use A Cricut Machine

S o, you have all your materials on hand, which is fantastic, but how do you use a Cricut machine? Well, that's what you're about to find out. If looking at your Cricut machine makes you feel all sorts of confused, then continue reading – here, we'll tell you how to use your new Cricut machine in a simple yet effective manner.

Setting Up the Machine

First, you'll want to set up the Cricut machine. To begin, create a space for it. A craft room is the best place for this, but if you're at a loss of where to put it, I suggest setting it up in a dining room if possible. Make sure you have an outlet nearby or a reliable extension cord. Next, read the instructions. You can often jump right in and begin using the equipment, but it can be very tedious with Cricut machines. Make sure that you have ample free space around the machine itself because you will be loading mats in and out, and you'll need that little bit of wiggle room. The next thing to set up is, of course, the computer where the designs create. Ensure that whatever medium you're using has an internet connection since you'll need to download the Cricut Design Space app. If it's a machine earlier than the Explore Air 2, it will need to plug indirectly, but if it's a wireless machine like the Air 2, you can link this up to your computer, and from there, design what you need to design.

Using Cricut Software

So, Cricut machines use a Cricut Design Spaces program, and you'll need to make sure that you have this downloaded and installed when you're ready. If it's not hooked up already, make sure you've got

Bluetooth compatibility enabled on the device or the cord plugged in. To turn on your machine, hold the power button. You'll then go to settings, where you should see your Cricut model in Bluetooth settings. Choose that, and from there, your device will ask you to put a Bluetooth passcode in. Just make this something generic and easy to remember.

Once that's done, you can now use Design Space.

So, what I love about Design Space is that it's incredibly easy to use. They know you're a beginner, so you'll notice it's straightforward to navigate.

Now, I like to use the app for Design Space since this will allow you to have every design uploaded to the cloud to reuse your designs.

However, if you want to use them without having an internet connection, you'll want to make sure that you download them and save them to the device itself, rather than relying on the cloud.

When you're in the online mode, you'll see many projects that you can use.

For this tutorial, I suggest making sure that you choose an easy one, such as the "Enjoy Card" project you can get automatically.

So, you've got everything all linked up – let's move onto the first cut for this project.

Imputing Cartridges and Keypad

The first cut you'll be doing involves keypad input and cartridges, which usually do with the "Enjoy Card" project you get right away. So, once everything sets up, choose this project, then you can use the tools and the accessories within the project.

You will need to set the smart dial before you get started doing your projects. It is on the right side of the Explore Air 2, and it's the way you choose your materials.

Turn the dial to whatever type of material you want since this helps ensure you've got the right blade settings. There are even half settings for those in-between projects.

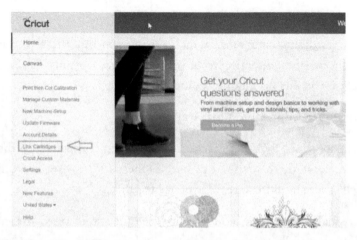

For example, let's say you have some light cardstock. You can choose that setting or the adjacent half setting. Once this chose in Design Space, your machine will automatically adjust to the correct location.

You can also choose the fast mode, which is in the "set, load, go" area on the screen, and you can then check the position of the box under the indicator for dial position. Then, press this and make your cut. However, the fast mode is incredibly loud, so be careful.

Now, we've mentioned cartridges. While these usually aren't used in the Explore Air 2 machines anymore, they help beginner projects. To do this, once you have the Design Space software, and everything is connected, go to the hamburger menu, and you'll see an option called "ink cartridges." Press that bad boy, and from there, choose the Cricut device. The machine will then tell you to put your cartridge in. Do that, and once it's detected, it will ask you to link the cartridge.

Remember, though, that you can't use it with other machines once you link this – the one limit to these cartridges.

Once it's confirmed, you can go to images and click the cartridges option to find the ones you want to make. You can filter the cartridges to figure out what you need, and you can check out your images tab for any other cartridges purchased or uploaded.

You can get digital cartridges, which means you buy them online and choose the images directly from your available options. They aren't physical, so there is no linking required.

Loading and Unloading Your Paper

To load paper into a Cricut machine, you'll want to make sure that the form is at least three inches by three inches. Otherwise, it won't cut very well. You should use regular paper for this.

Now, to make this work, you need to put the paper onto the cutting mat. You should have one of those, so take it right now and remove the attached film. Put a corner of the form to the area where you direct to align the paper corners. From there, push the paper directly onto the cutting mat for proper adherence. Once you do that, you load it into the machine, following the arrows. You'll want to keep the paper firmly on the mat. Press the "load paper" key that you see as you do this. If it doesn't take for some reason, press the unload paper key, and try this again until it shows up.

Before you do any cutting for your design, you should always have a test cut in place. Some people don't do this, but it's incredibly helpful when learning how to use a Cricut. Otherwise, you won't get the pressure correct in some cases, so get in the habit of doing it for your pieces.

Is there a difference between vinyl and other products? The primary difference is the cutting mats.

Depending on what you're cutting, you may need some grip or lack thereof. If you feel like your material isn't entirely sticking, get some Heat N' Bond to help with this since the issue with cutting fabrics comes from the fact that it doesn't adhere. But you may also need mats that are a bit thicker, too, to help get a better grip on these.

Selecting Shapes, Letters, And Phrases

When you're creating your Design Space design, you usually begin by using letters, shapes, numbers, or different fonts. These are the basics, and they're incredibly comfortable. To make text, you press the text tool on the left-hand side and type out your book. For example, write the word hello, or joy, or whatever you want to use.

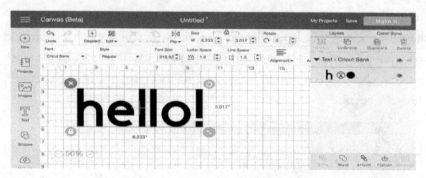

You can change the font size by pressing the drag and drop arrow near the corner of the text box or going to the side panel near the top to choose actual font sizes.

You can also select different Cricut or system fonts too. Cricut ones will be in green, and if you have Cricut Access, this is a great way to begin using this. You can sort these, too, so you don't end up accidentally paying for a font.

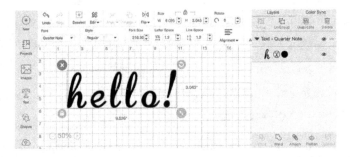

The Cricut ones are supposed to make for Cricut, so you know they'll look good. Design Space also lets you put them closer together so they can cut with a precise cut. You can change this by going to line spacing and adjusting as needed. To fix individual letters, you go to the advanced drop-down menu to ungroup the letters, so everything is separate as required.

Cricut also offers different writing styles, which is a great way to add text to projects. To do this, choose a font made with a specific style, choose only the Cricut ones, and then go to writing. It will then narrow down the choice, so you're using the right font for the essay.

Adding shapes is pretty easy, as well. In Design Space, choose the shapes option. Once you click it, the window will then pop out, and you'll have an incredible array of different shapes that you can use with just one click. Choose your body, and from there, put it in the space. Drag the corners to make this bigger or smaller.

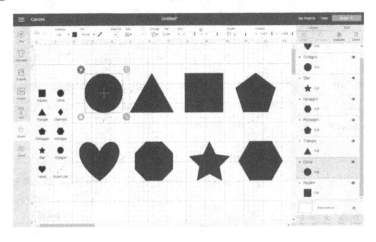

There is also the scoreline, which creates a folding line for you to use. Personally, if you're thinking of trying to make a card at first, I suggest using this.

You can also resize your options by dragging them towards the right-hand side, and you can change the orientation by choosing that option and then flipping it around. You can select exact measurements suitable for those design projects that need everything to be precise.

Once you've chosen the design, it's time for you to start cutting.

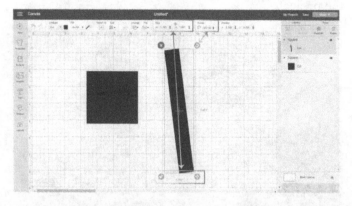

How to Remove Your Cut from The Cutting Mat

Removing your cut from the mat is easy but complicated. I ran into being more involved with vinyl projects since they love to stick around there. But we'll explain how you can create significant cuts and remove them, as well.

The first thing to remember is to make sure that you're using the right mat. The light grip ones are good for very soft material, with the pink one being one of the strongest, and only to be used with the Cricut Maker. Once the design cuts, you'll probably be eager McBeaver about removing the project directly from the mat, but one of the problems with this is that often, the project will ruin if you're not careful. Instead of pulling the project from the mat itself, bend the mat within your hand. Push it away from the project since this will loosen it from the mat. Bend this both horizontally and vertically so that the adhesive releases the project.

Remember the spatula tool that we told you to get with your Cricut machine early on? It is where you use it. Use this spatula to lightly pull on the vinyl until you can grab it from the corner and lift it. Otherwise, you risk curling it or tearing the mat, which is what we don't want.

Now, with the initial cuts, such as the paper ones, this will be incredibly easy. Trust me, I was surprised at how little effort it took, but one of the biggest things to remember is that you have to go slow with Cricut machines when removing the material. Do this slowly, and don't get rushed near the end. Taking your time will save you many problems, and it will even save you money and stress, too!

CHAPTER 8:

Complex Operations

Blade Navigation and Calibration

The blades that come with a Cricut machine are essential to understand, and you will need to calibrate your knives every time you use your device. Each blade needs this because it will help you figure out which level of depth and pressure your cut needs to be. Typically, each blade needs to calibrate only once, which is great because you don't have to spend time doing this each time. Once you've done it once, it will stay calibrated, but if you decide to change the blades' housings or use them in another machine, you'll need to calibrate it again. So, if you plan on using a knife blade and then a rotary cutter, you'll want to make sure that you do recalibrate – and make sure you do this before you start with your project. It is incredibly easy to do this, though, which is why it's encouraged.

To calibrate a blade, you launch the Design Space, and from there, you open the menu and choose calibration.

Then, choose the blade that you're going to put in.

For this explanation, let's say you're using a knife blade.

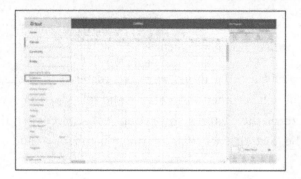

Put that blade in the clamp B area, do a test cut, copy paper into the mat, and then load it into the machine.

Press continue, then press the go button on the machine. It will then do everything you need for the item itself, and it will start to cut.

You can then choose which calibration is best for your blade, but the first one is usually good enough.

You can do this with every blade you use, and every time you use a new knife on your machine, I highly recommend you do this – for best results, of course.

Set Paper Size

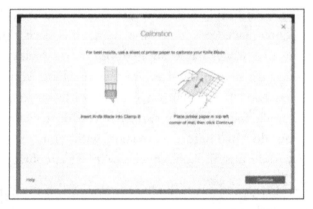

Setting paper size in a Cricut machine is pretty simple. You will want to use this with either cartridge or Design Space for what you'd like to make. It also comes with a cutting mat, and you'll want to load this up with paper so that you can use it.

To do this, you'll want to make sure that you have it plugged in, then go to the project preview screen.

Suppose you choose a more oversized material than the mat size. In that case, it will automatically change, and it'll adjust as necessary based on the size of the material you select. You can choose the color, the size of the material, whether or not it'll mirror – and you can also choose to entirely skip the mat, too, if you don't want that image printed just yet.

Note that the material size menu does offer sizes that are bigger than the largest mat available. If you're planning on using the print, then cut mode, understand that it's limited to a print area of 8.5x11 inches, but again, you can choose these settings for yourself.

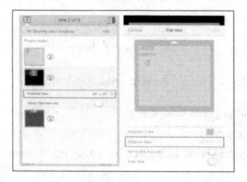

Load Last

To load that paper and image last is pretty simple.

Press that, and then go. You'll be able to skip this quite easily. It's one of those operations that's a little different from what you may use to, but if you want to cut design and don't want to work with it just yet, this is probably the best option for you to use.

If you're worried about forgetting it, don't worry – Cricut will remind you.

Paper Saver

Saving paper is something you'll want to consider doing with a Cricut machine because it loves to eat up the form before you even start decorating.

Explore Air 2 appreciates it if you save paper, and there are a few ways to do so.

The first one is, of course, to halve your mats.

But you don't need to do only that. You can also go to the material saver option on the machine, which will automatically adjust and align your paper as best it can.

Unfortunately, it does not directly state on newer machines, but there is a way to save paper.

You'll want to create tabbed dividers to organize your projects and save them directly there.

The first step is to create a background shape.

Make sure that the paper looks like a background.

Go to shapes, and then select the square to make the square shape. Once you have created the court representing the paper, arrange it to the back to organize the form to save the maximum space on each mat. Then collect the items on top of where the background is and arrange them to fit on a singular mat.

Rotating is your best friend – you can use this feature whenever you choose objects, so I suggest getting familiarized with it. You hide the background at this point, and you do this by selecting the square, and in Design Space, literally hiding this on the right side.

Look at the eyeball on the screen, and you'll see a line through the eyeball.

That means it's hidden. Check over everything and fine-tune it at this point.

Make sure they're grouped around one object, and make sure everything has measurements.

Move these around if they're outside of the measurements required.

Once they're confirmed, you attach these on the right-hand side of Design Space, which keeps everything neatly together – they're all cut from the same sheet.

Pressure Dial

Now, let's talk about pressure. Each piece of material will require different pressure settings.

If you're not using enough pressure, the blade won't cut into the material, and if you use too much pressure, you'll end up missing the mat, which isn't what you want to do.

The smart-set dial kind of takes the guesswork out of it. You simply choose the setting that best fits your material, and from there, you let it cut.

If you notice you're not getting a deep enough cut, you'll want to adjust it about half a setting to a better result.

From there, adjust as needed.

But did you know that you can change the pressure on the smart-set dial for custom materials?

Let's say you're cutting something very different, such as foil, and you want to set the pressure to be incredibly light so that the foil doesn't get shredded.

What you do is you load the material in, and you choose the custom setting.

You can then choose the material you plan to cut, such as foil – and if it's not on the list, you can add it.

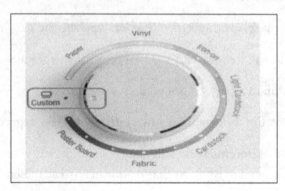

From here, you give pressure options. People will often go too heavy with their custom settings, so I suggest that you go lighter for the first time and change it as needed.

Several draggers go from low to high. If you need lots of pressure, obviously let it go higher.

Cricut Design Space

-Design Space lets you do many things with your Cricut machine.

-Here are a few things you can do with this convenient app:

-I am aligning various items right to one another.

-You are attaching items to hold images in place and lets you use score lines.

-I was arranging these to make them sit on the canvas in different layers.

-Canvas, a tool that enables you to set prints and vectors to use the various devices with them.

-Contour is a tool that allows you to hide image layers not to crop quickly.

-Color sync, which lets you use multiple colors in one project to reduce the material differences.

-Cut buttons, which will start cuts.

-Make it button: this is the screen that lets you see the designs cut.

-Draw lines: lets you draw with the pen to write images and such.

-Fill: lets you fill in a pattern or color on an item.

-Flipping items flip it horizontally or vertically by 180 degrees.

-Group: puts different text and images on a singular layer, and everything is moved at once so that it -doesn't affect the layout.

-Line type: Options that you can do with your piece, whether you want to cut a line, draws a bar, or score a sequence.

-Mirrored image: reverses it, which is very important with transfer vinyl, so everything reads correctly.

-Print then Cut: it's an option that lets you print the design, and from there, the machine cuts it.

Cricut Pens

Pens for your Cricut machine are essentially another way to get creative with your projects.

I love to use them for cards, handmade tags for gifts, or even fancy invites and labels.

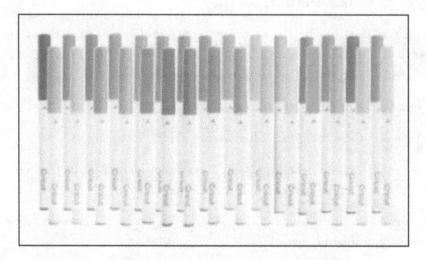

Now, each pen offers a little different finish and point size.

They aren't toxic, and they are permanent once they're dried.

You've got the extra-fine points for small lettering, up to a medium tip for making thicker lines.

To use these, choose the wording or design, or whatever you want to do.

You want to go to the Layers panel on the right-hand side and choose the scissors icon – change that to the write icon.

From there, you'll want to choose the pen color that you would like to use.

You can then have the design printed out on the material you're using. Some people like to use different fonts, whether it be system fonts or Cricut fonts, or the Cricut Access fonts.

However, the one thing with Design Space is that it will write what will usually cut, so you'll get an outline of that font rather than just a solid stroke of writing.

It can add to the design; however – you essentially change the machine from cut to write, and there you go.

You can also use the Cricut writing fonts, which you can choose by going to a blank canvas, and then selecting the text tool on the left-hand side, along with the wording you'd like for this to have.

Once you're in the font edit toolbar, you give a font selection.

You select the writing font filter so that writing fonts can use.

From there, choose the font, switch from the scissors to the pen icon, and then select the pen color. That's all there is to it!

You can also use this with Cricut Access – if you're planning on using this a lot, it might be worth it.

To insert the pens into the Cricut machine, you want to choose to make it, and from there, you'll then go to the prepare mat screen.

It will say draw instead of writing in the thumbnail this time around, so you press continue in the bottom right-hand corner, then put the pen into clamp A – you just unlock it and then put it in.

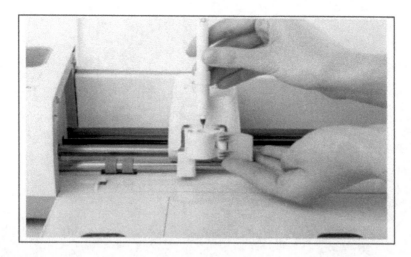

Please wait until it clicks, and that's it!

Cricut pens are super easy, and it's a great idea to consider trying these out.

As you can see, there are many different Cricut features and many functions that may seem complicated, but as you can see, you are not that hard.

There are tons of options for your Cricut projects, and a lot that you can get out of this machine.

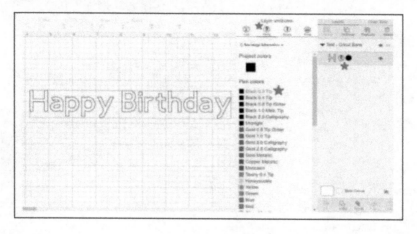

CHAPTER 9:

How To Connect Cricut To A Computer

The excitement of getting your brand new Cricut Machine is unique. It's not every day that you can get a machine that's as powerful as the Cricut Machine, well, at least as far as home DIY projects go. It is something that is both exciting and challenging. It assures that you are looking to get started as soon as possible. But before you can get your hands dirty, you need to set up your Cricut Machine.

Fortunately, Cricut has made it easy to set up your Cricut Machine. If you've ever installed a printer or any other external device on your computer, then you will find it easy to install your very own Cricut Machine.

There is just one crucial recommendation before making the installation: please ensure that you can devote the time needed to get the machine running. So, please take your time; it doesn't work at first. The last thing you want is to rush through the installation process. While it's pretty straightforward, there are times when running through installation; you might miss a step that keeps the device from working. It is what we are looking to avoid.

Installing On Windows Or Mac

To kick things off, we're going to look at how to install on a laptop or PC. You will find that installing the Cricut Machine on a computer or PC is just like setting up a printer. It's a pretty straightforward deal. So, do keep in mind that you will need about 15 or 20 minutes to get through the entire installation process.

Here is a breakdown of the steps needed to get the Cricut Machine up and running.

1. Check power. Firstly, plug your Cricut Machine and press the on button. It is essential, especially in the rare event that the machine defective. Otherwise, you might struggle to try to get the installation done with an unresponsive device.

2. Connect the machine to your computer. Secondly, connect your device to your laptop or PC. There are two ways to do this, using the USB cord (it provides in the kit, or you can also use one from a printer) or via Bluetooth. With the power cord, it's just a question of plugging it in, and that's that. If you choose to connect via Bluetooth, enable your computer's Bluetooth connection and then pair with the Cricut Machine.

3. You are going to the Cricut website. This step is essential, especially if you are setting up a machine for the first time. Go to design.cricut.com/setup on your browser. You'll be directed to the Cricut website and then prompted to create your Cricut ID.

4. Create your Cricut ID. At this point, you'll prompt by a set of instructions. Follow these instructions to create your Cricut ID. Now, if you already have a Cricut ID, then you can skip this step. Nevertheless, if you are installing a brand-new machine, it's always a good idea to start fresh.

5. Install Design Space. Design Space is "installed" on your computer via a plug-in. It is an addition to your browser of choice (Google Chrome tends to work best). It is what enables the cloud app to run appropriately. Please bear in mind that Design Space is a cloud-based application and

therefore does not install or save anything directly onto your computer.

6. You are getting started. It's always a good idea to test out various functions to ensure your device is fully operational and does not have any defects. Should things not work well for any reason, contact customer support?

With this, you are now ready to let your imagination fly! Do take the time to become acquainted with Design Space as this is the means that you can use to make your machine come to life.

Installing on Android Or IOS

To install on a mobile device (due to the screen size limitation, a tablet's operation mainly used for a smartphone may be significantly restricted). The installation process works the same as on a computer. The difference lies in the installation of Design Space and the connection of the machine itself.

1. You are pairing your device. The only means to connect your Cricut Machine with a mobile device is via Bluetooth. There is no physical cable that can use. As such, it's essential to make sure that your tablet's Bluetooth is enabled. You can pair the Cricut Machine just like you would any other Bluetooth device.

2. You are downloading the app. To do this, go to your mobile device's app store (Google Play or Apple Store). Do a quick search for Design Space. You will recognize the Cricut logo. It is the app that you need to get. You don't have to purchase the app as it is free to use. Click on "install" and sit tight for a couple of minutes.

3. Create your ID. The app installation process will prompt you to create your Cricut ID. Just follow the steps. If you already have an ID, for instance, when you set up your

machine on your computer, sign in with the user and password you created earlier.

4. Setup. Look for the "Machine setup and App Overview" menu. It is the menu that you need to finalize the installation of your machine.

5. New machine. Then, look for "New Machine Setup." Click on this to move the installation process forward.

6. Follow prompts. There is not much else to do here. Just follow the prompts, and you'll be all set to go.

7. You are getting started. You can go ahead and use one of the ready-made projects to help you test out your machine.

Voilà! Your Cricut Machine is now ready for use on a mobile device. It's a good idea to go ahead and set up both your computer and mobile device during the first installation. That way, you are all set to do whatever projects you want on whichever of your instruments. It will give you peace of mind in knowing that you are covered.

One last thing: please make sure to do a test project right away. While this doesn't necessarily mean that you have to do it immediately after finalizing installation, it's always a good idea to do a project to ensure that your machine is working correctly. In case of failure, you can call for a warranty. In this manner, you will feel confident that you won't have any setbacks in working with your brand new Cricut Machine.

CHAPTER 10:

Maintenance Of The Cricut Machine

All Cricut cutting machines fold away with protective faceplates. You should always make sure that these are closed when the cutting machine is not in use.

The Easy Press machines will need a protective bag to be stored, which is an excellent investment to prolong these presses' lives.

You should look at buying storage bags for the cutting machines and a bit of extra protection and move them without damaging them.

Changing Cutting Machine Blades

At times, the cutting blades will become blunt, especially with continuous use. You can purchase spare blades to maintain precise accuracy.

These blades are sold separately from the blade housing compartments and are not difficult to change.

Although care should always take as the edges may be blunt for cutting, they will still be considered sharp and cut through the skin.

For Cricut cutting machine blades that use blade housings like the Bonded-Fabric blade and the Fine Point blade:

- Press down on the dip of the blade housing cap.

- Pull out the blade (be careful as it can still cut).

- Hold the housing with the blade side up.

- Slide the new blade into position until it clicks.

- Cricut cutting machine blades that use the gear housing (housing with the gold gear on top) utilize blades like the Rotary blade or the Scoring blade:

- Like the scoring blade and the rotary blade, these blades are a little more complicated and require more assembly.

- The new blades come with a blade kit:

- The kit comes with an empty cap that contains the new blade and washer.

- The kit also comes with a small screwdriver.

- Each blade comes with a protective cap. Place the protective cap over the blade housing.

- You will note that the small screw at the bottom of the blade is accessible through the protective cap.

- Use the small screwdriver to unscrew this little screw and put the little screw to one side.

- Pull the cap with the bottom blade off of the drive blade housing.

- Place the blade housing into the new protective cap that contains the new blade and washer.

- Push the cap on tight and make sure that the screw holes line up.

- Using the little screw, you took out of the old blade, screw it into the new edge using the small screwdriver until it securely positions.

Caring for Cricut Cutting Blades

If you want to extend your Cricut cutting machine blades' life, you will need to take care of them.

- Always make sure to use the blade only with compatible materials. Trying to use the blades on materials that are too tough for them will blunt if not break the edge.

- Most blades come with a protective cap. When these blades are not in use, store them safely with their protective covers firmly in place.

- Make sure that you store them in a place that is free of dust and grime. The best site is in the Cricut's storage drawer, as these close away and protect the blades from dust and dirt.

- To sharpen the blade, you can use a crumpled piece of aluminum foil and poke the edge for two to three minutes.

But this is not ideal, and a blunt blade should replace to maintain the cutting machine's precision cutting ability.

Cleaning And Maintaining The Cutting Mat(S)

The Cricut cutting mats are sticky to keep materials cut firmly anchored to the mat during cutting. These mats can become clogged with particles, especially carpets used with the new Knife Blade that works with the Cricut Maker.

To clean the mats:

- Never try to scrape any leftover material from the mat. It can damage the mat and will remove its stickiness.

- Scraping materials from the mat may also embed them deeper into the mat.

- Remove any leftover materials with a tweezer or weeding tool.

- To remove dust or extra stubborn materials, you can wash the mat:

- Place the mat flat in a sink.

- Use only lukewarm water on the mat.

- Only use plastic-bristled scrubbing brushes to scrub the mat gently.

- Rinse the mat with lukewarm water.

- Leave it to dry lying flat and draining on the sink thoroughly.

- When the mat is dry, the stickiness should return.

- Keep mats stored in clean and dry areas where there is little dust. Any dust or particles can cause damage to the mat and projects.

- To keep them safe and sticky, use a piece of protective sheeting to keep them covered when they are not in use.

- It is best to store mats in a craft box or tote bag used to store other craft materials.

- Only use materials designed for the mat to prolong the life of the cutting mat.

- Use the mat with blades compatible with or damage the cutting mat and possibly the cutting blade.

Cleaning The Cricut Cutting Machine

The Cricut machine is going to get dirty as it cuts paper, cardboard, vinyl, and expose to everyday dust. The device is not difficult to clean either; all you need is a soft cloth and some glass cleaner spray.

Here are some cleaning tips:

- Never use anything that is corrosive or can damage the machine to clean it. Stay away from acetone (nail polish remover), strong cleaners that contain harsh ingredients such as bleach, or strong countertop cleaners.

- Always make sure that the machine is turned off and unplugged before attempting to clean it.

- If there is grease buildup on the rollers or dirt on any of the feeder bars or roller wheels, use a cotton puff with some window cleaner on it.

Caring For The Machine, Accessories, And Tools

The best way to care for the machines, accessories, and tools for the Cricut machines is to keep them safely stored away when they are not in use.

Most of the accessories and tools can fit into the Cricut's storage drawers (for the machines that have storage compartments, that is). It is advisable for the devices that do not buy one of Cricut's amazing storage totes.

Keep the tools clean by wiping them off before they are stored and after being used. You can even run them under lukewarm water, pat them dry, and let them drain before you keep them.

Caring For The Cut Smart Carriage In The Cricut Cutting Machine

The little carriage that houses the cutting blades and accessories is called the Cut Smart Carriage. From time to time, you may notice it getting a little stuck or not moving freely. It may mean that there is a little dust or goo on it, or it may need a little bit of grease.

Here are some tips on cleaning and greasing the Cut Smart Carriage:

- Ensure that the cutting machine is turned off and unplugged from the wall before you attempt to clean the carriage.

- To get the carriage to move to the side to clean it, simply push it to the side. Do not force it; be gentle.

- Use a piece of tissue to clean the length of it and remove grease or grime.

- Get the lubricant for the machine from Cricut or a Cricut dealer.

- Move the little carriage to the middle of the carriage barn.

- Using a cotton puff, some of the lubricant onto the tip of the cotton puff.

- You will need to swab a light coating of the lubricant on both sides of the carriage.

- Once you have applied the lubricant, gently move the carriage from side to side.

- Wipe off any excess lubricant with tissue paper.

Parts, Spares, And Services

Find your nearest Cricut supplier or dealer to learn about any maintenance or repair that may have to do on the machine. If your device is still under warranty, it is best to get service from your local dealer instead of trying to tinker with it yourself.

Cricut offers parts and spares for nearly all of its current and older machines. These can conveniently purchase online at their craft shop or your local Cricut dealer.

They include blade spares, roller, tools, and so on.

CHAPTER 11:

Easy Projects

Cricut Hello Greeting Card

Your Cricut machine will come with a green Cricut cutting mat, which comes with a protective plastic layer to cover its adhesive surface. Remove the plastic cover from the mat, setting the body aside in a place where it won't be lost or damaged. This layer is something you'll want to put back on top of your mats before storing them between projects, as it will keep stray dust and lint from collecting on the mat and ruining the adhesive grip. It will help you to have to replace your mats less frequently.

Taking the cardstock piece that came with your machine, line it up with the upper left-hand corner of the grip area on your mat, ensuring that the textured side of the card stock is facing upward. Smooth down your cardstock with your hands, rubbing any gaps, wrinkles, folds, or anything that forms.

Once the cardstock lines up with the corner of the grip on the mat, place the mat under the Cricut machine's guides. The guide is a small piece of plastic that juts out to keep the mat in place. Firmly push the mat toward the rollers while tapping the Load/Unload button, which is indicated by the double arrow on the top of your machine.

Accessory clamp A, which is inside the machine and labeled with an A, is where you will put things like pens and scoring tools. Open clamp A and take the cap off your metallic Cricut pen, which also came with your machine. To ensure it doesn't get lost, place the lid on the back of the pen, pushing it securely into place. Slide your finger up under accessory clamp A before sliding the Cricut pen into the slot. Once that is inserted, firmly get carefully push the pen into place until you hear a click. Once it clicks, you can close the clamp.

Now that your machine is loaded with the right materials and set up with the right tools, you are ready to get started on producing your design. When you launch your Cricut for the first time, this project should come up automatically. If you're having difficulty finding it or Cricut Design Space doesn't automatically pop up this project for you, you can click on the menu and select the New Machine Setup option. Follow the initial steps once again (you won't need to connect anything also; simply click through the prompts), and it should pull up the project for you.

Click the "Make It" button to check that your design is lined up properly with the materials as they arrange on your mat. If the screen shows that the materials should line up differently, you will want to unload your mat by pressing the Load/Unload button. Rearrange the materials on your mat the way they are shown in the sample screen, smooth everything down, and reload the mat. Once everything has been plotted out correctly and everything arranges, return to the "Make It" screen.

Set the dial on top of your machine (not applicable if you are using the Maker) "cardstock" setting to ensure that your blade applies to your materials with the right pressure. Using the appropriate set will give you the most exact, precise cuts without damaging your mat or your blades.

Once everything is lined up and set correctly, you will be ready to click the "Go" option. On the Cricut machine, once the Cricut C button starts to blink, press it to start the process. Your device will spring into action, and your design will shortly be cut and drawn to your specifications.

Once that's complete, tap the blinking Load/Unload button so you can remove your mat from the machine. Open accessory clamp A

removes the metallic pen and replaces its cap to ensure it won't dry out. Once your pen cap, you can place it in the storage compartment on the front of your machine. It's the part that folds down to hold your mat under the mat guides; you will see a little finger hold on the side facing upward when that portion of the machine is down in the usage position. Pull it open, and the pen will fit right inside. You will see that there is also a stage for your extra blades, tools, and additional accessories.

To release your cut cardstock from the mat, flip the mat face down onto your work surface so the back of your mat is facing you, ensuring the area is clear. Gently curl the corner of the mat back toward you until the cardstock releases from the sticky grip of your mat. Place your free hand flat on the cardstock to hold it to the work surface and assist it in pulling away from the mat. Be sure to apply pressure evenly to help your material stay flat and smooth.

Fold the cardstock in half widthwise to create the outer portion of your greeting card. Repeat this fold with the blue paper that came with your machine, place the form inside the menu, and you'll see that the report shows through the cut portions of your cardstock.

Wooden Welcome Sign With Vinyl Accents

For this project, you will need self-adhesive vinyl, transfer tape, weeding tools, True Control or other precision blade knives, scrapers or sanding tools, trimmers or scissors, and painted wooden plaques or stained according to your preference.

Open your browser and navigate to the Cricut Design Space. Logging in will be your first step if you do not already login. It will give you access to all your assets, designs, and elements. Once you logged in, click "New Project."

Select the "Text" option on the left-hand side. Once the text box pops up onto your screen, type WELCOME into the dialog box alongside the text box. Once you've typed that, you will see the text box populate with the same text.

Add any additional text you would like on your welcome plaque in a new line under your WELCOME. Your family name, or maybe a fun slogan, is recommended for this playful, decorative project. Once you've chosen that, resize it to the same width as your welcome. Both lines of text should be just slightly narrower than the width of your wood plaque.

Put both of your text boxes onto the same layer, picking the one with the weight that works best for your project.

Put some distance between the text boxes to leave enough room for a large monogram. This image will go in between the lines of text.

Click "Images" and set your filter for Single Layer Images, then search for the keyword "monogram." Select one that you like and click "Insert Images."

Place your monogram in between your layers of text and resize it until it all comes together.

For some added flair, let's curve the WELCOME text. Using a blank shape as a guide for this curve can help us line up our letters evenly. Select the "Circle" shape, stretch it into an oval with the desired angle, and place it over your monogram beneath your WELCOME.

With the text selected, click the "Advanced" tab at the top of the screen, then click "Ungroup to Letters." It will now allow you to place each letter individually along that curve. Be sure to adjust your letters' rotation, so the whole world place on that curve.

Delete your placeholder oval.

Review your text and image and make any last-minute changes you may need to make so your design is complete to your liking.

Once everything is in order, click Select All in the top menu, then click "Attach" at the bottom right-hand corner of your screen. The attach option will have a little paperclip icon beneath it.

Once that is finish, you will notice all layers combine into one. Edit the color of your—now single—image to match your material.

Click "Save," name your project, then click "Save" again.

Click "Make It" to start the cutting process. It will show you where your cuts will appear on the material on your mat.

Set the dial on your machine to vinyl. Line your vinyl up with the upper left-hand corner of the grip on your mat, ensuring that your vinyl's backing is face down. Smooth down your vinyl with your hands, so no gaps, wrinkles, or folds form in your vinyl.

Once you have that lined up on your mat, place the mat under the guides in your Cricut machine. Gently push the mat toward the rollers as you hit the Load/Unload button (indicated by the double arrow) on the top of your device.

Press the blinking Cricut C button and watch your project come to life.

Once the material is fully cut, press the Load/Unload button to release your mat from the machine. Using a precision blade, make an L shaped cut around your design to remove most of the excess vinyl from the mat. Roll up the excess and save it for later use.

Using your scraper tool, burnish the design before weeding. It will help the elements of your design stay stuck to the carrier sheet while you weed!

Now, holding the weeding tool at a slight angle, hook onto the blank vinyl around your design and gently pull up the pieces you don't need. You can collect them in a bind to the side or in the trash. Once you've removed all the small negative pieces of vinyl, you can remove the more massive vinyl sheet around your design.

Grasp the vinyl in the upper left-hand corner, pulling back gently and slowly continue to pull down diagonally toward the lower right-hand corner. Watch for any pieces of your design that stick to the blank vinyl you're removing. Using the back of your weeding hook, you can gently guide those pieces of your system back down onto the carrier sheet.

Once all that's left on your carrier sheet at the elements of design, it's time to cut the transfer tape! Carefully place the transfer tape over your entire system. Do your best to avoid bubbles, but a couple here and there won't do you any harm!

Use your scraper tool to thoroughly burnish your design into the transfer tape and then peel the carrier sheet away from the transfer tape. It will leave your system stuck to the transfer tape, with the adhesive side of your vinyl exposed.

Gently place your vinyl design onto your plaque, making sure to center it entirely before allowing the adhesive to touch the surface of your plaque. Once you have it lined up exactly where you want it, use your scraper to burnish your design onto the surface of your plaque.

Now, carefully peel the transfer tape from the upper left-hand corner down diagonally toward the lower right-hand corner. If any pieces of your design try to come with your transfer tape, simply lay it back down, burnish again, then resume peeling.

Your vinyl creation should now proudly display on the front of your wooden plaque!

CHAPTER 12:

Medium Projects

Leather Cuff Bracelet

Cutting leather with Cricut is a unique way to use the machine and create amazing projects and gifts for others.

The supplies you need for this project are simple and consist of:

A small piece of leather

A bracelet or piece of chain or cord, and small jump rings

Needle-nose pliers for jewelry

Deep cut blade for the Cricut Explore

Your first step is to choose the design image you would like to use on your leather bracelet. It can find inside the image files under Lace or any other design file that you already have.

Verify that the sizing is appropriate for a bracelet by cutting it on paper. You do not want to miss the leather and be wrong. It would waste the materials.

Once the size is perfect, you can begin your project.

Place the leather on the mat with the smooth side down and push the Cut button.

After the leather piece cuts, you will need to adjust your chain or rope to the appropriate size required for the person's wrist that it will be fitting.

Connect the leather to the chain with the jump rings. Attaching the leather links is perfectly fine, but it may tear the leather, so using the jump rings is a great alternative.

It is a simple process that anyone with a Cricut and a need to make leather goods can do.

Wooden Hand-Lettered Sign

Hand-lettered wooden signs are an excellent way to utilize your Cricut for creative projects.

- Acrylic paint for whatever colors you would like
- Vinyl
- Cricut Explore Air 2
- Walnut hollow basswood planks
- Scraper
- An SVG file or font that you wish to use
- Pencil
- Eraser

You will need to start by deciding what you will want to draw onto the wood.

Then, place some lines on the plank to designate the horizontal and vertical axis for the grid. Set this aside.

Upload the file that you wish to use to the Design Space. Then, cut the file with the proper setting for vinyl.

Weed out the writing or design spaces that does do not mean to go on the wood.

Using the transfer tape, apply the video to the top of the vinyl and smooth it out. Using the scraper and the transfer paper's corner, slowly peel the backing off a bit at a time. Do it carefully.

Remove the vinyl pieces' backing, aligning the lettering or design so that it is entirely centered. Place it carefully on the wooden plank.

Again, use the scraper to smooth out the vinyl on the plank.

Take off the transfer tape by smoothing off the bubbles as you scrape along with the wood sign. Discard the transfer tape at that time.

Continue to use the scraper to make the vinyl smoother. There should be no bumps since this creates bleeding.

Now, paint your wood plank with any color of your choice. Peel the vinyl letters off. Once the paint has completely dried, you can erase your pencil marks.

Framed Succulents Made From Paper

Framed paper succulents are a great way to appeal succulents without all that watering and killing of plants.

What you will need:

- Foam brush
- Standard grip cutting mat
- DecoArt acrylic paint for the frame
- Scissors to curl the succulent petals
- A piece of chipboard, cardstock, or cardboard
- 12x12 cardstock in assorted green colors

Glue Gun

Start with painting the picture frame that you wish to use unless you want to leave it rustic and old as I would.

Place your chipboard or cardboard to the inside of the frame. It is for placing the succulents on. Use the hot glue gun to put it in the structure properly.

Find the image of the file that you wish to use.

Press Go to cut out the succulents.

Once all the pieces have cut from the paper, you can begin to assemble the parts to make yourself succulent.

Once the succulents create, you can begin to glue them aboard.

Succulents

Succulents are a great addition to anyone's home décor. You can place them in a planter for decoration, or you can place them on a wreath or letter for the initials of your family or first name. It is a great way to decorate your living room or even a daughter's room. With paper designs, you can use your creative imagination to create new spaces and atmosphere within your home.

The steps to create the first type of succulent are easy.

Cut the leaves from the cards printed on them. Slice a slit in the leaf point at the narrowest end.

Cross your tips, overlapping each other to form a sort of cup, and then glue them together. Overlap the leaves with the same size and make a set of 6.

Using the glue, take the two sets of three leaves and curl them with scissors. It will form a small ball.

Place a floral pin at the center of the most massive leaf set.

Proceed to glue the sets of leaves to the inside of the other. Glue in order of largest to smallest. They were rotating as you glue them so that the leaves will be the opposite.

Once done, you will have a six-layer leaf with the ball in the center.

Attach this succulent to the item that you will be used to create the succulent craft.

Proceed to make the second type of succulent.

Cut the leaves of each succulent; there should be five sheets from the printed cardstock. There should be two succulents per page.

Curl your leaves with the scissors like you would curl a ribbon and place your floral pins inside the centerpiece of the enormous plate.

Glue the four sets together so that the center starts as the largest to the smallest. While stacking, rotate the leaves for each layer.

Bend the leaves out and arrange the leaves to fill up space. Using pins, you can attach the succulent to the décor that you are creating.

How to create succulent number 3 easily:

Cut out using the scissors the three larger pieces and the three smaller pieces for each of the succulents.

Using the scissors, like you would curl a ribbon, bend the leaves at the top. And then, again at the end to form an S shape.

Glue the large and small leaves together around the pin.

Using a floral pin, you can attach the succulent to the décor that you are decorating.

Succulent number 4 is super simple to create. Follow these steps to make it:

Cut out using the scissors the 11 leaf trio shapes from your cardstock.

Using the scissors, you can curl the leaves inward, forming a cup shape.

Glue your sets together in matching sets with one extra small piece. It should be six full floral pieces.

Place a pin at the center of the largest leaf.

Start gluing the largest to the smallest pieces together, rotating as you stack.

Use the pin to attach the pieces to the home décor that you are decorating.

Now that you have shown how to design the paper succulents, you can begin to create these fantastic DIY projects. You should find a pattern on many craft blogs for the succulents to use for the Design shop.

CHAPTER 13:

Difficult Projects

As you begin to get into the types of projects that require more skill, you will find that you will need to branch out to websites that offer their design and cut files that you can use to make more and more creative things.

Because of this, I would recommend looking at various online resources for projects you can do to broaden your horizons when it comes to more complex tasks!

To give you some ideas to get you started on where to look, here is a list of 100 crafts you can do with your Cricut system to make your skills unique to you genuinely!

3D Wood Puzzles

These are fantastic fun, and they make such an excellent final product when put together.

3D Foam Puzzles

Foam is just as sturdy for 3D puzzles, and you can take them apart, put them back together, knock them down, and more and they bounce right back. These make such a great gift for young children.

3D Wall Art

Art that pops off your wall and makes a statement about who you are to all your guests is something people pay a lot of money to have. Put a little piece of your creative self on your wall and show off your creativity!

Aprons

If you have a lot of passion in the kitchen, your apron is a great way to add a personalized touch to your experience. With a character you love, a funny saying, or just a monogram, you can own the kitchen.

Banners

Any occasion is made more official with a banner! With Cricut, you can use your materials to create a banner that is unique and which will beautifully commemorate the occasion at hand.

Beanies

For any outdoor activity that's going to be happening during the winter months, a knit cap is a great way to keep warm. Having one with your design emblazoned on the side is sure to not only elevate the style of the hat but to make others wonder where they can get one just like it!

Beer Steins

The dollar store will often have blank glass beer mugs calling out to crafters to decorate them. Make a memorable gift for the beer lover in your life!

Bookmarks

Bookmarks are such a simple craft, but they're almost always needed! Replace the grocery receipt in the middle of their book with something fun and personal!

Bumper Stickers

Something to occupy the drivers behind you in traffic will always be in style. Make some fun statements for you and your friends to put on the bumper!

Business Cards

Business cards that cut from premium stock and que shapes can be so expensive. Printing your designs on cardstock with a standard printer and cutting out dynamic systems is sure to catch the eye of potential customers.

Business Marketing Materials

Why stop at business cards when you can make standees, door hangers, and so much more?

Cake Toppers

Got a themed birthday party coming up? Use plastic or metal to make a beautifully themed cake topper that will blow away your guests!

Calendars

No matter how the times progress, you always need to know what day it is! See what unique calendars you can make for your desk or office!

Candles

Sure, you can't make candles themselves with your Cricut. But you could get a candle in a blank glass holder and put something PERFECT for any occasion on the outside of it. These make ideal gifts, let me tell you.

Canvas Tote Bags

Tote bags are one of the most useful accessories on the planet. Keep all your things together and add some style with your Cricut! Heck, if you felt like it, you could get some canvas and make your tote bag!

Car Decals

Got a business? Tell the world about it as you travel through your week!

Centerpieces

Any large-scale event could benefit from themed centerpieces to amuse and wow your guests!

Clothing

Put your creative flourish on anything you own with Cricut and the numerous materials they have to offer. Whether it's an iron-on decal or a fabric embellishment, there's no shortage of ways to impress!

Coasters

Like so many other things in this list, coasters can make such a great gift for housewarming or holidays. Everyone could use a unique set of coasters to keep their surfaces safe and dry!

Coffee Mugs

Coffee mugs are probably the one dish that I will always want more when I see them in my house. They're great for so many things, and having unique ones, you are the perfect addition to any office or kitchen.

Coloring Pages

Using the pen in your Cricut, you can download line art to make coloring pages of any style or theme for yourself or your loved ones! If you have children in your family coming to visit, this makes for a great group activity!

Commemorative Plates

Did you know that come Cricut materials that can adhere to ceramic could make an excellent embellishment for decorative commemorative plates? What occasions could you commemorate?

Craft Foam Shape Sets

Just like with the puzzle sets, you can cut just about any shape you want out of craft foam. Doing so on the foam sheets with an adhesive backing could allow you to make your own little crafting sets of any theme you desire! It includes letters as well!

Decorative Plaques

Decorative plaques are a breeze, and, as you gain more competence with the Cricut system, you can get more intricate and creative!

DIY Craft Kits

Making crafting kit components with the Cricut is a breeze. Let your imagination run wild on what pieces you could bundle together for someone to make their crafting projects! Let your mind run wild on this one as they make lovely party favors, gifts for children or crafters, and so much more!

DIY Decals

The decals you create can place onto a carrier or backing sheet to give out. If you don't want to put your decal right onto something, simply top with a piece of transfer tape and give away!

Doilies

Cricut's intricate designs can allow you to make doilies of so many different materials, colors, sizes, shapes, themes, and more!

Envelopes

Did you know that envelopes make out of one continuous piece of paper that cuts, folded, and glued in a specific way? It means that you can take any piece of paper you like, with any print you want, and make an envelope out of it! Go nuts!

Flowerpots

A flowerpot can be sort of a mundane piece. However, with some craft paint and a stencil that you made with your Cricut, or with a decal, they can transform into something that fits your décor perfectly!

Framed Affirmations

This life is tough! Affirmations that you can put in your font or style can make all the difference in the vibe you get from a personal space. Jazz up your own and put them all over your room!

Gift Card Envelopes

These can do with scrapbooking paper, construction paper, foil paper, or anything. You can elevate this tiny little gift into something truly personal that anyone would love to have.

Gift Tags

Going that little extra bit toward making someone's gift look and feel unique does make a difference.

Greeting Cards

Some of the gorgeous greeting cards at the supermarket these days can run you about $9 per card! With the materials to hand in your crafting station, you can make cards that are just gorgeous, multi-layered, and make them carry your message. It makes the whole gift so much more personal and meaningful.

Hats

There are patterns to make your hats and decals you can make that will make an existing hat pop!

Holiday Décor

I can't even be honest with you about how nuts I've gone into this category. You can make so many decorations for any occasion that you just can't even imagine doing all of them for every holiday!

Hoodies

Nothing is more comforting than a nice thick hoodie, sometimes. Put your personal touch on a hoodie or carry around the mark of your favorite characters or phrases.

Jewelry

Oh yes. You can make your jewelry with the materials available through Cricut. Leather, fabric, metal. It's all there.

Keepsake Boxes

No craft is complete if it can't, in some way, be tied back to keepsake boxes, right? They're all over the crafting world, and you can absolutely make keepsake boxes or just decorate them to the nines!

Key Fobs

Make your keys stand out by making an adorable or stylish fey fob!

Keychains

Got a favorite character or emoji? Make a keychain!

Labeled Kitchenware

From canisters to kitchen crocks, there's nothing you can't decal!

Labels

If an organization is your forte, using Cricut can help you make gorgeous labels for every room of the house!

Lanyards

Keep your keys or ID cards displayed with style and comfort.

Leather Accents

From scrapbooking to home décor, leather accents can elevate your designs from looking great to looking thoroughly professional.

Leather Accessories

Wristbands, wallets, lanyards, wallets, etc. Your Cricut can transform sheets of leather into your most gorgeous, stylish accessories.

Luggage Tags

Never be unsure of which bag on the carousel is you. Make a luggage tag that stands apart from the crowd as much as you do and claims your pocket in no time!

Magnetic Poetry Sets

By printing words onto a set of printable magnets, you can create a group to make magnetic poems and limericks on your doors, refrigerators, or metal tables!

Magnetic Puzzles

Puzzles are a timeless gift that is always fun. Print a picture of a loved one onto a printable magnet, make a jigsaw puzzle, and create a beautiful setting for the front of your refrigerator or a friend!

Makeup Bags

Personalizing a simple zippered bag can make all the difference in the style of that item! Make it yours! You could even make your zippered bag with your Cricut, and then decorate it!

Mandala Decals

Mandalas are gorgeous, and Cricut is the perfect tool to help you make decals to put on just about anything.

Conclusion

Thank you for making it to the end. Cricut machines are fantastic gadgets to own because they do not only boost creativity and productivity; they can also be used to create crafts for business. With Design Space, crafters can make almost anything and even customize their products to bear their imprints.

All over the world, people use these machines to make gift items, t-shirts, interior décor, and many other crafts, to beautify their homes, share with friends and family during holidays, and even sell, etc.

There are two types of Cricut machines; Cricut Explore and Cricut Maker. Both devices are highly efficient in their rights, and experts in the crafting world use them to create many items, either as hobbies or business.

Both machines are similar in many ways, i.e., the Cricut Maker and the Explore Air 2, but the Cricut Maker is somewhat of a more advanced engine because it comes with some advanced features Explore Air 2.

One distinct feature about the Maker that sets it apart from the Explore Air is that it can cut thicker materials.

The possibilities are limitless with the Maker, and crafters can embark on projects that were never possible with Cricut machines before releasing the Make.

Another feature that puts the Cricut Maker machine ahead of the Explore Air 2 is the 'Adaptive Tool System.' With this tool, the Cricut Maker has empowered to remain relevant for many years to come because it will be compatible with new blades and other accessories that Cricut will release in the foreseeable future.

Although both machines have several dissimilarities, there are also areas where they completely inseparable. Take, for example, the designing of projects in Cricut Design Space.

Please take note that Cricut Design Space is the software where all the magnificent designs make before they send it to cut. It is one of the most critical aspects in the creation of crafts in the Cricut set up. However, when it comes to Cricut Maker and the Explore Air 2, there is nothing to separate them because both machines use the same software for project design.

As a crafter, without proper knowledge of Design Space, you're not only going to cut out inferior products, you will also make little or no in-road in your quest to find success.

Understanding Design Space is important because it empowers crafters with enormous tools and materials to create generalized and custom products. It is a potent tool that just cannot be overlooked by anyone that intends to follow this path.

Thus, the understanding of Design Space is a MUST for people that intend to do business out of Cricut machines or even utilize it as a hobby. With the software, crafters can create their designs from scratch or use already-made methods on the Cricut platform. Those who have an active subscription to Cricut Access have access to thousands of images, projects, and fonts. They can cut out their products using these images or projects, and they can also edit them to suit their style and taste before cutting.

Cricut Design Space comes with some exciting tools and features that can make crafting easy and straightforward. These tools are not so hard to use; thus, to get conversant with them, you need to do some research and consistently apply the knowledge you gain from your research and reading. Expert crafters know all about the essential tools in Cricut Design Space and their role in designing projects. Some of these tools include; the slice tool, weld tool, contour tool, attach tool and flatten tool, etc.

Cricut machines do not function separately -when you purchase them, they come with accessories and tools required to work. Minus the tools and accessories that come in the pack can be purchased separately to boost the machine's functionality and output.

In terms of the Cricut Design Space software and app, some tips and tricks aid project design and production. The software is easy and straightforward to learn and design on, but it still has some related issues and problems like every other applications and software.

When problems arise, solutions naturally proffer, and in terms of Cricut Design Space, there are several ways to address app-related issues to improve user experience and functionality.

The Design Space software is web-based. Thus, some laptop computers are perfectly suited for the purpose. These laptops are suitable for several reasons, including; speed, Space and design, etc. In summary, the best five are; Asus Vivo book F510UA, Dell Inspiron 15 5575, Lenovo Ideapad 330S, Asus Vivobook S410UN, and the Acer Aspire E 15.

Everything on earth needs maintenance, including Cricut machines. These machines are continually cutting out materials of different textures, shapes, and quantity, etc. Thus, they need routine maintenance to boost their productivity levels and increase their life span.

The routine maintenance of these machines does not require a lot, and as a matter of fact, the hardware needs cleaning after cutting out materials. Thus, non-alcoholic baby wipes highly recommend for cleaning material residue on the machines. The cutting mat is another item that requires maintenance from time to time because excessive usage without proper care reduces its stickiness.

In terms of projects, there are so many items that can be designed and cut out from Cricut machines.

Also, these items can sell in the crafts market for profit. Although some people use machines for recreational purposes, many people use it for commercial purposes.

Commercial users of Cricut machines design and cut out items to sell for profit, and the machines have proven to be a blast.

People can sell items made from the Cricut machine to create custom and unique products that cannot found anywhere else.

CRICUT DESIGN SPACE

Master the Software, Create Flawless Professional Designs in Minutes &
Monetize Your Skills

Kimberly Maker smith

TABLE OF CONTENTS

Introduction

Design Space gives you many options for working with images. There are free images in the Cricut library. Upload your own, purchase images individually, or with an Access subscription.

The Cricut Design Space software enables you to obtain fonts and pictures on your devices, which means you can continue developing to do your project with no Internet.

You can make decorations for party and holiday jewelry, fashionable accessories, scrapbooks, wedding invitations, cards, and party, personalized crafts for kids and babies. Cut all the skills of yours with the Cricut Explore as well as Cricut Maker devices. You can publish your photos with the font you desire free of charge and create personalized designs. Cut a range of various materials like thicker materials, fabric, poster board, cardstock, iron-on, vinyl, and paper as leather.

How to use Cricut? You added the ink cartridge on the surface, then put the critical rubber covering across the computer keyboard, then turned on the system, and placed six pieces. Put the paper into the mat along with the order. Press the "load paper" button, and then moisten the mat/paper into the machine.

Press the (so); you can get anything you want to lower, and then press the "lower" button.

If you are a complete newcomer, you ought to grab yourself a record album having to protect sheets (they have been pretty inexpensive, then you never actually have to receive the costly types). A solid-color is commonly perfect, such as black, white royal blue. They have patterned/designed kinds.

You should receive any paper (12x12, 8x8, 6x6, etc.), perhaps not too pricey ($2 4 packs)

You should receive a few pliers to adhere photographs to the newspaper (do not utilize adhesive sticks, so they tend to elevate paper and jumble up it) (£ .99-3.99)

* Get both on the job vases (for instance, ribbon, stickers, brads, and so forth) (Ranges from $.99-4.99)

* Buy a newspaper trimmer: to cut extra borders from cut or photos paper into your particular measurement ($8.99-19.99)

All these are only fundamental matters. Do not allow shoppers to urge you to make the most effective of you personally. It occurs to us scrapbookers. We view something cunning we enjoy but not utilize. It doesn't desire it. Assess your earnings. Use vouchers if you're able to. Assess stores, for example, the.99 penny stores that additionally market rolling sheets for an affordable selling price & it's precisely the same item while the glue you'd find in Michaels for $4 7. Wal-Mart also includes a part of scrapbooking things more economical than neighborhood craft shops (Michaels, Jo-anns, Passion Lobby as well)

Assess e-bay at the same time. There are loads of inexpensive costly what to purchase.

How To/What to perform precisely:

Inch. Choose the document that you wish to use. 2. The photograph that you want to incorporate into the newspaper. 3. With your rolling up glue (or even "dots"), conduct it by way of corners of photos (do not require much only edges & Centre). 4. Put photographs in the paper exactly where you ever wis h to. 5. Set any embellishment you might need to beautify it. 6. Journal whatever great/fun to consider from anything come about or proceeded in this photograph. 7. When you've got any such thing such as brochures, ticket stubs, or anything, and then set them. Make webpages search a more excellent way too.

With Cricut Reducing Machines on The Craft Assignments

Increased numbers of men and women opt to produce their particular scrapbooking substances, invitations, and cards. These home improvement options make it possible for far more customization areas compared to their bulk created options. Maybe not just are they home-made invitations customizable, but they also cost less than shop-purchased choices. Circuit personal reducing machines ensure it is easy for all those who have minimal time and much more encounter to get professional appearing craft tasks everywhere.

Cricut-reducing machines have been available everywhere in art stores and a few malls that contain craft and art segments. Nevertheless, the very best prices finding on the web. For its sporadic do it yourself-er, the entry-level version, using available purchase prices around $100, is a lot more than satisfactory. It is significantly more than able to provide 1000s of diverse contour mixes and needs very little upkeep. More knowledgeable crafters, or even people who manage dwelling organizations that make customized paper goods, can detect that more substantial models tend to be somewhat more in accord by using their requirements.

These devices are mechanized and significantly less challenging to work with than manual paper cutters. Generally, in most instances, they could cut even very major paper inventory, enabling scrapbookers to generate layouts with a wide range of color and textures. Undoubtedly, many Internet sites provide ordinary amateur end users with information to guide you on the steps you should take to make the machine's best use. They can be an essential supply of inspiration and information, revealing how the system uses. When these sites are just the beginning of great vacation destinations, the home Cricut device's best/best feature will be your ability to generate a web page-experiment with new forms and shadow combinations-a kind of harmony Unforgettable.

Make Professional-looking Scrapbooks together with Circuit Personal Reducing Devices.

Even a circuit cutting tool is critical to have for any scrapbooker. These devices make it possible for end-users to lower paper to numerous intriguing shapes, generating personalizing just about every page at a record easy and more enjoyable. Built to become tiny enough to attract you whenever you were traveling, they may require up small space at the house. They will be performed together with you for almost any scrapbooking celebrations you could show up. They are the ideal device for everybody searching to get a user-friendly way of fabricating specific boundaries, inserts, or alternative page vases.

Cricut devices may cause contours that are everywhere from 1" to significantly more than 5" tall. Simple to alter alloy reducing patterns utilize to make smooth contours in craft newspapers. These sorts use to increase custom decoration, joyous contours, or intriguing boundaries that'll reveal every web page's material. Since cardstock of various thicknesses uses, scrapbook authors should remember that milder paper will make the blade punch faster. It follows this. You must continue to keep a tab on this blade's sharpness and exchange them if essential to keep fantastic outcomes.

Even a Cricut system isn't just a little financial commitment. But when considering the price of paying for packs of pre-cut letters and contours, many dedicated scrapbook buffs usually see the system will ultimately cover itself. It may likewise employ other paper-based crafts, like producing customized invitations, gift tags, and cards. Even the Cricut corporation includes a sound standing inside the trading globe, and also, their services and products are all known if you are lasting. Consequently, no substitute ought to be mandatory, despite significant usage.

Even a Cricut private cutting system is an excellent accession to almost any scrapbooker's tool kit.

CHAPTER 1:

Getting To Know Design Space

C ricut Design Space is a complement application that supports creating and cutting with Cricut Explore and other Cricut Machines. With this magnificent software, you are going to be in a position to put up a task from scratch or perhaps pick from a multitude of pictures, fonts, and prepared to print layouts of Make it today projects.

You can begin a task on a cell phone whenever the motivation strikes and choose it right up from your laptop because of the software program synchronizes across all your devices.

You can link the Physical cartridges to your Cricut account through Cricut Design Space. Digital ink cartridges are a collection of images sold only as digital products. So, don't expect to receive them by post!

If you are a complete beginner, you will like the following table. But if you are proficient with the Cricut Machine, you might appreciate and take this guide always with you for any doubt that might occur and use it as a reminder.

How to create an account on www.cricut.com

1. From the top right corner of Cricut's official site screen, select "Design."

2. From the bottom of the screen, a new window will come out, like "Create a Cricut Id."

3. Enter your personal information.

4. Accept the Cricut Terms of Use and "Create a Cricut ID."

5. You will drop to the "Design Space" landing page, and you will see the message displayed "New! Set your machine mode".

With these five steps, your registration completes.

Then, you click on the green button, and you will have to select the machine mode. You will have to choose the machine if the Cricut Maker or Cricut Explore Family for all the others. Then you are ready to create!

Please note that you need to select the Maker up above to the screen's right side to toggle the other machine. As you can, it is straightforward, so go ahead and register your Cricut account!

Design Space on mobile devices

The Cricut Design Space is available for Android, and you can download it from Google Store

And in the Apple Store for your iOS device. When running the Cricut Design Space for the first time, you will be guided from the App Overview to set up the app. It will also help if you need help with the application of your phone.

It will be like having a pc in your hand; there are so many things to do with your Cricut in your phone: you will get an image library, you can work on your new and old projects, you can work with text, editing, ungrouping and isolating letters as well, you have the panel control, projecting canvases, printing, cutting, sending to the mat, mat previewing, purchasing images, digital cartridges, linking physical cartridges.

Design Space Canvas

The Canvas is where you are going to design the projects of yours. On the Canvas, you can add and modify text, images, and projects. Here, you can turn your ideas into reality!

Getting started with your Canvas

Design Panel

On the left side of your Panel, you will find the toolbar with the following options:

New – By clicking on this icon, you can create a new project.

Templates – By clicking this tab, you will visualize your final project in the real-life background.

Projects – By clicking this tab, you can find, select, and modify any project.

Images – You can find several different ideas for free in the Cricut Image Library, including yours.

Text – Click Text to add your favorite words and phrases into your Canvas.

Upload – You can cut and modify all the images you wish, and you can upload format like .jpg, .gif, .png, .bmp, .svg, or .dxf image files without getting charged.

Header

On the top of the screen at your left, you can find the Menu to access features such as Home, Link Cartridges, Settings, Help, Etc. You can find the Sign Out option, too.

Page Title – To help you to keep in mind which page in Design Space you are on. If you click on the Page Title, you can close an open tab.

Project Name- Here to see your project's name, and if you have unsaved projects, it will say Untitled.

My Projects – Click and open one of the projects that you saved.

Save – By clicking on the Save tab, you can save your project, but you need to give a name to it; in this way, you can access your projects across any device because it becomes automatically saved into your account.

Make It – When you are ready to transfer your project to your Cricut Machine after you have prepared your mats, you can click Make it.

Zoom

Zoom In and Zoom Out to have a more or less detailed overview of your projects.

CHAPTER 2:

Project Design

N ow that you are more familiar with Cricut's "design space" layout, it's time to start Project Design.

Machine Reset

If you experience problems with the Cricut cutting machine, such as freezing, a blinking red light, or irregular cuts, your device may need a reset. When troubleshooting, the first thing to try is a machine reset.

How to Reset a Cricut Cutting Machine

To reset the newer Cricut cutting machines such as the Cricut Explore Air 2 and Cricut Maker, you hold down the Power button for 3 seconds.

Or power the machine off, unplug it, leave it for 5 to 10 minutes, and then power it back up again.

If the Cricut Maker's button is flashing red, you need to switch the machine off and clear any debris around the accessory carriage and the blade use. Make sure the surface of the material is clean and then restart the device.

Starting a New Project-the Basics

It will start a new project and work with Shapes, Templates, text, and basic object editing using the Edit menu and Layer menu functions. It will also cover the Prepare and Cutting Screens to cut out a project using Vinyl and Cardstock materials.

Working With Templates, Shapes, and Text

It will work through Exercise 2 to create a new project to develop a greeting card. When you are getting to know Design Space and familiarizing yourself with a new cutting machine, remember it is okay to make mistakes. Even the pros don't always get it right the first time around.

Creating Greeting Card Using a Template

This Exercise Covers the Following Topics, Options, and Functions:

- Templates

- Working with basic shapes

- Working with basic text

- Using the Rotate Function

- Using the Align Function

- Using the Cut Linetype Function

- Using the Draw Linetype Function

- Using Score Lines

- Sizing shapes

- Positioning shapes

- Using the Slice function

- Changing an object's Linetype color

- Selecting parts with point and click or right-click

- Working with Fonts

- Using the Make, it functions

- Navigating the basics of the Prepare screen

- Navigating the basics of the Make it screen

- Working with more than one material at a time

- Selecting Material for the cutting machine

- Changing accessories on the cutting machine

- Changing cutting mats between cuts

- Using the Weeding tool

Project Tools and Accessories:

- Active Design Space session

- PC with a Keyboard and Mouse

- Cricut cutting machine connected

- Red Vinyl

- White Cardstock

- Rose (light pink) Cardstock

- Clear Adhesive Foil Acetate

- Transfer tape

- Cricut Fine Point black pen

- Premium Fine-Point blade

- Stylus Scoring Pen

- StandardGrip cutting mat (green)

- strong grip cutting mat (purple)

- Glue or Glue Gun

- Glitter in gold, silver, and red

- Scraper tool

- Weeding tool

- Pair of scissors

  Builders tape

Directions:

1. Open a new project in Design Space.

2. Select Templates from the Design Panel on the left-hand side.

3. In the top right-hand corner, type Card in the Search box.

4. Select the Blue Card by clicking on it.

5. Design Space will warn you that Templates do not cut or draw; they are merely design purposes.

6. The Cards Template will appear on the Canvas Workspace.

7. The Edit menu will have changed to the Template menu.

8. On the Template menu, leave the Type as Bi-fold Vertical.

9. On the Template menu, change the card's Size to 5.5" x 4.25".

10. Things to note: The Canvas in the Layers Panel now displays the Cards template.

11. Select Shapes from the Design Panel on the left-hand side.

12. Choose the Heart shape.

13. The Heart shape will appear on the Workspace.

14. Click on the Shapes menu to make the menu close.

15. Select the Heart shape and Unlock it.

16. Change the Heart shape size to W = 1.796 and H = 1.7, then Lock the Heart.

17. Create a Duplicate of the Heart shape by selecting it and clicking on Duplicate in the Layers Panel's Top menu.

18. Move the duplicated Heart shape off the original one and out of the way.

19. There should now be two Heart shapes on the Workspace.

20. Change the size of the second Heart shape to W = 1.388 and H =1.314.

21. Position the small Heart shape on the larger Heart shape in the larger body's center.

22. To align the shapes to the center, select both bodies. To do this, click with the mouse just above the enormous Heart. Hold down the right mouse button and drag it. A box outline will appear. Drag the box outline over the shapes and let go.

23. To make sure they select, check that both shapes highlight a darker gray in the Layer Panel.

24. If not, you can select both shapes in the Layer Panel by clicking on the one Heart shape, holding down the CTRL key on the keyboard, and clicking on the second Heart shape.

25. Once the shapes select together, use the drop-down menu under the Align function on the Edit menu. Select Center near the bottom of the drop-down menu.

26. The small Heart shape will now be centered on the larger Heart shape.

27. Select both Heart shapes together once again.

28. You will use the Slice function to cut the middle out of the larger Heart shape.

29. You can use the "Slicing" function for this exercise in two ways:

-Select Slice on the bottom menu bar of the Layers Panel.

-Right-click on the selected Heart shapes and choose Slice in the drop-down menu.

30. You will note that the Layers Panel will have the Slice Results displayed in it once Design Space has finished slicing the object.

31. Deselect the Heart shapes by clicking anywhere on the Canvas Workspace.

32. You will peel away the layers of the slice to leave a hollow Heart shape.

33. Select the small Heart shape in the middle of the larger one.

34. Move the smaller Heart shape out of the larger Heart shape, move it away, and place it on the side of the screen. You will notice there is another small Heart shape leftover in the enormous Heart.

35. You need to remove the second small Heart shape slice the same way you moved the first one. You should have two small heart shapes put to one side of the Workspace.

36. You left with a hollowed-out Heart shape. The Slice function will slice an object into any form using the method you have used for the Heart.

37. Now, you want to create three duplicates of the hollowed-out Heart.

38. Create another Duplicate of the Heart shape by selecting it, right-clicking, and choosing Duplicate from the drop-down menu. Move the second hollow Heart shape out of the way.

39. Create another copy of the hollow Heart shape by selecting the form, clicking on the drop-down menu under Edit on the Edit menu bar, select Copy.

40. Click on a space on the Canvas Workspace, click on the drop-down menu under Edit on the Edit menu bar, and select Paste.

41. Move the second duplicate Heart out of the way.

42. There should now be three hollowed Hearts on the Workspace.

43. Move the first Heart shape to the following position: X = 9.894 and Y = 1.496

44. Rotate the Heart shape you moved into this position by 299.79

45. Move the second Heart shape to the following post: X = 11.433 and Y = 1.497

46. Rotate the Heart shape you moved into this position by 51.03

47. Move the rotated second Heart shape to the following post: X = the tips should join 11.472 and Y = 1.238 — The first and second Hearts.

48. Move the third Heart shape to the following position: X = 11.433 and Y = 2.914

49. Rotate the Heart shape you moved into this position by 149.4

50. Move the rotated third Heart shape to the following post: X = 11.269 and Y = the tips should join 2.802 — The first, second, and third Hearts with a slight gap in the middle, making the shape resemble a Shamrock.

51. Use the most comfortable method to choose three "heart" shapes.

52. Use either the right-click drop-down menu to select Attach or use the Attach option on the Layers Panel's bottom menu. Now, it will ensure that Hearts cut into the pattern of its layout.

53. With all three Hearts selected, use the Color Swatch to Linetype on the Edit menu to change the color of the Hearts to red.

54. Move the Hearts onto the Cards Template. If the template has disappeared off the Workspace, click on the Cards at the bottom of the Layers panel and change the Templates menu's color. The Template will reappear on the Workspace. Change the color back to white for this exercise.

55. Position the Hearts on the top middle of the left-hand side of the Cards Template.

56. They fit perfectly. Now it's time to create the actual card.

57. First, Save the Project and call it Exercise 2Select Shapes from the Design Panel on the left-hand side.

58. Choose the Square shape.

59. The Square shape will appear on the Workspace.

60. Click on the Shapes menu to make the menu close.

61. Select the Square shape and Unlock it.

62. Change the Square shape size to W = 7.514 and H = 4.847.

63. The Square is now a Rectangle shape.

64. Lock the Rectangle shape's proportions.

65. Move the Square to fit perfectly over the Cards Template.

66. On the Cards Template, a dotted line ran down the middle of the Template. This line is known as the Fold line, and Cricut

can trace this line with the Scoring Stylus Pen for the Cricut Explore Air 2 or the Scoring Wheel for the Cricut Maker.

67. To tell the cutting machine to make this line, you will need to include a Score Line on the card.

68. Select the Shapes menu from the Design Panel on the left-hand side.

CHAPTER 3:

Using Images In The Design Space

For starters, the Cricut Design Space library has over 60,000 images available for crafters to use in their crafts. Every update of Cricut brings about newly added images, so really, you are well equipped.

Selecting Your Project

As always, everything begins in your Design Space. Here, select New Project and then click on the Images tool located in your design panel. It will open up the images library to search for any image you want—either scroll or search for a specific image using the search bar.

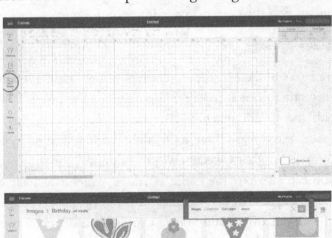

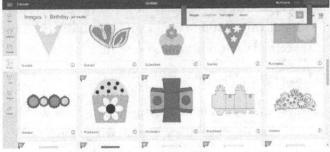

Search Using Category

To make your search a lot easier, you can also search by using the Category function. Search for images using the Free this Week, Most Popular, and Recently Added options.

As you scroll down, you can also see the list of categories that are listed alphabetically. So essentially, you have plenty of different ways and options to find the perfect image for your design.

Search Using Cartridge

Before the latest updates came in, crafters using Cricut Design Space and Cricut Craft Room software will remember the physical cartridge to use with the Cricut machine. But now, you can do this via the Design Space. Easy peasy. Practically, the Cartridge images arrange by theme, so this is another excellent way to find ideas for your project. If needed, you can also buy the entire cartridge, which is usually cheaper than buying a single image. Of course, this option makes sense only if you use the Cricut often, and you've explored all of those images on the Design Space and can't find what you want.

Filter Your Image Search Results

You can always use the Filter option only to show My Images, Uploaded, Free, Cricut Access, or Purchased at any point in your image search process. If you are not familiar with Cricut, you can easily find free images that allow you to test and try to design spaces before delving into buying prints.

About the Images

As you go through your Design Space, you will see some images that have the Cricut Access symbol. It's usually a little green flag icon with an A on it. The images and fonts with this symbol are available only if you have subscribed to the Access subscriptions.

Suppose you are a heavy Cricut user, and you've explored all the images on the Library, or the photos on the Library are not according to your likeness or taste.

The other thing you want to know about the Images library is the little italicized I on the right-hand corner for some images. After clicking it, you will see the image name, number, and the cartridge it belongs to. You can click on the link of the cartridge to see all images contained in the cartridge.

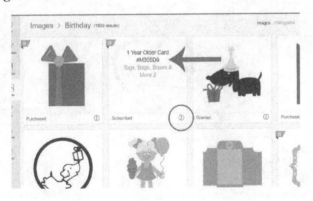

You would also see a printer icon on some of these images. It would mean that they design for ready-to-go use.

Adding Images to Your Project

To select one or more images for your project, just click on each image. All you need to do is choose the photos you want, as many as you would like, and then click on Insert Images to include your Design Space images.

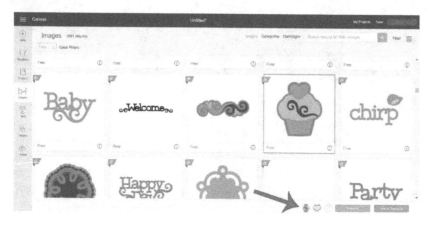

When the images are on your blank canvas on your Design Space, you can resize them or edit them according to how you want them on your design.

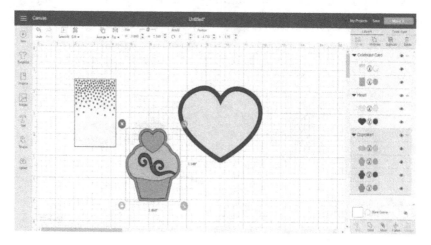

For any image that you select, there will be a box around it. You will see a red X mark in the upper left corner for you to delete the image. You can also rotate the image or even adjust the painting size according to your liking. You can also lock or unlock the image proportions. If you want to delete a photo, you no longer wish to work, just select the image, click the Red X in the left top corner, select the image in the layers panel, and click the Delete button.

Searching and adding images for your project is extremely easy with the Design Space. Before you subscribe to the Access or getting a Cartridge, explore what Cricut has to offer first because with 60,000 over images, you are bound to find something you like to do a beautiful project.

CHAPTER 4:

How to Browse and Search for Cartridges

First, select the 'Images' icon in the design panel to the left of the canvas. A new window should appear with the Image Library. You will select the 'Cartridges' tab at the top of the screen to browse all the available cartridges. There are over 400 cartridges to choose from. You should see the cartridge name and a sample of the image. It will tell you whether the ink cartridges are free, purchased separately, or part of a subscription plan. You don't have to search for a letter.

You can type all or part of the cartridge name in the search bar and click the magnifying glass icon. You then click 'View All Images' to browse your search results.

After making your selection, click the "Insert Picture" button, and they add to the canvas. Once added to the canvas, you can size your image(s) and move them around on the canvas. You can learn where you want to place the picture and how it will look in the final project. If your choice does not include in the free product, it may be more cost-effective to purchase the entire cartridge than to buy a single image.

Searching for Cartridge with Filters

If you want to search for cartridges with filters, you simply click on the 'Cartridge' icon and select the 'Filters' menu in the top right corner of the screen. It will bring up all available filters. There are three ways to search: Alphabetical Order, Cartridge Type, or by specific Cartridge. When you find the filter you want, select 'Apply' to transfer it to your canvas.

How to Purchase Images

- My Cartridges include all free cartridges, linked, purchased, and part of Cricut Access.

- Free – These cartridges use without a subscription or a one-time purchase.

- Cricut Access – These cartridges are accessible with your subscription.

- Purchased – These are the cartridges you have already bought and add to your canvas.

These are your four options for obtaining images. I have included how to access them for free, for those who do not want to spend money on pictures or have their own.

Uploading Your Images

You can upload your own images in the file formats .jpg, .gif, .png, .bmp, .svg, and .dxf.

Design Space will let you upload your images for free, and will convert them into shapes that you can cut.

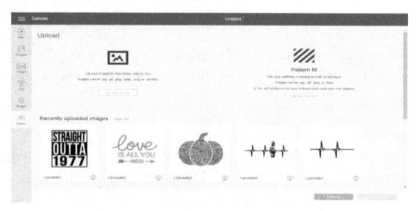

There are two different ways your images are uploaded, depending on the file type.

How to Edit Images Using the Slice Tool

To assist me in editing pictures in the Cricut Design Space, I used the Slice device. I am likely still going to use that method for photos that I have already uploaded to Cricut Design Space. Let me explain how to edit images using the Slice tool.

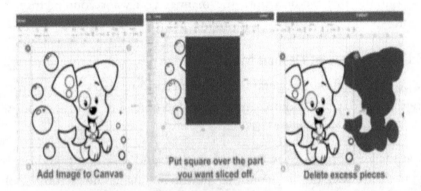

Add Image to Canvas   Put square over the part you want sliced off.   Delete excess pieces.

1. Click on the picture and then click 'Insert Images' to add your attached picture to your Cricut Design Space canvas. You can add multiple images on the canvas at once.

2. Make your picture a lot larger, so you can work on it by pressing and pulling it down a little bit on the right upper corner.

3. I want to get rid of the dog in the image I uploaded. I do not see any canvas-wiping alternative, so I try to use the Slice tool to cut the dog out. In the left-hand toolbox, press 'Shapes,' then press the 'Circle.'

4. Unlock the table by pressing below the square on the left upper panel. Do you see the icon of the lock? Click on that. Now, using the right top corner, you can transfer the square in any form you want. I placed the circle over the portion that I was about to wipe out, the dog.

5. Clicking or highlighting the circle, click and hold the 'Change key' on your keyboard. Click the picture of the bubble with your mouse. It emphasizes both of them.

6. Click the 'Slice' device at the right upper corner with both the circle and the picture outlined.

7. Start taking back your slice's parts. There ought to be three parts. They delete.

8. Continue this method until the manner you want your picture to print.

Editing images in Upload Mode

1. For this method to operate, you will need to upload a picture from your desktop. Click 'Complicated' once you upload it, and the window is where the magic takes place.

2. at the left corner of the top, look at the wand. Click on it and press on the hair. Click on the 'Continue' button and name the picture. Click the 'Save' button.

It is gone, and it has been so simple. Now, let us look after the flesh.

3. I got to upload her again. I am going to operate on erasing the corpse this moment. First, press back on the magic wand to remove the face, arms, body, and any hard-to-reach pieces.

Once you have finished that, take the eraser to wash the remainder of your flesh until it is gone.

Click 'Continue,' identify your picture, and then press 'Save' when the image is to your liking.

Insert both pictures into the surface of your Cricut Design Space. You can bring them back together once you have got them there. I am excited about this process because sometimes, like hair color, I want to change things. I could not change the hair color if I left the picture like it was. But I can do that now.

Create Layers and Separate Objects

There are many features for creating layers. It cannot be effortless if you are accustomed to using the many features your Cricut offers. You will want to practice before cutting your project.

Group/Ungroup: You can group multiple layers, images, or text using the group function. They will move and size together on your design canvas.

The ungroup function will let you move and size: layers, images, or text separately.

Duplicate: To duplicate an object, you copy and paste to create the same object's multiples.

Delete: Deleting will remove your selected object from the canvas. If you do this in error, you can undo this action.

Slice: Slicing will split two overlapping layers.

Weld: When you want to join multiple layers to create one object, use the weld function.

Attach/Detach: When you attach, you hold your objects in position so that items will cut, draw, or score separately from the other layers.

Flatten/Unflatten: When you want to convert an image into a printable image, use the flatten feature. It will merge the layers you selected into a single layer. Unflatten does the opposite, separating layers from one printable image into separate printable layers.

I will explain some imaging tips if you want to upload images from Photoshop and other illustration programs. You can upload your artwork from these programs to Design Space easily.

CHAPTER 5:

Advanced Tips and Tricks

A number of these tips and tips are elementary and therefore are for the complete novice to Cricut machines. But be sure to browse the entire list, because we guarantee that your title will prompt or have a prompt on top!

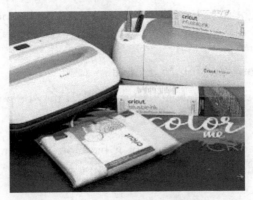

1. Register to Cricut Accessibility

We recommend that you subscribe to Cricut Accessibility. You can pay about $10 per month, and even prove that the monthly fee is a little cheaper.

Cricut access provides you access to 30,000+ images, 1000's of jobs, and more than 370 fonts. If you're likely to use your Cricut a lot, that can save a great deal of cash than if you should get every undertaking and picture separately.

Plus, it is less of a hassle to cover a set rate than stressing about just how much cash you are spending projects! It provides up! Make your money's worth from your Cricut by creating the fantastic Design Space jobs.

2. De-tack Your Cutting Mat

The green cutting mat is somewhat tacky when new! Once you peel off the plastic cap off, then you can put a clean, sterile t-shirt within the mat to be able to prime it to your very first job. It is quite tough to acquire that the cardstock off, even if you have all of the resources in its real stickiness! It's simple to hurt the project while attempting to get off it.

You should not have this issue with the grim light clasp mat, which means you might also buy that for your card and paper jobs rather than de-tacking the mat.

3. Maintain Your Cutting Mat Covers

The cutting mats include a Plastic shield. It may be pulled away and place back easily.

We maintained our pay and put it back on our mat. Once we do with this, it retains the mat tacky and clean longer!

4. Fixing the Cricut Cutting Mat

Occasionally (or even each use), wash the cutting mat with a few baby wipes. The non-alcohol water packs without aroma are the greatest. It can help keep it free from using cardstock and plastic residue out of cutting edge, and the average family dust and lint drifting around.

5. Get the Ideal Tools

It includes a useful instrument, also a scraper, tweezers, and a spatula along with scissors. It's particularly beneficial to have the weeding tool if you're considering cutting adhesive plastic or heat transport vinyl.

6. The Cricut Scoring Stylus

So a number of the card jobs ask that you get the scoring stylus. I didn't purchase one with my equipment initially, and thus needed a debilitating wait for it to arrive until I could go to a better job.

If you bought your system as part of a package, it might possess the scoring stylus contained, so double-check.

7. Start with the Sample Project

Once your device arrives, begin with the sample job.

The research air two and maker include sample stuff for an initial job. Unless you purchase a Cricut Bundle, you get the minimum number of things to do this small thing. However, it is ideal to begin simply!

Instead of attempting to do anything big and elaborate, simply start here to find a sense of how things work software and hardware-wise.

8. Evaluation Cuts

After doing your jobs, it may be sensible to perform a test cut before doing the entire thing. If the blade has been set too low, it will destroy your cutting mat. When it's too large, it might just cut marginally during your vinyl, cardstock, etc. and mess up your materials.

Doing a test trimming may involve asking your system to cut a little circle. Check the atmosphere is correct and make adjustments if needed.

9. Alter Pen Lids after Utilization

It is essential to have the lid it Asp after using it not to dry out. It is too costly to waste. The neat thing about the Design Space jobs is that it frequently prompts one to set the lid back!

10. Aged Cricut Cartridges

Do not forget to hook up any older Cartridges you might have obtained from a former device to your account. It is a relatively straightforward process, as displayed below.

Besides utilizing the right tools to eliminate your cardstock or plastic in the top mat, there's just another trick to getting off it.

Do not peel the item from the mat; otherwise, it will cause curling (or overall deformation), but peel the mat from the cause. Bend the carpet from the card instead of the other way round.

12. Purchase the Deep Cut Blade

There is nothing worse than placing your heart upon a project and then finding you do not have the ideal tools!

The massive cut blade lets one cut deeper leather, card, chipboard, and much more. This blade works with all the Explore Air 2. It's necessary not just to get the edge but the blade casing too.

13. Free SVG documents

You do not only have to use layouts in the design space shop. You may either make your SVG documents or utilize other free SVG documents that may be found all around the World Wide Web.

14. Alternative Pens for Cricut

You may use Cricut pencil adapters (such as that 1) to utilize any pencil with the Maker or Air Conditioning 2. Look at these Cricut Betsy Finds for much more weird and terrific inventions for Cricut!

15. Load Mat Correctly

Ensure that your mat fills before you begin cutting. It ought to slide beneath the rollers. Your device will probably start cutting ahead of the grid's cap onto the mat or perhaps not if it does not load directly.

16. Utilize Free Fonts

You will find so many free font websites for one to begin using!

Browse the internet to get a listing of free fonts for Cricut. You only download the font and install it on your computer, and it'll appear on your Cricut Design Space.

Regrettably, among the most awesome fonts, Samantha Font isn't readily available free of charge; however, check that connection to learn where you can get it to get the very best price!

17. Installing Themes

After installing a ribbon to your computer, you might want to sign up and back to Cricut Design Space before your font will appear there. You may even have to restart your PC to display it (this will not happen if you don't renew my PC).

For more information, read the way to set up fonts from Cricut Design Space.

18. Fixing Blades

Like that which, Cricut blades utilize out. If the reductions are no more so smooth and powerful, it is time for a shift. Other Indicators that you want a brand new knife to comprise:

§ Tearing plastic or card

§ Not cutting all of the ways through (ensure your trimming setting is right too)

You can buy brand new blades Amazon or see that Cricut Blade Guide for much more purchasing choices.

19. Whenever Your Favorite Loses Its Stick

Cleaning your mat is one approach for slightly more life from your cutting mat.

However, if it is beyond this, and you haven't purchased a brand new cutting mat still, you may tape off your plastic or card to maintain it in position.

You do not need to tape over a place that trims down. A few sides must perform the job. Even a moderate tack painters tape is ideal for this undertaking and ought not to harm your cardstock.

20. Cricut's Custom Cut Settings

The Explore Air two includes seven preset Choices on the dial:

§ Paper

§ Vinyl

§ Iron-on

§ Light cardstock

§ Cardstock

§ Bonded fabric

§ Posterboard

If the material you're cutting is not on this listing, there's a customized option that you'll be able to pick on the dialup. Visit Design Space, choose your project, and click 'Make It.' Then you will have the ability to select your content by a drop-down menu.

Or you may produce a new custom made cloth. You may find more info relating to it on in Cricut's site.

21. Various Blades for Different Materials

Some folks swear by using different Blades for cutting every substance.

That is because the variety of stuff will wear otherwise on your blades. Cutting plastic is more straightforward on edge compared to the cutting cards.

Having a committed blade to get vinyl means that it will remain sharp and ready, instead of having an edge to get all that immediately goes dull then lifts your vinyl!

22. Mirror Your Pictures for HTV

If you're cutting heat transfer vinyl together with your Cricut, then you'll have to mirror your design!

Once you choose 'Make It,' there's a choice to mirror your layout (as seen below), and you'll need to pick this choice for every individual mat!

23. Set HTV the Perfect Way Up

To lower heat transport vinyl, you'll have to set your polished vinyl side down on the outer mat.

This way, the carrier sheet is. Beneath, along with the dull plastic side, is at the top.

It is difficult to determine which side the carrier sheet is around, so remember the polished side down, and you are going to be OK!

24. Weeding Boxes

If you're cutting a little or intricate layout, or you're cutting a lot of unique designs on a single sheet of vinyl, so it can help use weeding boxes.

Use the square instrument in the Cricut design room to put a box around your layout and set both components together. Unlock the silhouette at the bottom left corner, manipulate it in a rectangle.

It makes weeding easier than weeding several layouts simultaneously on the one sheet of vinyl. It is even more superficial than attempting to observe where your designs are cutting them out individually using scissors.

25. Don't Forget to Establish the Dial

This suggestion sounds like a no brainer; however, how often have I forgotten how to alter the material placing?!

This straightforward thing to overlook -- Particularly once you have finally completed your layout and wish to get clipping edge! What's interesting is that Circut Design Space can tell you precisely what kind of watch face you want to put in the watch face. If you're going to cut the layout, it is not unforgettable! Save the mistake of cutting on Right through to a cutting mat, or perhaps through your cardstock -- check your dialup!

. And today we have a bonus tip!

26. Keep a Source of Materials

CHAPTER 6:

Working with Text

There is a lot to working with text, and at first glance, it looks dizzying, but really, it's not. Let's start with adding text so you can personalize your projects.

Adding text

You'll want to begin by inserting text onto the design screen. You do that by clicking the "Text Tab" located in the design panel on the left. You should get a blank text box with a text edit field. If you've worked with PDF editing, you'll know how to use this feature. Type your text into the text edit field. It will appear in the edit field. Once you've typed the text you want, you can size it, move it, or rotate it.

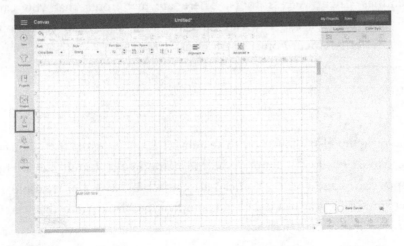

Now you can move, size, and rotate the text by clicking the black area of any letter. The "Bounding Box" appears around your text when it is selected, and you can make an edit in each corner if you prefer to do any editing. You can then click the concrete area of any letter to view the Bounding Box.

By clicking the red "x" in the Bounding Box's top-left corner, you can remove text from the design screen.

If you want to change the width and height while keeping the text proportional, use the closed lock icon at the bottom-left corner.

The Sizing Handle is used to size the text by clicking and holding its icon in the Bounding Box's bottom-right corner. You can drag it in any direction to see the text change.

The Rotation Handle allows you to change the orientation of the text in 45-degree increments.

Text Edit Bar Overview

The Text Edit Bar is located at the top of the canvas. The Font menu allows you to change your text to one of the hundreds of font choices, depending on whether you have Cricut Access. A green "a" symbol identifies Cricut Access fonts. There are also fonts that you can purchase individually. You can filter the font library, so you know System Fonts, Cricut Fonts, or All Fonts.

The program also allows you to search for fonts by name if you know the name. To do so, simply type the name in the search bar in the upper right-hand corner. You can also search by style. For example, if you want a font available in bold, simply type "Bold" into the search bar.

A neat feature is that you can mouse over some sample text to preview the alphabet and numerals for that particular font.

The Style menu allows you to select your style from regular, bold, italic, or bold Italic. Not all fonts have all styles. You may find some that are only available in regular or only regular and bold. You can adjust the size of the font with the "Font Size" menu.

With the "Letter Space" menu, you can adjust the spacing between each letter within the text. The up and down arrows are for increasing or decreasing the amount of space between each letter. You will be able to see how this looks on your canvas. You can adjust paragraph spacing with the Line Space menu.

With the "Alignment" menu, you can align a paragraph to the left, right, centered, or justified.

If you've used MS Word or Apple Pages, you'll notice the toolbars and functions are almost identical. If you regularly use these features on a word processing program, you should have no problem using them with your Cricut Design Space.

For more advanced features, head to the "Advanced" menu. There are many options for you to choose from, such as rotating, resizing, coloring, and deleting.

Text Sizing

You'll be using the Bounding Box around the text to define the image size. You can also size the length and width separately. You can choose three options to size your text with a constant ratio or keeping it proportional.

Size text using the Bounding Box (in a Locked state)

Size text by changing the dimensions in the Edit Panel

Once image sizing is complete, the Edit Panel will show the updated image size.

Size Text by Changing the Dimensions in the Edit Panel

Click on the text, so the Bounding Box appears. Select your image, and you will see the size in the Edit Panel. Next, you need to click in the box next to "Width" or "Length." You will then type in size. It will change your size within the Edit Panel.

Size Text in the Edit Panel

Click on the text to bring up the Bounding Box. Selected your image, and you will see the point size (pt) in the Edit Panel. Click in the point size field and type in the number that you want.

Working with Multiple Lines of Text

Another nice feature of Design Space is that you can add multiple lines of text to your project, allowing to personalize with a favorite quote, the names and dates of birth of your children, your surname and the names of all your family members, the names of your pets, and most anything that will fit in your designated space.

If your child plays a sport, you can add their team name and jersey number and even their stats or a quote related to the sport they're playing.

You can sell personalized beer koozies, calendars, etc. to businesses and make a tidy profit. You can make ornaments for your family and friends as gifts.

With so much you can do with your Cricut, you want to take advantage of all the features, and with the ability to add multiple-line text, it opens a whole new world whether you Cricut for profit or yourself.

What's even more fun is that you can edit the text using a single font style or multiple styles.

Here's an example:

Merry Christmas

From

Susan and Stephen

So, you see how we can change the font on our example. Of course, you can make yours better looking than my example. I just wanted to give you an idea of how you can switch it up.

Here's how:

To edit the text using a single text box and only one font style, you must first go to the "Add Text" box to bring it to your screen. Your text should appear as a single image in the Layers panel.

By default, the text will align to the left, just as with any word processing program. You can realign the text by clicking on the Edit tab, which will open your Edit panel. Choose the alignment option that you prefer.

Your text will appear on the Mat Preview and should show as you arranged it.

First, you need to click the add text icon to add a text box to your screen.

Type your first line and each subsequent line. Each text box should appear in the Layers Panel.

You can arrange them here if you'd like.

Next, open the text edit bar and select your font and make all your adjustments. You can adjust the alignment and the size or style. If you want to move your letters, you can also do so now using the letter-spacing option.

While your text is in the Layers Panel, it is attached, and you'll no longer be able to edit.

If you are ready to cut, you can begin the process by clicking the "Make It" icon. Be sure you have everything as you want it. Your text should be as you arranged it on the mat and cut in the same manner.

Writing on Your Project

Design Space has fonts designed to be drawn with a pen. They will look like handwriting, and it provides a friendly, homemade look to your finished product.

These script-style fonts find by searching "writing" in the font search bar. You'll be able to pick a style and color from the drop-down menu. Your new font will display.

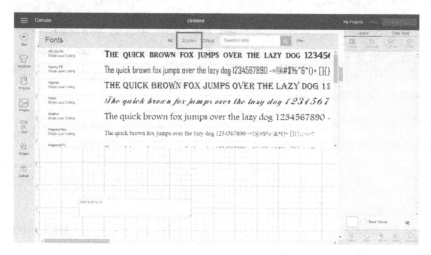

Using the attached feature, you need to select which layer the text should write on. When your images have been selected, click "Attach." At this point, your text should be converted to an image and written on the layer it's attached to. You can now click the "Make It" icon to go to your preview screen.

Your images should appear on the preview screen in the same manner as you have arranged on your project.

When you begin the cutting process, you will need to insert your pen.

CHAPTER 7:

Working with Color

Images are divided and placed according to color on the mats, layers of the same paint place on the same mats.

Color Sync Panel

You are using the Sync panel to combine a project's colors to reduce the amount of different necessary materials. You can synchronize colors by dragging and dropping an image layer onto another layer in the color you want to match.

Example
The term "Fairy" is red before synchronizing color, and the wing is magenta.

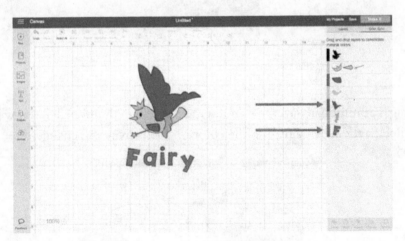

Change it to the color of the word "Fairy Tale" by dragging the first letter "F" of the text, which locates to the "Sync Panel" wing

Color Syncing Images

Within your project, the Sync Panel lets you combine colors to reduce the number of different materials required and the number of mats to cut.

Tip: Photos are isolated and color-based on the mats. Layers of the same color are put on the same mat. If you have layers that even have slightly different colors, they're putting on other mats.

Changing a single layer color individually

Step 1

Press the sync tab to open panel.

Step 2

Drag a thumbnail layer to another color. The thumbnail layer will switch to the new paint, and the color on the canvas will change.

Tip:

Click the Undo button in the top menu to go back to a move to reverse your color changes. You can use Undo more than once.

Changing a Color Row to a Different Color

tep 1

Press the Sync Tab.

Step 2

Press on the left side of the row color bar and hold when moving the color bar to a different color. The row will be highlighted in gray to indicate that it chooses. All tiles on that row will switch to the new paint, and you can see the changes on the canvas. Changing color for cutting images. By choosing colors for each image layer, you can imagine the final product and determine its layout on the cutting mat. Images are separated and placed according to paint on the mats, layers with the same color place on the same mats.

There are three ways to pick new colors for the cut and print layers using the Layer Attributes Panel.

1. Basic color swatches

2. Custom color picker

3. Hex values

The Sync panel can also use to reduce the number of cutting mats used in a project.

Tip: Inside a clustered image, you can change colors of individual layers without unbundling the image.

Option 1

Basic Color Swatches

Use one of the 30 standard colors available in the primary color swatches to choose a color.

Step 1

Press the layer thumbnail.

The primary color swatches find on the Layer Attributes Board.

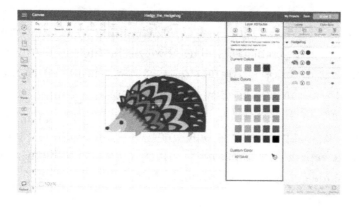

Step 2

Tap on one of the standard color swatches to choose a color. The new color mirrors in the Layers Panel and the Canvas.

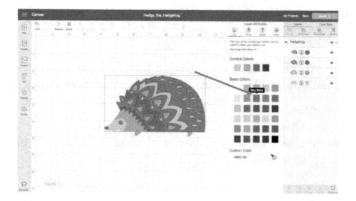

Tap outside the Attributes Layer Panel to close.

Option 2

Custom Color Picker

If you use the custom color picker, you have several more color choices for your designs.

Step 1

Press the layer thumbnail.

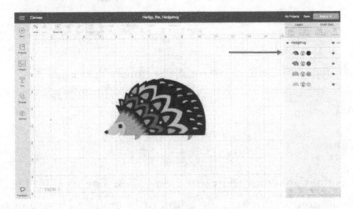

You can find a custom color picker on the "Layer Property Panel." Click the "Custom Color Picker" eyedropper icon light up.

Step 2

To change the color over the spectrum, move the vertical slider up or down. The new color is mirrored in the Layers Panel and on the Canvas.

Tip:

Consider selecting the primary color similar to your background color if you are trying to suit a particular shade of the background. It will put you in the estimated range of colors. The custom color picker can then uses to refine the color match further.

Step 3

Select a particular color in the color family by shifting the circle inside the square color region.

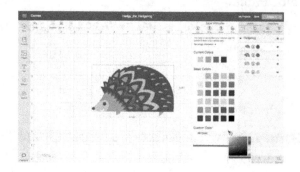

Clicking outside of the Layer Attributes Panel will close it.

Option 3

Hex Values

The hex values are color representation codes. The six-digit Hex value can include numbers, letters, or a mix of both. The Hex values allow you to select a specific color for your images in the custom color picker.

Step 1:

Press the layer thumbnail

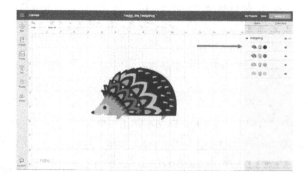

The Layer Attributes Panel shows the Hex Value Field, in which you can enter the hex code.

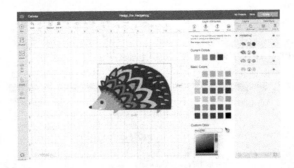

Step 2.

The layer properties panel displays a hexadecimal value field where you can enter a hexadecimal code.

Tip:

Open the Color Sync panel once the paint has been added to one layer and transfer additional layers to that color.

Change the color of images with printed line styles

The color on the Canvas represents the color, which will be printed for Print then Cut pictures. Before flattening the picture, all changes make to the layer's color; when you want to change a flattened image's color, you must flatten it first.

There are three ways to select new colors for images with a form Print line.

1. Basic Colors scheme

2. Custom Color picker

3. Hex values

Use one of the 30 Basic Colors provided in the Simple Colors swatches to quickly pick a picture layer color with a Print line style.

Step 1

Press the layer thumbnail.

Step 2

Click on one of the Simple Colors swatches to choose a color. Click outside to close the Layer Attributes Panel.

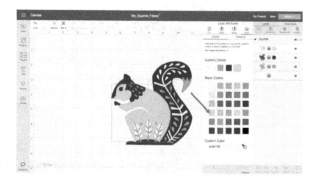

Tip:

You will flatten the image into one layer for printing once you finish changing the colors. Click on the Layers Panel to flatten.

CHAPTER 8:

How to Make Multiple-Layer Vinyl

What you'll need:

- A cutting machine

- Craftables Permanent Adhesive-Backed Vinyl

- Weeding devices

- Squeegee

Layering vinyl is simple; it likewise takes your tasks to the following level and truly makes it pop. The vinyl layering technique is somewhat not the same as different crafters; anyway, it will work for you and work extraordinary for you.

My vinyl cutting programming is the Cricut Explore Air. The initial step to layering vinyl is to transfer a picture with numerous hues and layers into Cricut Design. When your image transfers, the time has come to choose a picture type. If you have a mind-boggling picture and you pick necessary, you will see that the shading change and the subtleties may get lost.

When your picture transfers, it's an ideal opportunity to think to layer. When layering vinyl, generally think base up. You need to consider the basest layer of your picture. You need the blue vinyl to be underneath the white. In this way, you are going to proceed with the print similarly for what it's worth.

Circuit Design gives you an alternative of a Print and Cut picture or only a cut. For vinyl, you need to pick the cut alternative on the right.

It isn't required for you to name your view. Anyway, a tip to use is to document the shading vinyl image you will remove it off. It can help you input vinyl records.

The picture has two layers-a naval force blue base and a dark top on to the top layer. Utilizing the enchantment wand apparatus, you will erase all the blue on my image. It will abandon the skinnier dark letter that you will lay over my blue vinyl. The enchantment wand device truly is enchantment and makes life much simpler when you isolate your hues. Ensure you get all the blue, even the ones within your letter circles.

When you cut the vinyl and arrange it through the shade, weed it to evacuate all the rich vinyl.

Recall that you are going to think in reverse when applying vinyl. Start with the base and work up. The base layer of my Welcome is naval force blue. Since you utilized clear transfer tape, you are virtually ready to see where you set the vinyl on our item.

Utilizing a ruler, you can put the second piece of your welcome precisely where you needed it. You expect to ensure that your crab would fit superbly between the two arrangements of letters. Guarantee your vinyl is on easily and reliable. You will utilize Clear Vinyl Transfer

Tape to put vinyl on top of the vinyl. The other thing you need is for your Clear Vinyl Transfer Tape to draw up your current vinyl.

It is the ideal opportunity for the fun part. You will directly add the second layer to your vinyl. It requires a decent eye and an enduring hand. Thank heavens for Clear Vinyl Transfer Tape, since you certainly need to perceive what you are doing in this progression. You will put the second layer on vinyl directly over the leading segment of vinyl. Take as much time as is needed because it is practically challenging to draw up once it is down. Afterward, not exclusively will your top layer be destroyed yet additional your base.

Those letters look so tremendous and mind-boggling. Presently for the last advance. However, the potential outcomes are unfathomable. You could choose to utilize a pineapple, a blossom, or even the diagram of your state.

The crab is your third and vinyl layer of your project.

You currently have to possess a personalized layered bloom grower. Also, it looks such a significant amount of superior to one shading. Be imaginative with investigating vinyl layering!

Have you, at any point, been threatened by a design that you need to cut in vinyl? However, it has a lot of layers? It's a little nerve-wracking attempting to assemble every one of the pieces and layer vinyl. What's more, the odds of having it line up on each layer entirely are relatively thin.

Go ahead and discover lots of adorable SVG on Etsy, and you truly needed to put it on a sparkle tumbler for my niece. It has eight, tally them, eight hues. Rearranged it down to a couple of less and get the chance to work, making sense of the ideal approach to layer them.

Step by step instructions to Layer Vinyl Using Registration Marks

Select Image, Resize and Ungroup

In this advanced guide, while transferring an SVG record, the idea is equivalent to design from Cricut Design Space.

When the design brings onto the canvas, select it, and resize it to whatever size you require for your undertaking. After determining the size, you need to go to the layer board and select "Ungroup." Ungrouping allows us to move each layer independently instead of the entire design.

Adding a Shape as a Registration Mark

Embed a shape. You can utilize a square, yet have seen it finished with stars and triangles also. After that, add the court and snap the 'open' so you can control the picture into a square shape. When you have the rectangular shape the size you need it, copy it.

Line every square shape up under the first picture. These will be your enlistment denotes that will be on each layer to keep the design arranged.

Copy Original Image and Registration Marks

After the first picture has the enrolment stamps set up underneath it, select everything, and copy it. You will do this for each shading you have. On the off chance that you have six hues, you will copy multiple times at that point.

Erase Layers Leaving A Single Color

For each picture, you copied, erase each layer, each one, in turn, leaving just a solitary shading. If you didn't have light pink for the inward ears, so chose not to cut that part. The various layers find underneath.

Append each Set of Images

Select each layer picture (not the main image), and it's comparing enlistment stamps and afterward select 'append.' This will keep the photo and the enrolment checks set up when you go to cut. Something else, Design Space will attempt to spare you materials by setting them as near one another as would be prudent. That won't support us.

You will see that when you select 'append,' the enrolment imprints change to the shade of your layer.

Shroud Main Image and Make It.

Before the layers slice, you have to shroud the primary picture. Else it will attempt to cut every one of its pieces also. Select the main image and its enrolment marks. Select 'gathering' and after that, in the layers board, click on the little eyeball. It should make that main picture covered up, and it would not cut.

Select 'Make It' to send the task to the tangle. Each shading individually tangles. Cut each shading, and after that, weed the picture.

SIDE NOTE: If you lean toward utilizing scraps and not stacking and reloading with each shading after you conceal the central figure, select the majority of the images and the select 'join.'

They will all turn dark, so you should recall what shading you needed for each piece. When it proceeds to the cutting mat, it will all be on one tangle. You can put every one of your shading scraps where the knot demonstrates they will cut.

Weed Vinyl Pieces and Apply Transfer Tape

Weed each layer leaving just the design and the enrolment marks.

Make sure you connected the exchange tape to the purple bow first since it is most distant to the side front of the design.

Add or include each layer to the Transfer Tape from the Top Layer Down

The main issue that needs to emphasize when traversing the layers is the square. For whatever length of time that they organize, everything else will be as well. I want to state it's so natural, yet it indeed wasn't to me. It helped colossally, yet realizes you may not arrange every square shape merely flawless. It's alright. Modify and continue onward.

In the photograph beneath, you can see that instead of expelling the whole paper sponsorship of the vinyl and afterward layering, just collapsed back the paper backing where just the square shapes appeared. That may enable you to arrange the square shapes all the more precisely. Whichever route works for you is okay. There's no 'right' or 'wrong' way.

Alright, readers, that is the bit by bit of how to layer vinyl utilizing enlistment marks. Presently snatch some vinyl and demonstrate to me what you make!

Cricut EasyPress: Layering method

Make a kaleidoscopic and finished perfect work of art with an iron-on strategy called layering.

How to layer iron-on design

1. Many Cricut images are designed with different layers that fit together to frame a composite picture. Design and cut your layered picture on your Cricut machine.

2. Plugin and control on your Cricut EasyPress.

3. Set the Cricut EasyPress temperature and clock to the setting that suggests for your base material. Utilize this Interactive Quick Reference Guide to locate the correct settings.

Firm pressure means utilizing two hands and free bodyweight. It's ideal to use a table at midriff stature for straightforwardness in applying muscular weight.

The cement won't be totally "set" as of now, yet as you apply more warmth with each extra layer, the glue for all layers will appropriately set.

4. Repeat stages 5 and 6 for all the remaining layers except for the top layer.

Before applying warmth to each new layer, ensure that the uncovered iron-on movie from each past layer is secured by a liner or other defensive hindrance to shield it from direct contact with the warmth plate. "Uncovered iron in movie form" alludes to the iron-on regions that won't be secured by the new layer of iron-on film.

5. Top Layer: when including the top layer of your picture, apply healthy weight with the Cricut EasyPress for 15 seconds.

6. Flip your base material over and apply warmth and healthy weight for 10-15 seconds.

Note: If utilizing Foil Iron-On for the top layer, apply warmth using healthy weight for 10 seconds.

What sorts of iron-on would be able to utilize while layering?

All Cricut Iron-On items utilize in layered activities. Pursue the alerts and proposals underneath for the best experience layering with iron-on.

CHAPTER 9:

How To Add Shadows To Letters

Decorative shadows can add such beauty to a product. Have you ever wondered how it was doing?

For those using programs such as Photoshop, it can be simple, but not everyone has an illustration program.

Fortunately, it does with Cricut Design Space and a smartphone app called Phonto, available on the Apple Store.

Photo is a free, easy-to-use app with over 400 fonts and interchangeable text sizes. You can also add your fonts if you'd like.

Don't let the "free" part scare you into thinking there won't be much you can do with it. On the contrary, it has impressive features, and you can do many things with it, so it is worth taking up a small amount of space on the device.

There is a video tutorial that is worth watching. It will guide you through all the functions. To begin, open Phonto and click the camera at the bottom of the screen. You'll see options, and you'll want to select "plain image."

You will see the white square on the top right-hand corner, and it is to a black court. It is hard to see. Select the white square and click the "upload icon" in the top right-hand corner of your screen.

You need to tap on the white square and then tap "add text." Write your text and click done once you've added what you want it to say.

Click on "style." Three options will appear text, stroke, and background.

A gray highlighted area will appear, and this is where you'll start.

This part might make you nervous because you will change the text color to white in the color box. Your text will turn white, and you might not be able to see it. Don't panic! It's still there.

Now it's time to add the shadow. To do this, you need to select the "Stroke" box. It highlights in gray. You want to change the stroke to black.

Scroll to the bottom of the screen until you see the "Width" slider and then slide it up until you get the desired shadow. Select the shadow you want and click "done."

Your shadow saves, so now it's time to save the text inside of the shadow.

Click on your letters and select "style" again. This time, go to stroke. Pull the width slider back down to remove the shadow.

After you remove the shadow, select "text" again and turn your text back to black, select "done," and then select the "upload icon" to save your image.

You now have two images, and you need to transfer them from your phone to your computer or transfer to the Cricut app. Open Cricut Design Space and upload your pictures to a new project.

Cricut advises the following: "Make sure you're only deleting the white background around the shadow and not the inner white part. For the word, you'll delete the white background and all the inner parts of the letters just like normal." Itis important, as you don't want to delete the inner white part. If you do it by accident, you should restore it.

With your new project started, you'll want to make any adjustments, such as resizing or rearranging. You can select your colors, and you're ready to cut. Your letter shadows as you determined, and your finished project should be excellent.

The Photo app makes shadowing very simple to do on your phone, and you shouldn't have any instability when transferring to your computer or the Cricut app.

You can now make beautiful shadowed letters, just like the Cricut pros make!

Mirroring Images for Iron-on

You'll want to avoid the mistake of having your mirrored image is wrong when you go to iron it on, so I'll explain how to prevent this.

Iron-on material is fun to work with, and you can do so many projects with it. Nothing is more frustrating than ironing a design onto fabric and having it reversed. For some systems, you might think, "Hey, this doesn't look so bad" because the image does look good either way, but for letters, there's only one way to go!

So, let's begin to design our iron-on images. You'll create it the way you create your other photos, and when finished, double-check the direction of the image and click the "Make It" icon in the top-right of the design screen.

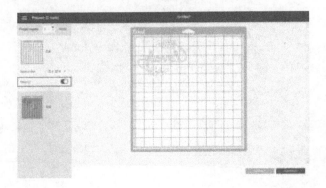

Select the mat you will use, check the "Mirror Image" box, and make sure it's for iron-on. After selecting the mirroring option, the image will reflect the changes on the "mat preview." If you set the Smart Set dial to be ironable, but the photos do not mirror Mat Mat Preview, you will receive an alert on the cut screen. If you want to reflect the images, go back to the Mat Preview pane, and check "Mirror." You can now continue, and your image will reproduce correctly.

CHAPTER 10:

Tips for Using Images From An Art Program

Sign in to Design Space. On the homepage, you can navigate directly to the design canvas by clicking the main menu (the three lines to the word "Home"), and then select "Canvas."

Or click the green New Project button at the top left corner of your screen or the New Project + icon. It will pull up the canvas.

On the left side of the screen, you will see the following options:

New

Templates

Projects

Images

Text

Shapes

Upload

When you want to use the saved project, click the "My Projects" button from the canvas and scroll until you find the project you wish to.

If you click Images, you'll see previews of available images. These are called tiles. The ones with a green A mean they are part of the Access Subscription. You can select from these images as long as your subscription to Access is active.

When you purchase an image, it will say Purchased in the bottom left of the tile. You can continue to use that image, whether you subscribe or not, you now own it. Clicking on the square grids in the upper right corner to Filter lets you see a few image tiles in larger sizes or to see more, smaller images on your screen all at once. It's easy to search for specific categories of images in the search box like cats or types of projects such as cards. When you find the image or images you want to use, just click on them. At the bottom right, you'll see a green Insert Images button. Click on that to pull the images onto the Design Space canvas.

You'll see options across the top of your screen. You'll not see the options across the top until you've clicked on an image and bring it into the canvas.

These options include:

Select All: Puts a blue box around every image on the canvas.

Edit: This allows you to cut or copy your images.

Align: Rearranges multiple images when they are selected.

Arrange: When one image is selected, its layers reorder.

Size: You can resize images by clicking and dragging it to make it bigger or smaller. Or you can use the size boxes to type the exact size you want the image to be or use the arrows to adjust the size. There is a box for height and width.

Flip: This allows you to flip your image horizontally or vertically. It is essential to create projects that need to be reversed or flipped like some vinyl projects.

Rotate: You can type in a number to turn your images, such as 90 degrees or 45 degrees.

Position: Use the arrows to move the image in small increments or type where the image repositions.

Layers and Colors

On the right side of the screen, you will see the "Layers" panel, which use to divide the image into separate layers. If your image makes up of many layers, you can choose to Ungroup your image. It gives you the option to use each layer individually to change the color or function like changing the layer attribute (Line Type icon) from a cut to a write.

Color Sync: Takes the guesswork out of matching the color of one layer to another.

Duplicate: If you want to make an exact copy of your image, just click this icon.

A Blank Canvas square, when clicked, will change the color of the canvas to whatever color chose.

Below that you have the following options:

Slice: Use this to separate two parts of an image.

Weld: This allows you to connect images or letters, so they are not cut apart.

Attach: This has two functions. Use it to fasten a score or write a line to an image. They are attaching items on the canvas to maintain their position on the mat.

Flatten: Use this to turn a multi-layered image into one layer for printing.

Contour: With this function, you can remove unwanted cut lines.

On the toolbar to the left-clicking, the Shape icon to add a shape to the canvas

It is also where you select a scoreline to inserts into an image.

Note: If you're working in Design Space and you accidentally delete something or make any other action and then say, Oh no! I didn't mean to do that. Never fear. In the upper left corner of the screen is a curly arrow called the "undo" icon. Click on it, and your last action undo. Keep clicking, and it will keep undoing your previous steps. If you go one too far, then click the Redo icon to go forward.

Uploading Images

You can now upload your images into Design Space. Users have been asking for a long time, so it's a significant improvement to the software.

These are the file types that can upload jpg, bmp, png, gif, svg, and dxf. Images are either Basic or Vector.

Necessary images upload in a single layer. You can edit the image to some extent during the upload process. These images include the following types of files: jpg, BMP, png, and gif

Vector images will upload as they were designed and separate into layers, making them easy to manipulate. These include files in the .svg, and .dxf format.

On the left sidebar, click Upload, and then click Browse. It will open the file for you to select the image you want. There's also the option to drag and drop to import the file. If you're going to use this option, it's a good idea to save the files in a folder on the desktop, so they're easy to find.

To upload a Basic image, select the file and click Open. Click Preview to show the image with your cut lines. If it's not correct or sees a gray box instead of the image, click Hide Preview and continue to work with the idea; remove the background until it appears as you want it.

Now name the image and save it. You can save as a Print and Cut image, which will keep the colors and patterns. Or you can save as a Cut image, which will save only the outline of the cut path. Click Save when you're ready. Remember to use descriptive names when you save images to make them easier to locate.

When you return to the upload screen, the image will appear in the Upload Images Library shown on the screen's bottom. To place it in your project, select the image by clicking on it. Add it to the canvas by clicking Insert Images.

If you've selected a Vector image, you take through a simple process, just follow the on-screen instructions.

Save the image using tags and a descriptive name.

Return to the Upload screen, and your new Vector image will show up in the library. Select an image by clicking and then click "Insert Image"; it adds to your design canvas.

One of the most popular things to do is convert a cut image to a printable image using the Layers Panel on the right to change the scissor icon or Line Type to the print icon.

You can change multiple layers to print together by using the Flatten tool.

Note: Some images you upload will not work as well as others. Design Space has to trace the uploaded image to map out or define the outline to print or cut the designated area. To make the process easier, look for images with high contrast between dark and light colors, an image with well-defined lines, and not many intricate details that will work best.

The best format to save files

When saving their files for uploading into Design Space, the users I've talked to all prefer the SVG format. They find it easier to work with since it's already layered. Print and Cut projects work well with a PNG since it has a transparent background, which requires less editing.

You might want to try working with several formats and see which you prefer for specific projects since they edit.

Should you save as a Print and Cut or only a Cut file?

I prefer to save images I upload as a Print and Cut. If I choose to cut the file, I can change the function to Cut only in Design Space. However, after saving the image as a cut file, I will not recover all the lost color details. So if you're not sure how you'll use the file in the future, always save as a Print and Cut file.

Tagging Your Files

You have an option to tag your files and give them a name when you save them. Use these tags to identify the type of project, the kind of image in the file, the designer's name, or any other information you might find useful when searching the file in the future. File sharing do's and don'ts

When you save your projects, you have the option to share them with the public. It means other Design Space users can see and use the scheme.

If you want to make the project private, make sure that the "Public" box is check when saving.

If the images are no longer available, you will not save the project as a public file or upload your photos to create the design.

Some files will note whether they are allowed for commercial use. It means you may be able to use the file for personal use, but you're not allowed to use the image for a project you want to sell.

Shared files alter. Rename it and Save As to keep the changes.

CHAPTER 11:

Slice, Flatten, Weld, Attach, and Contour Info-Graphic Slice

The slice tool is ideal for cutting out distinct forms, text, and other elements. When I chose both shapes and clicked on slice, you will see that all the original files cut up; to show you what the final result was, I pasted the "slice result" and then divided all the parts from slicing.

Weld

The welding tool combines two or more forms in one. When I have clicked on Weld and chosen both shapes, you can see I formed a new body. The back layer determines the color, so the original condition is pink in color.

Attach

Attach operates like grouping layers, but firm. When I have chosen both forms and clicked on attach, you will see the layers just changed color. However, the conditions are linked, and this attachment will stay in location after I send my project to be cut.

Flatten

This tool supports the Print and then Cut Fill environment; if you alter the fill from no fill to print, it only applies to one layer. However, what if you want to do various forms at the moment?

When your design finishes, pick the layers you want to print together as a whole, then click on flatten. When completing your plan, select the layers you want to publish together as a whole, then click on flatten.

In this case, the element will become a **printed design** and then cut, **so** it no longer shows the black edge that the blade passes.

Contour

The Contour tool enables you to conceal unwanted parts of a design and only be allowed if a model or shape has elements left out.

For this instance, I combined the initial design in one form with the weld tool; then, I wrote the term contour and cut it against the new way, using the Contour tool to conceal the two letters O's inner circle's letter R's inner part.

Color Sync

Color Sync is the last panel choice.

Every color on your canvas is a different material color. If your structure has various colors of yellows or blues, do you need them? If you only need one yellow shade, like this instance. Just click and drag the tone to get rid of and drop it on the one you want to maintain.

Cricut Design Space Canvas Area

Canvas Area

There you see all your designs and elements. It's intuitive and user-friendly.

a. Canvas Grid and measurements

A grid separates the canvas; this is good because every little square you see on the grid helps visualize the cutting mat. Ultimately, this helps maximize your room. You can alter the readings from cm to inches by clicking the top panel toggle and selecting Settings. A window will open with all choices.

Design Space Settings

Turning off-grid and turning off-grid and

b. Selection whenever you select one or more layers, the choice is blue and can be modified from all four angles.

The "red" delete the layers. The upper right-hand corner allows you to rotate the picture (if you need a particular angle, I suggest using the editing menu tool). The selection's reduced right button, "the tiny lock," keeps size proportional when increasing or decreasing your layer size. By clicking, you can now have distinct proportions.

c. Last but not least, zoom in and out. If you want to see in a smaller or larger scale without modifying the original size of your designs, then you can do it by pressing"+ and-" signs on the canvas' lower-left corner. That's it— you're no longer a beginner.

CHAPTER 12:

New Features For Design Space

Save the project in Cricut Design Space Desktop

I've lost many last minutes learning my exercise, along these lines, it would be ideal if you spare as you go. Note: I save changes on my venture like clockwork or somewhere in the vicinity.

When you start using the new shiny canvas, the "Save" option turns gray, but it will begin as soon as the picture includes.

To spare your project, place the main thing (picture, content, shapes, and so on.) you will use on your canvas.

In any case, if you utilize your pictures, "The general population" alternative won't show up. Try not to stress; however, you can even now share your manifestations from the "My projects" window that will I show you.

Note: When you share ventures, you should acknowledge Cricut's Term and Conditions; so ensure you concur with them. You can read their terms here.

In the wake of naming your project, click on Save. A blue standard will show up over the window, educating you that your project saves.

Now, you can begin changing your plan by including content, evolving colors. Right now, I turned the shade of the record.

Not all that much.

Make sure to spare your venture each three to five minutes; trust me, you would prefer not to sit around if the program crashes.

If you need to make another undertaking, ensure your venture saves.

Open a project in Cricut Design Space Desktop

To open a task you've just made, you have to clean and fresh out of the box new canvas.

Right now, there's not a path for you to consolidate ventures. How about we trust Cricut includes this usefulness soon.

You can discover your plans in two distinct manners.

The first and quickest one is tapping on the "My Projects" alternate route connect situated on the window's right-hand corner.

This method is to click on the "Project" option on the left panel of the canvas, then go to the drop-down menu and select "My Project" (check the various decisions of the drop-down menu to find the ready cut project)

As should be evident on the screen capture directly over, the venture I made is in that spot. The request for the activities it depends on the last spared date.

From the "My Projects" see, you can alter, erase, modify, and cut your as of now made ventures.

There are better places you can tap on a specific venture; on the off chance that you click on the "Offer" choice, you execute to include a portrayal, photographs, and so on. Also, there is little chance of connecting the three DABs (bottom right corner of each item); you can choose to delete it.

If you need to alter your task or remove it right, you should tap on the included picture of your structure.

After clicking, a little window will open, and you'll have the option to share and observe the entirety of the data about the undertaking, including the textual styles, shapes, and pictures you utilized.

By the by, if you need to alter the presence of your plan, click on modify.

Presently how about we perceive how to alter your task!

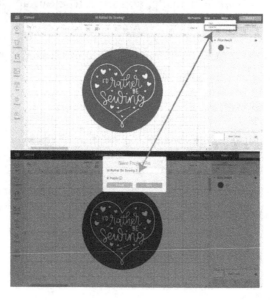

At the point when you click on "Save As," you will be incensed to change the name of your unique undertaking; right now, just included a "two" to the title.

Simple, isn't that so?

Presently, if you choose to use either structure once more, return to your ventures and see that any of them are accessible.

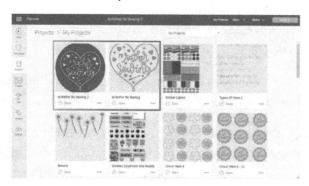

Save a Project in Cricut Design Space App

As a rule, when you first open the application, the view will be set to "Home." To begin dealing with another undertaking, click on the enormous blue square with the sign, or tap on "Canvas."

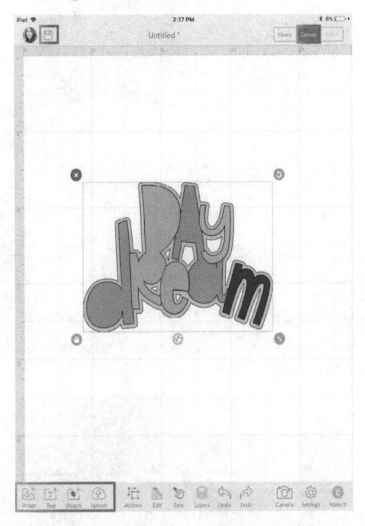

After putting a thing, tap on the Save symbol situated on the upper-left corner of the application, and pick the option "Save."

Pick "Save to the Cloud" on the off chance that you need to get to your projects from your PC, and you have a stable Internet

Connection. Pick "Save to Ipad/iPhone" if you don't have dependable Internet and like having the option to work without disconnected.

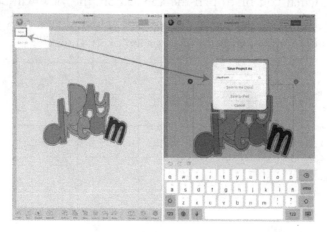

While picking "Save to Ipad," you won't have the option to see those ventures on your PC. In any case, you'll have the opportunity to utilize that project over and over without the Internet. I generally pick "Save to the cloud" since I like approaching my activities on my PC. However, choose whatever meets your requirements the best. Save changes as you chip away at your plan in such a case that the application crashes, you will lose the entirety of your challenging work.

An interesting point is how to begin another undertaking when you have something on your canvas.

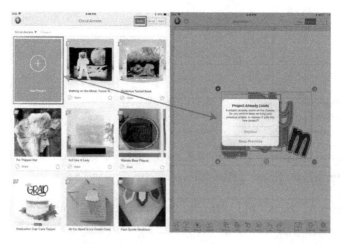

If you, despite everything, have unsaved changes, the application will bring a warning. Select Previews and spare the entirety of the progressions and rehash a similar procedure to dispose of any sign.

Try not to trifle with this notice; if you don't spare, your project lasts.

Open a Project in Cricut Design Space App

First, to open a made task, ensure your canvas is spotless (no different undertakings, content, structure, or shapes) and go to the "Home" perspective.

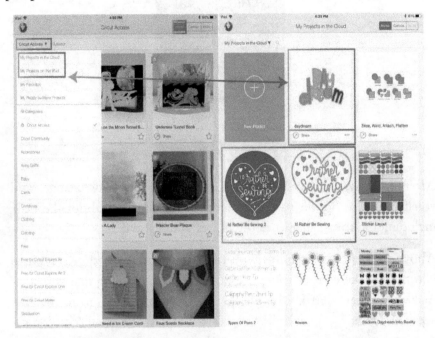

From the "Family/My Projects in the Cloud" view, you can do two or three things on each task.

If you tap on the "Offer" choice, you provoke to include a depiction, photographs, and so forth of your projects.

Furthermore, if you click on the three specks (base right of each task), you will have the option to erase it.

If you need to redo your task or remove it right, you should tap on your structure's included picture.

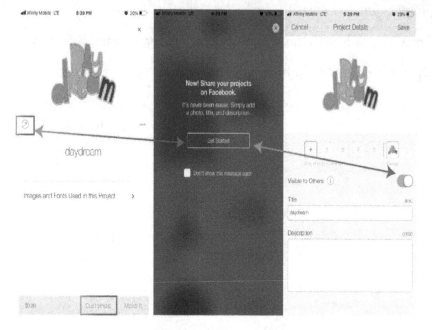

After drawing, the perspective on your telephone will change, and you'll have the option to see the entirety of the data about the task, including the fonts, shapes, and pictures you utilized.

Above all, from this window, you can tweak your extend or send it to cut; this "Make it" easy route is extraordinary supposing that your task makes, you can skirt all the Design Space process and go to the Mat see immediately.

If you need to alter the presence of your plan, click on the redo.

Presently how about we perceive how to alter your project!

Edit Projects in Cricut Design Space App

When you tap on redo for any undertaking, you will have the option to edit and change things around.

Look at the accompanying screen capture to see the progressions I made to the first design.

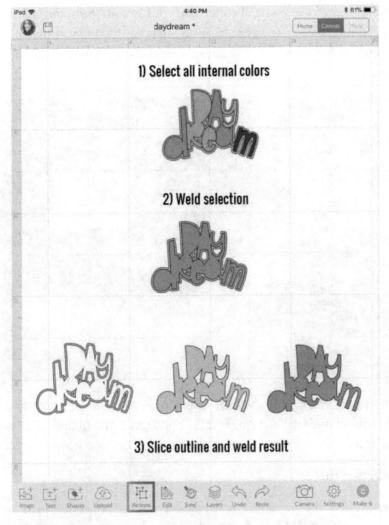

1. Select the entirety of the letters within the "dream layout."

2. Weld the whole of the inward letters.

3. Slice the layout of the layer with the welded letters.

Note: Slice and Weld are inside the activities menu.

This altering is fundamental; I am sure you can improve; however, I needed to tell you the best way to continue altering a made project.

If you tap on spare, you will supersede your unique plan and the thing you need incredible. However, despite the countless opportunities, you still need to continue your business. Please click "Backup" and select "Save As."

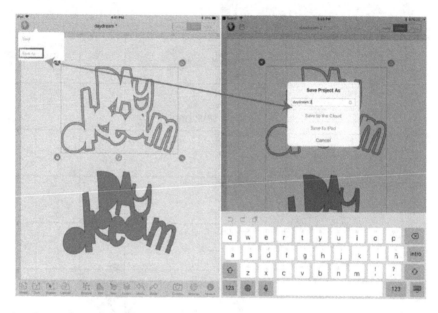

At the point when you click on "Save As," you will be provoked to change the name of your single task; right now, just included a "two" to the title.

Simple, isn't that so?

Presently, for the situation, you choose to utilize either plan once more, return to the "Home" view.

And see that the two are accessible.

CHAPTER 13:

Selling For Profit

The lower the craft, the more lucrative it is when selling art. It turns out. Fewer expenses for shipping, less material, everything works out. Therefore, my main concern is the cost of equipment, overall size and transport aspects, effort (as time is money!), and popularity.

Material cost— Material expenses are usually priced, but overhead expenses are something you might want to consider. Most individuals must pay the cash first to purchase products. Some unused scraps and materials will also be available when you buy bulk. You can always try and buy only as much stuff as you need, but it is never optimized correctly.

Shipping–Many reports publish that shipping is free, and individuals purchase only more. It is generally feasible for the seller by folding the transport expenses into the price of the item. It is okay if you have a high-cost product, but it doesn't make sense to the end customer if the article's original price is 5 $, and the shipping costs 50.

Effort–It is mostly a work of love for most artisans who sell their goods. But when you make crafts for orders, your life gets away from the fun. It just has to be remembered. Do you want to weed it for an hour and sell only for $5 if you sell a complex vinyl piece?

Popularity–fads are coming and going, never hurts driving one.

Let's begin with the list:

Vinyl crafts are the most lucrative Cricut vinyl projects, the ideal material for company vendors in Cricut. It's comparatively cheap, lightweight, and effortless to ship, and most importantly, you can do so much.

Wall Art Here is endless opportunities. Even with Fixer Upper presently not showing, the decoration of the farmhouse's wall remains powerful. Pinterest searches for farmhouse wall arts are over half a million per month. Don't miss actions. Don't miss them.

Custom decals Custom stickers are great, as they apply from parties to home décor for many end applications. It is a difference that large retailers cannot compete with when you offer a tailor-made service.

Children Related Wall Decals

The decorations of the children occur throughout the year. There's a constant need to decorate babies and children from kindergartens to birthdays to baby showers.

Do not miss the unicorn trend! DIYUnicornKit See this FREE SVG texts and printouts unicorn decor kit.

The wedding industry is alive and well. The wedding industry that's not unexpected. The back yard marriages are on the increase, according to Pinterest. It has increased by 441% in the search. All try to save their friendship a little.

DIY Gift favor box Check the boxes you can create with FREE paper food bags for this adorable wedding. So your material costs are 0! Of course, it includes the free SVG model.

I began with the Cricut Air to make cash from a Cricut Air 2. After I got my Cricut Maker on the Cricut Explorer, I discovered that most of my stuff accomplishes. So many products sell with the Cricut Explorer. Paper flowers' popularity is at an ever-high level, just like farmhouse decor, with over half a million searches per month on Pinterest. They are fantastic for every opportunity, from Mother's Day to Baby Shower's weddings. They're on-demand, no wonder.

Cricut Cake Toppers —Customization is a crucial case, and the toppers of the cupcake can be the most straightforward and most economical. Parents always try to raise their games at birthday parties for children with various personalized decorations and favors.

These adorable earrings do not have graphic design abilities to produce. Leather Earrings If you only want to test the water, go to a shop and use a batch of free leather swatches to create an original quantity.

How to sell Cricut maker projects The opportunities are truly infinite now with the top cutting machine like Cricut Macher.

There are so many materials to work with, from paper to textiles and wood.

According to Pinterest, the search for Felt and Fabric Flowers Cactus arrangements increased 235% in 2019. Go on with Felt Succulents on this trend.

Felt floral napkin rings In my resource library Wood Letters, Pinterest searches for over one million a month for rustic signs. It was a perceived decorative napkin ring model. You can cut your Cricut maker wood by coincidence!

Custom wood characters are a safe bet.

Cards deserve their category because they are very economical to create, and it takes one from birthdays to thank you for weddings on every occasion. Furthermore, transport cards are not cheaper.

25+ Goal Ideas For Craft Businesses

Financial

$xx in weeks / month revenues.

Reduce your business expenses.

Keep business accounting up to date.

Make your company a city, state, or county official. While I can't tell you precisely how to do this, there's an excellent starting point here–different in every country.

Keep purchasing impulses at a minimum in your company. In this post, read more about cash wasters.

Pay off the debts of your company and avoid liability. Debt is no good–see how you can keep your company out.

Set up a company savings account automatically draft your company bank account.

Post to social media regularly.

Create and begin using a profile on a new social media network.

Start with a calendar of content. In this article, I have more info on these calendars.

Network to encourage your goods jointly with other tiny company owners.

Begin marketing for a new population. If you are presently producing goods mainly for mothers, broaden your marketing to include other groups of individuals.

Get out of the market and launch your website.

Buy a loyalty program for your clients.

Note that you have the most straightforward client to get! It is my loyalty sample program.

Enhance your branding. You may have your logo, brand colors, packaging, etc.

Register for a course related to business.

I often hear from owners of small businesses that "my product photos are bad." Make it a better objective!

Contact your customers more to find out what they want. Whether social media or surveys, the best product is that which meets your requirements.

Start something new.

If you produce and sell wood signs, consider hosting guests, too. At this link, pick up my 15 Party ebook.

Create pop-up stores all year round to increase your company knowledge. Think of how many people you might attend for the year when you set a target–a month? A quarter by one?

Here are a few ideas.

Time Management

Enhance your balance of working life by setting and adhering to regular office hours.

Hire your company's assistance. Hire assistance. Take some of your burdens from social media support to creation and packaging.

Plan your holiday. While it may appear counterproductive, it takes time to escape reality and charge all business owners. If you haven't been on holiday for years–this year, plan on it. Even better? Even better? Use artisanal cash to finance it.

Productivity

Set several goods each week or month to be produced. These can be products that are digital or tangible.

Switch your custom store to the vessel ready. What do I believe about custom goods?

Clean the things you don't need from your craft and maintain them tidy this year. Although this may be a good idea, you can increase productivity through a clean, structured workspace.

There are two main components to set objectives:

1. *The goals that you set must be realistic and achievable. If you're just beginning, sales of $100,000 in your first company month are not practical. But in the first month of the company, it is feasible to set a $1,000 sales target.*

2. If you set them and forget them, the objectives are not right. Instead, it must assess continuously and adjusted.

Draw some targets for your company, Silhouette or Cricut today.

Great Cricut Ideas to Bring in Some Cash

By using the innovative design of different Cricut cartridges, you have become an expert. Talk of your colleagues is your creative scrapbooking. Your wonders of creative Cricut concepts are your personalized greeting card collections. Friends say your invention can compete with any card or scrapbook sold in your local stationery store, which commercially manufactures.

So, did you think you would make cash from your incredible and kind of craft? There are excellent ways to make your love cash.

Although there are thousands of craftspeople, who like to use their Cricut die cutting machine, the software they don't know how to operate. Take this opportunity to provide your custom order service and to create cut files that can be used by your customers. Craft forums offer you the chance to see what other people want, and then make those cut files, especially on eBay, and sell them on the internet.

Show custom cards in the local arts and crafts shop and invites them to you. It sells to its clients. A customized card or invitation likes for special occasions like a birthday, anniversaries, birthdays, etc. Because of infinite Cricut concepts, your creation can be unlimited and distinctive.

Infinite theme parties for children organized. Parents enjoy celebrating their child's birthday with topics such as a Disney costume feast or a Pokémon party. By creating decoration packages for such events, you can easily make some money. Prints and cut off a variety of décors, makes custom names or play cards for children, even after the party, to collect and trade with each other.

As scrapbooks become more popular every day, scrapbook enthusiasts will sell them using the Cricut machine to cut scrapbooks' page layout. You will undoubtedly have lots of designs and thoughts, as passionate as you are about scrapbooking.

Did you know that you can also sell your ideas to interior designers or homeowners who love home decoration? You can spread your money to home shops, wallpapers, and paint stores and leave them with your business cards or flyers to publicize your wall art services.

Interior decorators can also recruit your services if you show them your home decoration projects. You can use the Design Studio and the Vinyl Sheets to create any design, art words, character cartoons, or symbols you have made.

With your endless Cricut ideas, you can make additional money using Cricut software and technological innovation with your skills and experience while continuing your passion for creating beautiful crafts for everybody to enjoy for years.

Five pure vinyl cricuting projects you have to try

Did you listen to vinyl Cricut? If you own either a Provo Craft personal electronic die-cutting machine, you have an excellent opportunity of hearing it. Nevertheless, you may not want to use your vinyl cutting machine if you are like many craftsmen and do not realize the many projects this useful item can produce.

CHAPTER 14:

Using the Contour Feature

With this feature, you can successfully hide parts of an image, thereby adding more features to your images.

Using the Contour feature in hiding part of an image can also be used when you don't want to cut out any part of the image. For instance, you have a rainbow rose flower with different colors with varying layers, and based on the design you have in mind, you don't want the red color to show. Hiding the red color might make the flower turn out, not how a flower should as an essential part of the flower be lost. To get around this, a Contour is used.

To get started, the different layers of the flowers are ungrouped, sequentially.

After you must have done that, you then pick the layer of interest, which is the red petals. Choose the red flowers and tap on the Contour in the bottom right corner, all the cut lines available for the part highlights seen. Click on the highlighted sections and hide the areas. Tap on the close screen icon on the sub-screen on which you are currently working.

You can carry out the same procedure for multiple parts of the flower. And just like that, you have added the Contour and hidden the red petals without distorting the real image of the flower.

Adding Fonts

A lot of folks have the misconceptions that they need to add fonts to Design Space. The truth here is that you don't need to do that. To get your desired fonts, you will have to download them to your PC and install it. The downloaded fonts will only be available on the system you downloaded and installed on and not on any other system in which you log into your Design Space account.

Go with the following steps to download and install fonts to the Design Space on your PC

1. Get a site where you can download the fonts from. Here are some of the sites you can use; esty.com, fornsquirrel.com, fontspace.com, creativemarket.com, datfont.com. Note that some of the fonts are free, while others are not. If your finished product is going to be sold, you should obtain the license or get commercially free fonts. On any of the sites you choose to get your font from, you can browse through the catalog available to pick the one that best suits your current project. Click on download when you have decided on the font you want to go with. It will download straight to your PC.

2. Search for the downloaded file on your PC, or better still, go straight to the Downloads folder. It will most likely be there. The data comes in a zipped folder; unzip it (right-click on your mouse or the touchpad, and select the unzip option) to get access to the fonts.

3. When you are in the file, tap twice in quick succession on the .ttf file. A prompt will initiate the installation of the fonts and tap on confirm to begin the process.

4 .Open your Design Space and open a new page, and from there, click on the text tool. Enter a sentence or a word and then move onto the font selection option. You can tap on the system option to look at all the fonts installed on your PC or simply enter the name of the font you want.

CHAPTER 15:

All You Need to Know to Become a Professional Cricut Designer

The scrapbook business has exploded, releasing an ever-increasing number of devices that help you transform your photos into works of art that cement your memories for a lifetime.

As a scrapbooker, there are a couple of instruments that you need to enable you to make the simplest to the most dynamic scrapbook pages you have ever seen. You should have devices for journaling in your basic package, following your photos and components, paper, adornment, and a trimming instrument. As your expertise grows, you can include further developed devices, like the die-cutting apparatuses.

The purpose of scrapbooking is to recount a tale about the occasion that prompted the image. Journaling is a component of each page. To journal effectively, you should select markers or pens that are not corrosive. They ought to be quality. Pens and labels come in numerous hues that will make your pages come to life. Make sure to check the tips. A few markers are for shading and are less successful as composing instruments.

Glues. Glues ought to be clean and not corroded. Office tape or paste can harm your photographs and yellow your pages. A tape sprinter would be a fantastic essential instrument for a beginning scrapbooker. Tape sprinters can be refilled or discarded. You should check that your tape sprinter can accompany strips, dabs, or more extensive groups. Your tape sprinter could likewise accompany a lasting or repositionable glue. If you are experimenting with your page, use repositionable adhesive. If you are content with your plan, use lasting bonds. You can get cement machines that will transform paper or other slim materials into stickers for experienced scrapbookers. Glue gadgets can handle things from one inch wide to several inches wide. Similarly, these machines can use repositionable or durable cement. A portion of these machines will likewise work with attractive mediums or act like laminators.

Editing devices can be as necessary as many scissors or paper trimmers to circle and other shape cutters. A paper trimmer will enable you to edit your photos by removing foundation areas that discourage the film's genuine significance. Paper trimmers are likewise useful for resizing your papers to mount pictures. Paper trimmers can cut straight lines, and some can also go with additional edges to cut scallop and wavy edges.

Each scrapbooker will have a wide assortment of pages. Paper jams will be helpful. Cardstock is a bit clumsy, but it is incredible for making cards and installing pictures. The cardstock will appear in the most basic colors and designed, finished, metalized, and flashed. The paper also has different loads and styles. There is vellum, lighter weight papers, mulberry, and more. Paper turns out each day in various loads and mediums. It is the thing that makes scrapbooking so energizing because the options are endless. Papers come in 12x12, 8x11, or 5x5 configurations. Collections likewise come in comparable measurements with the goal that your scrapbook pages will fit.

Embellishments incorporate stripes, eyelets, catches, stickers, brads, chipboard, and die cuts. Anything is possible with components, but a few designs require different apparatuses. To use eyelets, you will need an eyelet locator and a hole punch.

Die cuts acquire, or you can utilize electronic machines like circuits or manual instruments like snappy slices to cut your die cuts. Manual and electric die cutters are for the more experienced scrapbooker.

For any individual who is an enthusiastic scrapbooker or simply appreciates making expert-looking signs and specialties, you have the Cricut Expressions.

If exactness and supreme accuracy are absolute necessities, the Cricut Expression machine might be for you.

Lately, they have released many units with various components that consider the customers' different needs. In addition to the necessary machines, they've included items that can further improve the Cricut machines.

The Cricut Expression is the most widely used choice for clients. The fundamental explanation is size. The Cricut Expression can fit increasingly vigorous tangle sizes of 12" x 24", which means it is possible to give more structures to a solitary cut. It will be simpler to make more cuts using a solitary tangle by running the machine once.

The bigger tangle size likewise encourages you to make bigger plans, room designs, or even standards, for example. It is the best quality machine since increasingly complex structures frequently require more space, and the Cricut Expression can deal with it effortlessly.

In any case, this bigger unit also has its drawbacks. For example, it loses its transportability. Along these lines, it intends to remain in one spot rather than having the ability to move around like the other cutting machines.

The Cricut Expression also packages with new presets, which will make your work simpler and help accelerate your creation. The Mix 'n Match highlight empowers you to program distinctive imaginative cuts for each character, and it will all fit into only one cutting project.

On the off chance that you wish to redo a structured design, use the AutoFill highlight - this will copy the plan to fit in; however, many iterations expect onto a solitary piece.

Another paper-saving element is the Fit to Page preset. It'll increase the plan's size as large as conceivable to change by the majority of the page.

When you need to make cuts in bunches, the Quantity highlight will ask you what number of patterns you need and take you through each stacking mat.

Pictures and shapes flip just by only choosing the Flip element.

Thick paper cuts are additionally not an issue, given that the Multi-Cut element will gradually shape the cutting edge. Like this, it is precise each time it cuts.

A few cuts need an alternate beginning position. The Center Point choice will situate the cutting edge to the center of the tangle.

To have the option to keep taking a shot at a recently cut paper, you may choose the Line Return, and it will situate itself to the following line after a cut makes.

Different highlights incorporate language determination and changing the metric estimations. Likewise, an Xtra catch can be customized to work with components that will eventually be released.

If you wanted to make yourself a Cricut Expression for work, or maybe for some reason without special consideration, we have conducted a detailed review, and you may want to read it carefully before buying these machines.1. What the hell is a Cricut?

A Cricut is a cutting machine that you can use for a wide range of creating ventures. It takes plans that you make or transfer (like those you get free from us) into their Design Space programming and removes them.

It sounds simple, but I promise you will be surprised by the number of activities you can perform in a short time compared to handmade. I'm talking sewing designs, organizer stickers, and wooden signs for your home, monogrammed mugs, and much more!

This machine is ideal for the inventive individual who consistently needs to do DIY projects but lacks the time, so they sit on your Pinterest page. Also, if you have a custom made business or Etsy shop, you could get a tremendous amount of incentive out of this machine.

2. Can I transfer photos to Cricut for use?

Of course! You can transfer your pictures, or any of our free SVG and Me cut records that now arrange to be good with Cricut Design Space.

There is a wide range of picture document types out there. The best kind (that we give) is SVGs, which stands for (lemme put on my geeky glasses here) versatile vector realistic. It utilizes numerical recipes to make the picture focus between lines. Try not to stress – I can see your eyes staring off into the great unknown, so that I won't go into more detail than that.

The advantage of this is the SVG designs amplify without getting that hazy, pixelated look you see with other record types, making them incredible for making tasks of any size!

3. What various materials would I be able to cut with Cricut?

In general, everybody will consider Cricut machines as cutting paper or vinyl, yet the matter is there are a LOT more things that a Cricut can cut.

For example, it can cut chipboard, balsa (excessively slight) wood, magnet material, aluminum (like the kind soft drinks package in), and much more! You will need to move up to the elevated cut sharp edge for the best cut quality for thicker materials.

You can also take advantage of the Cricut frequent-buyer system, which rewards clients for their buys. Brilliant organizations can issue prizes to keep clients steadfast and returning to them, over and over again. Offer your creative ventures and get great tips to decrease your vinyl expense for your specialty shaper drastically!

Cricut prizes are impressive because they explicitly target cutting machine clients. We adore our art cutters and are always acquiring different kinds of products. The Cricut vinyl, for example. Vinyl has become prominent because of its usability, assortment of hues, and availability of sizes and lengths. The same number of us is significantly cost-aware; we need the best appreciation when acquiring our Cricut supplies. Reward projects help decrease our provisions' general expense while rewarding our faithfulness to the organizations that notice our buys.

Vinyl Cricut prizes are increasingly accommodating. Since vinyl has such a significant number of employments in the art showcase, Cricut vinyl merchants reward their clients with bonuses based on the number and frequency of their purchases. Some vinyl Cricut providers offer partner programs that pay clients for advertising their Cricut vinyl supply sites to their friends and family. Everybody loves rewards, and what arrangement is superior to FREE vinyl for your Cricut. Sharing takes only a moment and little energy for such an extraordinary advantage.

Inventive Cricut vinyl supply organizations are offering credits to their clients who are eager to share. Credits are earned as Cricut clients transfer and show the exciting Cricut documents they have made using Cricut vinyl. This method successfully decreases vinyl supplies' general expense and advances the Cricut vinyl supply organization as a reliable hotspot for other Cricut clients to buy their vinyl supplies. Organizations with vision are executing Cricut reward programs and will keep on making long term, win-win relations with their clients.

In summary, Cricut prizes are perhaps the most straightforward approaches to set aside loads of cash on the general expense and responsibility for the Cricut shaper or individual specialty vinyl shaper.

Imaginative record sharing is fun and prizes the individuals who are eager to give others a chance at the very Cricut vinyl ventures they made. As you invest energy making souvenirs for yourself, you can likewise get Cricut rewards that help pay you back for your time!

There are a few die cutting machines available, including the Cuttlebug and Sizzix. These machines utilize the conventional technique for die-cutting, including setting paper over a format, covering it with a defensive board, and running it physically through a press machine to punch out the shape. This strategy is compelling and can cut numerous impressions of a picture without a moment's delay. However, there are a few confinements concerning determination, stockpiling, and size.

Conclusion

Thank you for making it to the end. I hope it was informative and this book has given answers to your questions about the Cricut Design Space. When it comes to sustaining the DIY movement, it's tough to think of a better brand than Cricut. Although the Cricut brand is in the US, Canada, and the UK, this brand is slowly becoming widespread worldwide. Nowadays, more and more people are disgusted by the quality of mass-produced products, so they only like old-fashioned handicrafts. Therefore, it seems that mass consumerism has affected the quality of the products we are buying. It is what indeed encouraged the DIY movement, arts, and craft.

Plus, if you think of the wide variety of products nowadays, some people simply want to be different, to distinguish themselves from the others. So why buy a product that is used by everybody else? There's nothing wrong with being different, and purchase something different can only encourage the small manufacturers to develop their businesses. They can survive in the market more quickly if consumers don't spend their money on a gigantic company's product. Just think of the beer market, as crafted beer is way better than mass-produced beer.

However, Cricut is not about crafted beer, and it's about other arts and crafts. Since the development of the Amazon platform, more and more people have started to develop their products using Cricut technology. We've all told to look for products on the Chinese markets, buy massive quantities, and get the products at low prices. Some people prefer to use the Cricut machine to create their decorations, while others can even make some money out of their projects. Just think of customized T-shirts or mugs, as these items are trendy today.

Slowly, Cricut is expanding its user base, and more people are becoming fascinated by these machines. Whether we are talking about decorations enthusiasts or just people who are very good at crafting, this brand has become a niche market leader. Since the machine is being sold on different sales channels, not only on the Cricut Shop, this brand expects to become a lot more popular. Cricut has a few models that are in use nowadays. The most important ones are the Explore Family (Explore, Explore One, Explore Air, and Explore Air 2), and the premium Cricut Machine, or the ultimate one, the Cricut Maker.

If you are not familiar with any Cricut machine and are curious to find out how these machines work, it's better to start with a lower version like the Explore Family ones. However, Explore Air 2 has become an exciting machine, as it offers plenty of features for just a small amount of money. If you use the Cricut Access subscription, you will have access to most of the designs, images, and other files shared with this service. Trust me, the Cricut Access subscription is worth it, but you need to go through all possible resources if you want to learn how these machines function genuinely. It should be the perfect guide for using these machines, the Design Space application, or the Cricut Access subscription. Therefore, you will need to apply all the tips, tricks, and information provided by t to make better use of these machines.

CRICUT PROJECT IDEAS

Over 33 Beautiful Holiday & Household Projects,
Fully Illustrated with Step By Step Instructions and
Tutorials for Design Studio & Cricut Techniques

Kimberly Maker Smith

TABLE OF CONTENTS

Introduction

Everybody can acknowledge what an extraordinary picture can do for you. If you take a look at a beautiful shot that you took a couple of years back during your child's secondary school graduation, you will understand better. You see that image, and it appears as though you were transported back in time and right over into the graduation of your child and begin to relive it once more. Pictures can express a million words and bring out an ocean full of emotions. Thanks to technology and innovation, we can now preserve each extraordinary moment that we had either in still mode or in motion. Cricut design also has a vital role in this.

Making design has been around for quite some time, and this is considered a very meticulous process. You see, people revere scrapbook making as an art and a heightened manner of preserving pictures. The materials and photographs are selected so that they may stand the tests of time. If you make a good design, chances are it will last for hundreds of years, and even your great grandchildren's grandchildren will be able to see and relive each moment that their grandparents had. Now isn't that something?

Making designs makes more convenient and faster thanks to the Cricut cutting machine; the Cricut cutting machine is a tool that is responsible for cutting out the techniques you specify. When you select the plan for your scrapbook or what have you, you should always consider the theme. If the pictures that will be housed by your design centers on a reunion that you had with your family, then think of a system that will highlight the theme.

Back in the day, once you had finalized the design, the next challenge that you will face now is how to create the design. There is another tool that eases your burden on that, and that is the Cricut Design

Studio. This bad boy is a software program with hundreds and hundreds of designs that you can choose from.

Another great thing about this software is that it gives the program the ability to edit the designs and even create new ones. Now that is technology at its finest.

Cricut Machine - Beyond the Scrapbook World

Presently the vast majority imagine that the Cricut machine is exclusively only for making designs for scrapbooks.

They are very wrong if they think that way. This tool has helped not only scrapbookers but also makers of gift cards as well. Yes, you heard me right when I said gift cards. The Cricut cutting machine is obviously by and large made for the novice to advanced scrapbooker.

This machine is responsible for cutting papers and different materials into the pattern or design that you need. The print or system can acquire with the assistance of programming devices.

An exceptionally renowned software apparatus called the Cricut Circuit Design Studio has a vast amount of pre-stacked designs.

The best part of this software tool is that it lets you edit the design they already have in place, and if new designs are available, you can update it. That is so cool! Cartridges also come loaded with a lot of methods that you can also choose from.

The Cricut machine can use to make gift cards. I'm sure everyone has had this bad experience in the past of getting frustrated because the store that you visited did not have the design that you wanted. It can cause a lot of stress facing that fact, especially when the person you want to give the card to is extraordinary. With the Cricut Design Studio's assistance, a Cricut cutting machine, and a computer, you can develop the design you need for your card and make that special someone happy. In addition to greeting cards, this tool can also make hangings for walls and calendars.

If you think of anything else that you can do with the Cricut machine, please implement it. There is no confinement to what you can do. If you decide to purchase one, which I urge, you need to invest $300 or more. If that seems a bit too tight for you, you can always look for a good deal on a Cricut machine. Watch out for sales in your local mall or try to purchase online from eBay or Amazon. But remember that you do not necessarily need to go for something new. If you know someone with a second-hand machine but is still in pristine condition, go for it. You need to be a wise buyer and spender at the same time.

INNOVATIVE CRICUT IDEAS FOR YOUR CRAFT PROJECT

How does a Cricut machine work? It's effortless. Just load a Cricut cartridge into the engine, select what color card stock you want to use for your particular design, and cut away. Each cartridge has various themed designs, from seasonal plans to favorite cartoon characters. You can choose from the cutout designs to use for scrapbooks, picture frames, personalized greeting cards, wall hangings, calendars, and many more.

One of the awesome Cricut ideas you can make as your craft is the Cricut calendar. Each month can create on a separate page, and you can decorate these pages with different designs. Wouldn't it be lovely to make your February page using the Love Struck Season Cartridge? The Easter Cartridge can provide you with unlimited plans for the April page calendar. Your May calendar can design from the Mother's Day Cartridge. How fun is it to develop your July page with trimmings created from the Independence Day Season Cartridge? December can design with the Joys of the Season Cartridge and Snow Friends Cartridge. You can choose to your heart's content.

Another great idea you can make is the scrapbook. This well-loved craft project is the reason why the Cricut Cutting machine invents in the first place. With the Cricut cutting machine, you can personalize scrapbooks for your children, mother-daughter, father, and son keepsake. Cricut created cartridges that every little kid would enjoy making, such as the Once Upon a Princess Cartridge or the Disney Tinker Bell and Friends Cartridge. Your little superhero would love the Batman design from the Batman: The Brave and the Bold or Robotz cartridges. Cricut gives you humungous designs to choose from for your scrapbooking ideas.

The Cricut designs laid out ideas and fonts and alphabets from the Sesame Street Font Cartridge and the AShlyn's Alphabet Cartridge. Use these exciting tools when creating your personalized gift, such as a wall-hanging picture frame with a photo of an unforgettable event of the recipient of your gift. Embellish your wall hanging with pretty cutouts made by the Cricut cutter.

CHAPTER 1:

What Is The Cricut Design Studio?

The Cricut Design Studio adds a new measurement to your Cricut experiences, regardless of whether you possess the first little Cricut or the more significant Cricut Expression. Just by connecting your Cricut to a USB port on your computer and introducing the Design Studio software, you'll enter an energizing new universe of design potential outcomes. Perhaps the best part is this program is easy to understand and use. It's not necessary to be a computer wizard to make use of this device, and you can do a large number of creative impacts with the expansion of this one piece of software.

How Will Design Studio Help You?

The Cricut Design Studio enables you to blend pictures from any of the cartridges you claim and mix them into one design. You can plan your system before you even put it in a cartridge. It's possible to weld letters together, expand or shrink pictures, put a picture on a diagonal, and stretch, turn, or flip images. You can even stop and save your structure before it's finished; at that point, return later to complete it. When you have the plan, only how you need it, slip in the primary cartridge required, and push a single button. When the Cricut arrives at the point where it needs an alternate cartridge, it will caution you to change the cartridges. When you finish, you can save your design to your flash drive or computer, and you will be able to share it with your companions.

Another advantage of Design Studio is that you can analyze each accessible design in the whole Cricut library, regardless of whether you possess the cartridge or not. Type in keyboards to scan for a specific picture or expression, and you can see precisely how it would look in your projects. It will assist you with choosing if you need to buy a specific cartridge or not. You can even preplan your structure and spare it until you get the essential cartridge or get it from a companion.

One disappointment to individual clients is that the Cricut Design Studio isn't compatible with Mac. As of now, you can utilize this product with Windows XP or Vista. The main other concern is that you are limited to using Design Studio in an area where you access a computer. If you have a laptop, that's not an issue.

By and large, the Cricut Design Studio is an incredible expansion to your Cricut assortment. Your creative mind constrains you.

In case you're a scrapbooker with a ton of extraordinary thoughts and ideas that you simply don't know how to get out on paper, consider the investment of Cricut Design Studio. This magnificent programming software will assist you with transforming the entirety of your extraordinary thoughts into enchanted manifestations directly before your eyes.

You can make the absolute best scrapbook themes and designs around.

You can find out about cartridges and utilize them just to utilize more than one cartridge in your design. Please find out about the cutting mat and how to use it to make the best structures for all of your scrapbook themes.

Organize everything in your cartridge library, and you will always have it there. Arrange everything in your cartridge library, and consistently have it there when you need it. You can add keywords to your library to make it simpler to discover what you need, thus considerably more. These are only a couple of instances of what the Cricut Design Studio can accomplish for you.

There is a bit of an expectation to absorb information about learning the program, and the manual doesn't work admirably to clarify everything. Fortunately, there are some extraordinary, accommodating instructional exercises and manuals out there composed by others who utilize the program to assist you with making Cricut Design Studio work for you.

It's significant to ensure your computer meets these base prerequisites before putting resources into the software. When you realize you meet the necessities and get the program for yourself, you should utilize it to make the best structures around your scrapbooks.

CHAPTER 2:

Why Get The Design Studio

Cricut Design Studio is a software program that offers you more incredible design energy with Cricut content.

Suppose you stuff your Cricut design studio program. In that case, you will observe four primary components: the virtual mat. Your work shows the Cricut cartridge library, the virtual keypad overlay, and the design qualities window.

As more come out, you will have the ability to upgrade your library to ensure you can usually have new tools for your creations.

You are free to develop with all the cartridges in the design studio library, though you can lower the cartridges you have. The library may allow you to explore articles out of the cartridges that you do not own, so put it to use as something to enable you to find everything you enjoy!

Browsing through the library is not difficult. The Cricut cartridge library allows you to show cartridge set in any order you select from a drop-down menu. You can arrange your library checklist alphabetically by favorites, category, or cartridges you have.

You can browse through the library by using keywords (tip: if you perform a search by keyword, the less complicated the search term, the better!), and the auto filler feature anticipates that which you could be searching for and provides you with tips.

As you cycle through the search results, the virtual overlay modifications indicate which cartridge set and feature your search result is. This method makes it simpler to find what you would like fast. You can personalize what shows in the virtual overlay if you choose that what it offers for your keyword is not exact.

On the left, you will find the six characteristic buttons, the "shift lock" button, so space/backspace buttons.

When you hover the mouse pointer over the image keys, they will zoom in to show the image keys you intend to decide. Dealing with a virtual mat is as intuitive as it becomes. When you have selected the form you wish to work with, it will show up on the virtual mat with choice manages. Selection handles are the eight circles which show on the corners and sides of your shape.

The bulk of your respective picture crafting accomplishes using these handles; as you play with them, you will discover the options that opened up for your creative mind.

The Cricut and Cricut Expression house cutting printer has grown to be an interesting vital to almost any scrap and crafter booker's supply closet.

With the device's potential to chop numbers, shapes, and letters at the touch of a switch, the Cricut is a straightforward method to produce scrapbooking pages, display boards, and cool wall art!

This application takes the Cricut printer to soar amounts of imagination. The application enables you to connect your Cricut to the home computer and make countless new shapes and designs for the device to cut.

The application consists of a searchable database of every letter, number, and shape in the entire Cricut Cartridge library, placing a considerable number of designs at your fingertips. And, Cricut provides internet posts to add to the library collection continually.

With the resources provided, you can have complete command over your Cricut, enabling you to meld (called welding) letters into a single word and structure and condition products on a virtual cutting mat before your machine starts its work.

The recognized Cricut program, likewise referred to as Cricut Design Studio, is a software type uniquely created to make slicing pictures easier.

With a thumb drive unit (USB), you will have the immediate benefit of producing All the models that you like, which may be effectively cut by making use of a Cricut machine. It is merely the quickest & most well-organized link you can have for both your Cricut and computer.

With all the Cricut program's assistance, you will be ready to create different designs for any project you have in mind. You will have the gain of welding, resizing, reshaping, combining, and twisting images of your choice.

These features by themselves can provide you with more flexibility and freedom than you have ever thought possible. Best of all, you don't have to become an expert or a genius to have the ability to achieve and create your Do-It-Yourself crafts.

Cricut Design Studio means to present everything craftspeople with tremendous advantages. One of those advantages will be that the program has been pre-loaded with each cartridge readily available for the Cricut cutters.

It means about 1000 of various designs and patterns you can use as it is or combine to make a far more excellent, extravagant, and unique cutting patterns. Consider the endless possibilities you can formulate, 1000 of designs you can develop. You can also do combinations with your friends.

CHAPTER 3:

Knowing The Materials To Use With Cricut

There are hundreds of different materials that can work on with Cricut machines. To be precise, Cricut machines can cut through many materials that are precisely or below 2.0 millimeters thickness. Users with Circuit Maker models have the more cutting force and size advantage. The Cricut Maker model cuts ten times faster and can put up with materials that are up to 2.4 millimeters thickness.

Many materials can be cut with a Cricut machine, even though it is mostly known for cutting paper or vinyl. The type of material to use depends solely on the kind of objects you want to work.

Main Materials

The type of materials you will choose for your cut will significantly depend on the kind of projects you want to engage in. Some of these materials work with different blades and use with more than one Cricut blade—this makes them the essential materials associated with Cricut cutting and are the primary materials for your Cricut Explore machine.

To be more organized, we will mention some of them by category. However, you can choose new materials from these categories and start experimenting with new projects. Paper and Cardstock: It seems somewhat necessary to begin with this category because they are the most popularly used class material when designing. They have over thirty-five different kinds of materials under them, making them the type with the highest resources.

Paper is another primary material you can use for cutting. You can make homemade greeting cards and envelopes from cutting paper with different designs. You can always choose from various types of writing from corrugated cardboard, kraft paper, foil, glitter paper, and many more.

Types of Paper or Cardboard:

- Construction paper

- Cardstock

- Kraft board

- Metallic paper

- Copy paper

Transfer Tape

It is a clear, medium-strength adhesive tape that comes in sheets. It is an invaluable step in the process. I will tell you that the Cricut brand transfer tape comes in a single, rolled 12" x 48" sheet. You can cut pieces to your liking and use them multiple times before disposing of them. These sheets from Cricut are currently $8.99 at a local crafting retailer, while other brands offer a 12" roll of six to ten feet for a similar price.

While transfer tape is an integral part of the process of using your Cricut machine, the brand is not nearly as important. Do some shopping around, find a sample size that works for you and your price point, and get started!

Like with any new type of crafting project, it will take some time to get used to the supplies and products and find the things that work the best.

Now that a lot says about different materials used on Cricut machines, you should be inspired to try new projects with these materials. However, only a beginner would stop here. We're not even close to unfolding the fantastic parts of the usage of Cricut machines.

Vinyl: Professionals use vinyl materials a lot because they find it very useful and outstanding for making graphics, stencils, decals, signs, etc. There are about 11 materials made from vinyl that uses on Cricut machines.

Iron-On: This is also a vinyl product, but with a different framework. Some people know it as heat transfer vinyl. You can use this type of vinyl to design and decorate tote bags, t-shirts, caps, and other clothing items. There are around nine iron-on materials that are usable on Cricut machines.

Iron-on vinyl is also one of the treasured materials to cut with Cricut Explore Air 2. You can use the iron-on vinyl to design bags, t-shirts, and any other items.

Types of Iron-on:

- Printable iron-on

- Glossy iron-on

- Metallic iron-on

- Foil iron-on

Fabric and Textiles: Fabrics are naturals on Cricut machines; they work seamlessly on almost every Cricut machine model.

There are about 17 different materials under this category. However, they, most of the time, need stabilizers to be added before cutting.

Textile or Fabric is not an unusual material for some Cricut users. Still, because the variety of Fabrics available to choose from is complete, it needs to be mentioned again because some techniques and materials are a little more unusual. For example, cutting a lace-like pattern into fabrics can immediately add a color-palette of fancy lace to any project. It also makes it possible to have the same lace pattern on various complementary materials or colors.

There is a fabric blade specific to the fabric material; all you need to do is keep the Fabric set in place on the settings dial. Cricut has some fabric materials online that you can cut.

Types of Fabric:

- Leather

- Canvas

- Duck cloth

- Silk

- Linen

Infusible Ink: Infusible ink is an exciting material from Cricut, allowing heat transfer on white and light-colored fabrics. It comes in different colors, patterns, and gradients and designs to be resistant to peeling, flaking, and washing. It uses for shirts, totes, coasters, etc.

CHAPTER 4:

Tips To Help You Start

While the Cricut's website offers many tips and techniques, there are some tried-and-true ways of using your machine and saving money and time.

10 Top Tips and Tactics for success:

1. Freezer paper is ideal for creating custom stencils.

2. Label blades for use on paper, vinyl, Fabric, etc. only use those blades on that medium. It helps preserve the lifetime of the edges.

3. Learn the proper cutting methods and approved materials by reading the cutting guide on Cricut.com.

4. Spray paint is an excellent tool for coloring vinyl if ever in a pinch and do not have a required color on hand or the time for it to arrive.

5. Free fonts can be uploaded and used in the Cricut Design Space.

   Find free fonts on websites such as dafont.com, fontsquirrel.com, or 1001freefonts.com.

6. Personal images and pictures can use for Cricut projects if the image saves on the computer as a PNG, JPG, or SCG.

7. Test out materials before printing and cutting a final project to be sure it will work as planned.

8. Pens other than Cricut pens work with the machine. Some brands to try to include Sharpie, American Crafts, and Recollections.

9. Avoid paper curling by pulling the cutting mat from the project and not the other way around.

10. Lint rollers are great for removing leftover materials from cutting mats. If the carpets need further cleaning, use soap and water and gently rub clean with a soft cloth. Rinse with clean water and let air dry.

Cutting with your Cricut

Masking tape or painter's tape is excellent to place on the edges of materials when they do not stick well to the cutting mat. Thick cuts sometimes will not be cut entirely through. To avoid having to do it by hand, keep the material in place when it finishes cutting the first cut without pressing the arrows button to remove it and then cut it again by selecting the "Go" or "C" button.

Print and Cut

An inkjet printer works best for printing. A laser printer sometimes heats the toner too high, making it hard for the Cricut machine to read. Internet Explorer or Safari is best for working with large images because these browsers support about 9 inches high and about 6 inches wide. Chrome and Firefox cap their heights around 8 inches tall and about 5 inches wide.A white paper is best for printing the registration marks for projects. If the project is any other color, print, and cuts on white paper first, attach them to the colored paper before putting it into the Cricut.

Writing with your Cricut

Pens work best when stored cap-side down. It keeps the ink at the tip. Thin pens can have their barrel widened by winding tape around it.

The electrical or painter's tape works well and does not leave a sticky residue behind.

Scoring with your Cricut

Folding materials are made more comfortable using the scoring tool when placed in the machine's pen holder.

Deepen the score lines in a custom design by doubling up the canvas's score lines in the Design Space.

Embossing with your Cricut

It can do! Use the accessory adapter in the place of the blade housing and insert the scoring stylus into it. When the Cricut tells of cutting, it will instead emboss.

Badges for your Cricut

Sharpen blades with aluminum foil by cutting a basic design into the foil on the cutting mat.

Designing for your Cricut

Firefox and Safari are best for using Design Space. Google Chrome does not work well with it.

Save the free designs Design Space offers by saving a new project with the design and name it with a design description for easy access.

Cut the canvas exactly how it is laid out by selecting "All" and clicking on "Attach." It ensures everything stays where they place without the machine defaulting to individual cuts. Instructional handbooks are available for Cricut Access members. This link is a functional place to learn how to assemble cartridges. (www.home.cricut.com/handbooks)

Cut the most massive layer last to avoid the material from moving around during the smaller cuts. It means placing the most massive layer as the topmost layer and the more delicate elements at the bottom in Design Space.

CHAPTER 5:

Why Should You Get A Personal Cricut Cutter

A Cricut personalized electronic cutter is a Cricut machine that allows you only to cut single-touch forms, letters, pictures, and words. Also, you don't have to use any computer since this type of machine can stand alone. You can use this for materials such as cardstock, vellum, vinyl, and any other paper or carton.

Cricut Has Many Benefits And Advantages

Some Of Them Are As Follows:

1. It's easy to use. All you need to do is access the machine by placing the material plainly on the chopping mat, loading it in the personal electronic cutter, putting the cartridge you like, choosing your chopping style, and pushing the "cut" button. Your best personalized and customized result will follow in this comfortable and easy way.

2. It's convenient and functional for everyone. Each one of us has different talents and skills, so that this machine transport from place to place. It weighs only 7 to 9 pounds and is easily monitored and managed by any of your friends, particularly for outdoor and indoor parties.

3. It is beneficial in crafting and scrapbooking. This computer will produce papers, scrapbooks, greeting cards, and much more. It usually cuts about 1 inch to 5 1/2 inches in height.

4. It modifies the cartridge material in up to six specific ways. Cartridges contain hundreds and thousands of art icons and styles that can always use.

The positive thing about personal electronic cutters is that a hundred versions and icons can personalize using a few acceptable methods.

5. It offers a free user guide and startup manual. For beginners and consumers such as you, a user manual, fast start guide, adapter, blade mount, 6 x 12 -inch cutting mat, necessary cartridge binder forms, manual and keyboard overlay will provide whenever you purchase any of these Cricut personal electronic cuts.

Cricut mats are often somewhat underrated because people don't give them the kindness and gravity they deserve. When someone buys a Cricut machine, they will undoubtedly spend on a new device an average of $300. This person would most probably worship Cricut as a half-god and treat him like a shrine. Could it be treated like this because it costs $300? The floors, on the other hand, are not adequately valued. Most of the time, people leave them unprotected and lie like unwanted.

It has got to stop! But first, let's get to know these two titans.

The Cricut machine is one of the essential devices for the development of scrapbooks. Its tool is responsible for cutting paper, vinyl, or fabric into the design you select. Where is the system coming from?

It can come either from a software tool similar to the Cricut design studio or from cartridges. You plug it into a computer, choose the design, and cut it off! When technology was still in its infancy in ancient times, the cutting stage was extremely tough, and you needed very hands.

But things were very convenient now with the tools in place. In addition to the Cricut machine, Cricut mats are another set of tools that are also very important. When you choose your design and are ready to have your machine cut, these bad boys are the ones who must put their papers in place to make the cuttings accurate. How much is one mat expensive? The average price is $9 and can be increased depending on the mat size you want.

One challenge facing most people is that they live longer than expected. What causes this? One of them is irresponsibility. After using them, many scrapbookers fail to cover their mats. It leads to the loss of adhesiveness. One great way to combat this is to protect your mat with transparent plastics after being used. There is also a chance that excess paper is left over, and you need to remove it. Wonders will work if you use baby wipes on your Cricut mats.

Cricut projects do with your Cricut cutting machine. It can be anything that can give your pleasure in simple activities to help you make an income. In the past, this machine was only considered a scrapbooker tool. But with humanity's growing ingenuity, ideas grow as crazy.

People understand that the Cricut cutting machine is just a die-cutting tool and is not directly responsible for the design. Software tools and cartridges provide the methods. The Cricut machine cuts the applications or cartridges the user selects and nothing more.

The Cricut Design Studio is the software responsible for creating designs for the numerous Cricut projects. This bad boy has hundreds of designs from which you can choose. You can also create your template and edit the ones already in your collection. Once you've selected your system, cut it off, and you're good to go for prime time. Welcome cards are a project for which the Cricut machine uses. Most people often have their designs that they have crafted and imprinted upon their minds. The mall you go to most of the time doesn't have the system you are looking for. Often, they may, but this is a leap of faith. With the Cricut machine, you can build and be proud of your design.

You can also sell the cards you create and earn money. It is now the attitude of businessmen for you! This move will reduce tension and anger and allow you to achieve a degree of peace or quiet. Calendars take into account. Calendars have 12 months a year, each of which has its name. You can help give life to those months with the help of a

Cricut cutting machine. Make sure you create or select designs that can help paint the mood or the month's associated moods.

Invitations are great projects for Cricut, too. You choose a design that matches the occasion and then cut it through the Cricut cutting machine. The key is never to relax your imagination. Make sure you keep things going, and you're going to work on more projects.

Scrapbooking is the craze of the new art. Photo albums have been left behind with the innovation of digital cameras. You've got a better way to keep your pictures. Cricut ideas for creating scrapbooks are as simple as a button with the advancement of technology. Cricut's Personal Cutter was the answer to your scrapbooking needs, with Cricut Expression. It allows you to create some of the most exciting and attractive forms to enhance your most simple paperwork projects.

The Cricut is a lightweight machine that can be transported everywhere, including artisan parties. During the journey, the device comes with a travel case that contains padding, wheels, and handle. You can start to create beautiful crafts with electrical power and passion for scrapbooking.

The Cricut looks like a picture printer and can help you design and create creative techniques in your scrapbooking projects.

It can make different shapes and sizes up to 24 inches. The Cricut is used to cut any paper-like plastic, vellum, and chipboard.

The Cricut Expression machine is an excellent tool for making your projects fun. A cutting system that needs a computer to work is easy to use.

It can cut small or large letters, phrases, and shapes. The paper products can be cut and thin magnets, and some fabric and etched glasses cut.

This improved machine can save your paper and even make several copies of your selected design or shape.

It definitely can bring your scrapbooking project to the next level of different Cricut ideas. If you buy it from retail stores, it could cost you over $350 to own a Cricut Expression machine. However, you can buy a cheaper, more expensive machine for $150 via the internet. Cricuts can cost you up to $80, but online deals are less than $30. There are more than 2000 images that each cartridge uses extensively.

Create beautiful scrapbooks, greeting cards, calendars, posters, banners, handmade decoration, teaching resources, commercial, promotional products, and ads in minutes.

With its multi-function capability, crafters like you can turn your innovative ideas into unique works of art. With the Cricut Machine, you can develop your status as a professional crafter. Now you can unleash your original creations to admire and even by others.

The Cricut computer is a marvelous human device. Since the invention of the Cricut cutting tool, the scrapbooking world has never been the same. This tool has revolutionized the way we cut paper, vinyl, and textile designs.

The art of preserving memories was primitive back in the days of wood and metal. The man only used sculptures, drawings, and writing as instruments to capture memories and to make sure future generations saw them. At the time, there was no way to record movement and voice. As the years went by, things changed.

Technology had a massive boom due to the brilliant minds of the late 18th and 19th centuries. You look around and what used to be a dream is now real. The scrapbooking technique was a method or process introduced in the 19th century and considered a unique way to preserve memories. This process involved the creation of a book containing images that shared a common theme.

When scrapbooking was relatively new, it was also challenging to achieve what it was. The design was easy, but the cutting stage was the challenge of scrapbookers since the process alone required the planet's steadiest hands. But the cutting phase was straightforward with the introduction of the Cricut cutting machine. In reality, there are many Cricut projects out there that you can use your Cricut computer.

Cricut projects can help you achieve personal satisfaction or earn income. Most people on the Cricut machine are only a scrapbooking tool. The Cricut cutting machine uses for many things. Remember, the designs in your software tool or cartridges use for many things.

CHAPTER 6:

Tools And Accessories

Must-Have Cricut Tools

You are great because you just bought a Cricut machine for yourself and are looking for the tools and accessories you need for beginners. You will want to look at the essential Cricut, whether you have a Cricut Explore, a Cricut Maker, or any other die cutting machine.

All right, not all of these are necessities, but they make you're crafting a lot easier. Let's take a look! Let's take a look!

Weeder Tool

There are several tools for weeding, all of which work to lift vinyl from the back panel. Cricut Weeder Tool is the most popular tool, but I recommend the Weeder Toolset to have more nuanced points.

Pin Pen–This tool works wonders on the smallest pieces and can even pop those vinyl bubbles without tearing. Although it's comfortable and sharp, it doesn't help keep the vinyl down while it is peeling.

Dental picks– users who wear dental picks by themselves. They're fantastic, but the handles can't be as convenient.

Exact knife–The sharp point is small and sufficiently precise to get into the little detail. Combine this with tweezers to ensure that the project is not damaged.

Experiment with various types and find out which weaving tools work best for you.

Scraper Tool

A clean mat is essential for smooth cutting and ensuring that you don't move your material during cutting. The spatula tool can help remove the small parts, but the scraper tool does a lot quicker.

The scraper I suggest is the extra big scraper. Holding is much easier and faster and better than the smaller one. It also helps to remove all the vinyl bubbles.

Spatula

Cricut Spatula is another tool you need to have is a spatula. When you lift the material from the cutting mat, you don't have to worry about tearing the fabric. The spatula can solve this problem quickly and satisfactorily, lifting the material from the mat. The spatula can also use to keep the carpet clean and the spatula free of debris. For an excellent price, Cricut sells the spatula and scaper together. No reason not to have them!

Tweezers

They're super helpful if you don't have tweezers yet. I like to carry two types, one for vinyl and one for picking up small items.

All right, this isn't a Cricut tool, but it's too good not to share! The Pazzles Needle Point Tweezers are the tweezers I like for weeding. These tweezers are sharp and excellent for vinyl. These points are intelligent enough to collect vinyl right from the center without using the edges. It can also order the smallest scrap!

The other tweets that I like are mainly for collecting and holding items. The Cricut Tweezers did not sell separately anymore. The EK tools Craft Tweezers are vital if you're still looking for a good pair! They are ideal for collecting rhinestones and other enhancements with reverse action. The opposite is excellent, so you don't get sore hands.

Scissors

The right scissors can make a difference in the world for the job—the Cricut Scissors made of hardened stainless-steel blades, which even cut while remaining lasting. The scissors are rather sharp and come with a microtip blade, making it easier and cleaner to work on smaller areas' fine details.

Paper Cutters / Trimmers

A paper trimmer is just great for getting straight cuts. Do not use a ruler and scissors anymore. A paper trimmer facilitates cutting, primarily if you work with vinyl.

Cricut has its trimmer, but the Fiskars SureCut Paper Trimmer I like is a little more advanced. It even can score these perfect folds.

Brayer

One of the most common errors of beginners is not to fully stabilize the material before cutting. A brayer fixes this by holding the material on the Cricut mat without hurting it.

Extra Mats

Something you should also have mats back up. When you are in the middle of the project, there is nothing more annoying and realize that you are no longer sticky. There are ways to restrain your cutting mats from saving money, but additional mats are always a good idea. For the types of mats, you use most often, you will want extra mats.

LightGrip (Blue) - For paper and cardstock projects

StandardGrip (Green)

For iron and vinyl

StrongGrip (Purple) — For posterboard, thick cardstock and other thicker materials

Fabricgrip (Pink) for Fabric

Must-Have Cricut Explore Accessories

Cricut Explore Blades

The Cricut Explore features a super sharp German carbide blade that is a fair point so you can get a cut right away. It is housed in the Cricut and can be easily changed if it is painful. You may find that when you cut rough materials, you have to change them more often. Silver (old machines) or gold (newer devices) are the boxes on this blade.

Finally, a bonded fabric blade is available, which you will use to cut Fabric stabilized by Heat N Bond or another stabilizer.

Note that the Cricut Maker has a blade of cords, a rotary cutter, a wheel of scoring, a perforating blade, an engraving tip, a wave tip, and no tool is compatible with Cricut Explore.

Cutting Mats

Cricut also has 12x 24 mats when you cut larger projects. I love it for more significant vinyl projects — I recently cut iron-off vinyl for 15 bags with this larger size on one vinyl sheet, and things went even quicker.

Regardless of what cuts you use, I suggest you break them a little before using them. Remove the transparent mat protector and stick the mat several times onto the front of your shirt. It picks up some of the lint and, believe it or not; this helps to remove your project from the mat after it cuts. It is almost impossible to remove a project from a brand-new carpet cleanly.

CHAPTER 7:

Cricut Hacks

Pegboard Tool Storage

Every proprietary Cricut machine you have come at the end of the device fitted with a convenient eyelet. It makes storing their accessories very simple by hanging them up. In a crafting room, a pegboard makes it so incredibly easy to hang your tools in your crafting room.

You can have all your resources arranged and laid out right in front of your eyes over your room. No more searching through drawers or bags, no scuffing up your tools, and any thinking about any edges throughout or chipping.

The more available your resources are, the more comfortable I find it would be for inspiration to reach me with unique projects.

IKEA Grocery Bag Holders as Material Organizers

IKEA offers reasonably priced plastic dispensers for grocery bags, which feature circular slots positioned symmetrically, making them suitable to carry several rolls of Cricut materials each. These cost only $2.99 each, so you can keep all of your rolls of fabric from folding, creasing, wrinkling, or even being ruined with one or two of them.

Plus, with how cute all the materials are, they make a pretty great decorative piece independently.

Use a Lint Roller

When I've clarified this one a little, it may seem a bit simple, but I guarantee it's a lifesaver that can save you a lot of trouble as well as keep the grip on your pad. Little pieces of dust and dirt will find their way onto your mat as you do more and more tasks. You'll see, as they do, an abundance of dust, ashes, paper scraps, glitter, cloth, and more. Since Cricut strongly advises against cleaning your mats to maintain its grip, proper care must exercise to make them last.

This technique swears by a significant number of crafters and says that it brought weeks to their Cricut mats' lives. It's better to stop using this hack before you're sure you'd like a new rug anyway so that if it doesn't perform well, you can get a new one without thinking you've missed something.

Use Non-Alcohol Wipes to Clean your Mats

Nonetheless, this hack test by a decent number of people found it a perfect way to give their mats a few extra weeks of life.

Using baby wipes or non-alcohol wipes on your mats can loosen stuff catches in your mat's grip, clear away dirt or paper leaves, and can give you a few extra weeks of grip power in your carpets!

Wash Your Mats with Soap, Water, and a Gentle Scrubber

Because Cricut strongly encourages you not to clean your mats, you must know you're doing this at your own risk. A large number of Cricut artisans, however, have said that this little trick has saved them at least for a couple of weeks from having to buy a new mat.

You can gently clean the adhesive grip side of your mat using warm water (don't go too hot, or you might melt the adhesive on your carpet) and a mild dish soap like Dawn, Fairy, or Palmolive, and the soft side of a kitchen sponge.

Don't add too much pressure if you don't want to ground debris any further or even scrape the adhesive entirely off the surface.

Rinse the meat and dry it thoroughly with a linen dish towel or high-quality paper towel without leaving any residue. Schedule the mat to dry completely for an hour or two after you have done so, and then give it a shot to see how much the wash has helped you out.

Doing all these hacks over time should give you an idea of what works, what doesn't, and how much you need to swap your Cricut mats.

Clean your Blades

You can find that your blades are snagging on your materials after some period of continuous use or that the cuts aren't as sharp as you would light them up to be. If this is the case, remove the housing from its attachment clamp and push the button at the housing top. It will stretch the blade beyond the casing but will also give you a comfortable grip on the edge while you clean it up.

If there is some gunk visible on the blade, pinch around the blade shaft using a very careful grip with your opposite thumb and forefinger, and bring it back, making sure you don't go against the blade angle as you do. It will remove any foreign material from your blade tip and make your cuts more accurate.

You may also take a ball of tin foil and poke the blade a few times into the cup, which will remove debris while also allowing a minor sharpening on them.

Leave the Material Dial on your Explore Set to Custom

One of the issues many Cricut Explore users have is to recall setting the dial to the top of their computer for the correct material they've loaded into the system. If you do this, you might find your blade pressing too hard for the material you've loaded into it or not hard enough.

Leaving your computer on the setting you last used to be very familiar, causing trouble when doing the other one. Many craftsmen make it a practice at the end of each project to set their dial to "Custom" because you won't know what material you might use for your Cricut.

Leaving your dial set to "Custom" will cause the Cricut program to ask you at the start of a single project what sort of material is in the unit. That removes the risk of cutting too much or too little because of this issue.

CHAPTER 8:

Producing Cricut Stencil Using Stencil Blank

DIY Cricut Stencil Using A Stencil Blank

When it comes to creating a Cricut stencil, there are different ways this achieves. However, this tutorial will dwell on how to cut a stencil with the Cricut Design Space.

Supplies for Cricut Stencil

- Stencil blank
- Paint tray
- A standard green grip or a standard purple grip
- A paintbrush
- Woodcraft frame
- Sponge brushes
- A transfer tapes

Directions for creating a Cricut Stencil

- The first step is to make a stencil in Cricut Design Space.

- Create a new project design from your Cricut Design Space. On the left side, click upload and navigate the system you created. Click "Save" to save the configuration.

  - Select the file you uploaded, and to bring it into your canvas, click "insert images."

Hint

You can always create your stencil design using the Cricut Design space instead of downloading from the SVG file.

- To start by creating your stencil file, click on shapes located on the left part of the Cricut design.

- Select your preferred form for your stencil project.

Resize the shape you chose to fit in the design text frame.

Hint

It is advisable to measure the shape to be half in size of the frame so that you will have room left when you tape your design to the backing board without a shift in Space.

- Arrange your shape and image in good order using the edit toolbar or align tools under the Arrange menu.

- What you are going to do is now to slice your stencil design. Click on the image and the shape of your stencil design and click "slice" located at the bottom of the layer panel.

Hint

Slicing is the process of splitting your stencil design into different layers until left with only your stencil piece.

- Click "Make It" to send the stencil piece to the Cricut machine for cutting. Then click continue to start the cutting process. Besides, on the "make screen," click on the browse all materials and select stencil.

- On your Cricut machine, set the dial to "Custom."

- Press the blinking "C" button to start cutting your stencil.

Hint

Before you try to eject the cutting mat from the machine, make sure your stencil cuts through the layering piece; if not, press the "C" button again. The device will repeat the cutting process.

DIY a Banner with Iron-on Vinyl on Cardstock

Out of all the primary materials you can use iron-on vinyl with, paper and cardstock are the most inexpensive of them all—and you can create a beautiful project with them.

The following steps will show you how to use vinyl on cardstock by creating a banner used for engagements, as gifts, weddings, and parties.

Supplies for Banner

- Cricut Easypress or household iron
- A white cardstock
- A gold glitter iron-on vinyl
- A ribbon

Directions of using iron-on on cardstock to create a banner

- Download the banner SVG cut file. And you can design your banner file or upload the downloaded file to Cricut Design Space.

Hint

Note that the banner file usually comes with a measurement of 5 inches x 7 inches, but you can resize it to your preference. Do not forget to mirror your iron-on vinyl so that your letters will face the right direction when you iron them to your cardstock or any other material.

- Once the Cricut machine has cut your cardstock and glitter iron, then you can weed out the negative area from the iron-on vinyl.

- Line up all the iron-on pieces over the cardstock pans. You can use household iron or Cricut EasyPress to press the vinyl to the cardstock.

Hint

For cardstock, low heat requires for adhesion. Press for a minimum of 30 seconds and flip to press for 15 seconds from the back.

- Peel off the plastic liner after the heat press and keep the paper from curling by placing them under a heavy object like a book.

- Use ribbon to string together your newly made banner pieces.

CHAPTER 9:

Cricut Stencil Directions

Stenciling is a popular way to add patterns to walls, floors, furniture, clothing, glass, mirrors, Fabric, paper, ceilings, or almost any other object.

You can use paint, glaze, metallic powder, gold, silver, copper leaf, Gesso, plaster, joint compound, or molding paste. Using stencils, you can take an everyday piece of furniture or a dull wall and make it a unique decorative item in your home.

You use the stencil like a pattern to help you decoratively paint a design. Much like an artist would freehand it. With stencils, everyone can be an artistic genius even if you can't draw.

Another favorite stencil material is Mylar. The big difference between this polyester film and vinyl is that it does not have an adhesive backing. It is reusable, durable, and resists tearing. Mylar can also cut using your Cricut; the settings will vary depending on the thickness of the sheets you buy.

When working with stencils, you have options. You can remove the backing and stick the vinyl on your project's surface or leave the support and secure the vinyl with tape or a light spray adhesive. The advantage of being your stencil is now reusable when you keep the backing paper intact. It is also easily repositioned.

With other vinyl projects, you pull away from the negative parts of the vinyl. In other words, if you're using a flower, you weed out anything that is not the flower and then applies the height to your project.

Stencils are, of course, just the opposite. You pull the flower part away and leave the negative Space. It's the negative space that is the flower's image that you'll fill in with paint.

When working with a reusable stencil, you'll have to adjust the setting on your Cricut machine to cut through the vinyl AND the backing. For a one-time use stencil, use the kiss cut and weed your image.

Remove your stencil from the mat. Clean the surface of the area you're going to paint and let it dry. Apply the stencil using whatever method you choose, making sure places where you want it. Tape the reusable stencil securely in place. You don't want it to move, or if you've removed the backing, make sure all the edges of the design adhere firmly, or paint will get under the edges.

Pat the paint on as opposed to brushing. You don't want to paint anywhere except inside the stencil area. You can also use a foam pouncer or a foam roller. You want to apply the paint evenly but assure that none gets under the stencil. If it bleeds, lift the stencil and wipe it off. When working with paint, don't overload the brush with too much color. You'll get better results applying two thin coats and waiting between coats for the paint to dry.

Don't think you have to use only one color of paint for each design. You can add strokes of different colors or blend them for a shaded look.

Use touches of white paint along the top of designs to give the appearance of highlighting.

Use a touch of dark paint to achieve a look of depth or a 3D shadow effect.

When making a continuing pattern, always use at least three or four of the designs in a row. This way, you can overlap the last shape and make sure the pattern is even with the same distance between each body.

Relief stenciling

Instead of flat design, you can add dimension to simulate carved wood or plaster relief decorations on walls, ceilings, or doors using a joint compound or a host of other products that are easy to work with and achieve extraordinary results.

Using a mixture of Gesso and glue instead of paint will make a textured stencil that stands out from the surface in relief. You can then sand the image carefully to make them smooth and even.

Paint can add to the Gesso before uses, or you can paint the designs after it has completely dried.

Use glue in the stencil and then place sand on top. It makes another textured design. You can use bare sand or colored sand, depending on the look you want to achieve.

Favorite stencil projects include:

Borders on walls are usually at the top or in the middle of the wall, acting as a chair rail. If you're stenciling walls around a corner, you may need to cut a notch in the stencil so it will bend around or into the corner.

If you like the look of inlaid wood or parquetry floors but not the hefty price, tries stenciling a center medallion, geometric patterns, or a floral border. Adding patterns on wooden furniture can make any thrift store look new and exciting. Chairs, tables, dressers, desks, and entertainment centers can give a whole new look.

Glass jars or decorative dishes can stencil. Depending on the type of paint you use, they may not be suitable for use as tableware, so you cannot eat them. Besides, painted dishes are generally not dishwasher safe. Turn that old glass tabletop into a family heirloom with reverse painting on glass, the centuries-old art form you can recreate with stenciling.

CHAPTER 10:

How To Use A Cricut Machine Properly And Easily

U sing a Cricut is easy and can be even utilized by most DIY craft beginners. When you purchase your Cricut machine, you will receive a machine; a storage bag to store everything in; a blade that uses for the device.

A power cord and USB cord connect it to the computer system you are using; the samples; a user manual; a silver pen; and your cutting mat, a standard grip mat. It will get you started using your Cricut. However, if you want to make the best out of your new Cricut machine, then you should consider purchasing one of the many starter packs.

As you get into using a Cricut machine regularly, you will need to invest in some other items to help you be more efficient with your device. For now, I will walk you through the use of the standard kit.

By locating the power button, you will be able to turn the machine on. Then, you can start to learn the other parts of the device. You will need to understand the cartridge port, the accessory cup, how to use the dual cartridge, and the Smart Set Dial. The button that you push to open the lid locates in front of the machine's left-hand side. It is directly in front of the cartridge port, which is where you will place the cartridge that you are using at the time. The power button is located on the machine's right-hand side at the back, indicated by a circle with a line through it—similar to other power buttons found on most devices. Itis located directly in front of the power button and directly behind the buttons that go with the Smart SetDial. To place the blades and pens in the housing, you will need to open the machine like a printer and place them inside the machine's compartment. It will resemble the ink compartment of a printer. You will have the accessory cup located at the backside of the cartridge port. It will be a helpful spot to use along with the accessories drawer on the machine's Front.

Using your Cricut does not require a large amount of Space. However, you will need to have a bit of a designated space for using the machine. It can be a flat surface that has an easily accessible power source. You will need a free space located around your Cricut so that you have room for the load mats to go inside the machine and easily come out of the device. Now that you have your Space set up, you will need to open the machine's front. Make sure that you have your computer close by for setting up your software and designs. It is not necessary to use a desktop or laptop computer.

Both are sufficient to use Cricut machines and software. You can even use a tablet or a cell phone. As long as the device has internet capabilities, you should be fine. You will need to download the Cricut Design Space app to design the images you wish to cut out.

The new Cricut design is wireless, making the studio easy to access, without the need for enough space to create for your creative center. There is no need to link the machine with your computer. You will simply log in to the DesignStudio, and it will automatically connect with your Cricut machine.

When you purchase your Cricut machine, you will receive a link to download the DesignStudio form online. Itis where you will design your images that cut out with the Cricut. However, if you are purchasing your machine from a person, you can log in to https://design.cricut.com/setup to start creating images with your Cricut. On this site, you will get a step-by-step process that shows you how to set up the program and how to plug in the machine's power, as well as how the Cricut machine works. Ensure that the device used for

DesignStudio has Bluetooth enabled so that Cricut machines and tools can talk. It locates in your settings. You will then need to press the power button on your Cricut to connect the devices. You will see the Cricut machine will pop-up as a connected device on your screen. You may get a message that says to type in the passcode. It can merely type as 0000.

If the connection is not working through the Bluetooth connection, connect your Cricut to your computer using the provided USB cable and begin this connection process. After you have linked the device and the Cricut, you are ready to start creating.

Since you are reading this manual, you are a beginner in the world of Cricut. That is perfectly fine; we all start somewhere. When you start with your Cricut machine, you direct to complete the project that comes with the device for beginners. It is the "Enjoy" card project. This card project will help ease your way into using the Cricut and beginning your crafting career or hobby. It will also teach you about different aspects of the machine.

Once you have linked the Cricut machine and the computer or DesignStudio device, you will ask to start this beginner project. It will take you step-by-step through the process and teach you the steps needed to design your images.

There are a few features that you will need to know when using the Cricut Explore Air 2. One of those features is the Smart Set Dial. As we mentioned before, this dial locates on the top of the Cricut machine's right-hand side. This feature designs to help you have an easier time using the Cricut. This dial enables you to select the material that you are using so that your machine has a pre-programmed setting for that specific material. You will notice that they have a pre-programmed set for cardstock, Fabric, poster board, paper, vinyl, and many other options.

CHAPTER 11:

How To Make Personalized Plates And Mugs

Create your mug with vinyl

10 minutes (time spent performing things)

5 minutes (time spent around)

15 minutes (total project time)

Tools

Cricut Explore Air and fundamental tools

Scissors

Materials

Exterior glue vinyl in whatever colors you would like (I used silver, slate grey, and dark blue)

Transport tape

"Baby it's cold outside" layout (you can find my Cricut layout here)

Rubbing alcohol

Cotton balls

This Valentine's Day cocktail job is ideal for "first time" plastic undertaking. Therefore, if you got a Cricut device for Christmas, now's the time to get it from the box and begin creating!

Here is what you will have to create these cute mugs.

- Cricut system (I used my Cricut Explore Air Two) could use any Explore device or the Maker. -- does not stress silhouette users, I still have not forgotten about you! You might even use the SVG document)

- Heat transport plastic -- yes, I will place HTV onto a ceramic mug! What??? Stick around -- you will see!

- Better collectively SVG document (you can find this here)

- Mini handheld iron or heat media using a mug attachment

Here are the ways for the best way to decorate mugs with iron-on vinyl along with a Cricut.

Directions

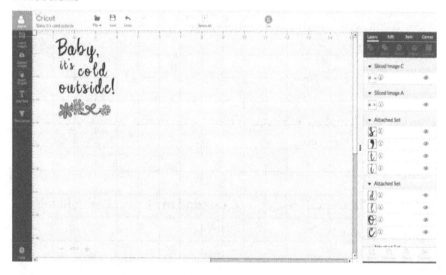

Begin with opening Cricut Design Space on your browser and begin a new project.

Click on the "insert text" button on the left and right type your text to the original text box.

On the right, below the "edit" tab, you can change the font and size, and orientation of your text if you want.

I changed the font to the wildflower.

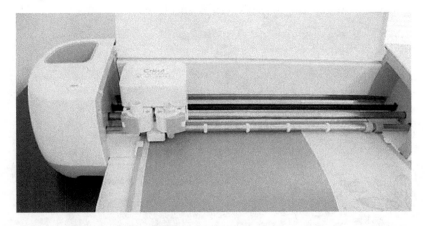

I then clicked "insert images" and discovered a cute snowflake I enjoyed and added it. I resized the picture so it would match on the mug and put it under my text.

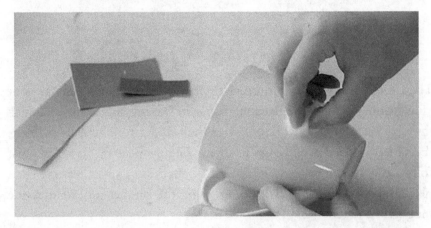

That was it; it is ready to cutback! Just click on the go button, placing the dial in your Cricut device to vinyl, along with the program, will help you through the remaining steps for cutting and loading every distinct layer of vinyl.

When cutting vinyl, use a cotton ball dipped in alcohol to clean the cup into which the vinyl will place.

Once your vinyl cuts, weed off any desktop vinyl using the weeding tool, leaving the backing paper's letters and layout.

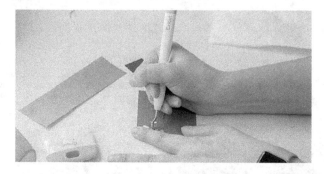

Then trim a slice of tape to precisely the identical dimensions as your vinyl layout. Remove the backing paper in the transport tape and stick the tape onto your vinyl layout. Use the scraper tool actually to press the video onto the vinyl, so it sticks. Gently peel the tape; it must follow the vinyl nicely enough to lift the backing paper's letters. Then place the vinyl layout on your mug, using the scraper tool to stick the mug's vinyl letters.

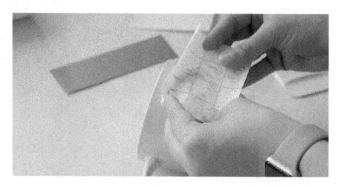

When the vinyl stocks onto the mug, gently peel back the tape, leaving the mug's vinyl letters. And you are done!

Fill it with your favorite hot beverage and revel in it!

CHAPTER 12:

More Cricut Machine Activities

How to Design Onesies with Cricut Machine

Supplies needed:

- Cricut machine
- Iron-on vinyl
- Iron
- Onesie
- Muslin cloth
- Transfer tape
- Weeding tool

Steps on how to design onesies with Cricut:

1. Get and save the image you want to use online. You can also create your image personally.

2. Log in to the Cricut design space and start a new project.

3. Click the upload icon and upload the saved image.

4. Click on the image and drag to the next page, then select the image type.

5. Select the parts of the image you do not want as part of the final cut.

6. Select the image as a cut image. You will get to preview the picture as a cut image.

7. Approve the cut image. You would redirect to the first upload screen.

8. Click on your just finished cut file, highlight it, and insert the image.

9. The image is added to your design space for size readjusting. The idea is ready to cut.

10. Highlight the image and use the Flatten button to keep the design together.

11. Place the shiny side of the iron-on vinyl down on the cutting machine.

12. Mirror the image before cutting.

13. Cut the image, and remove excessive vinyl after the image cuts with a weeding tool.

14. Carefully peel away the paperback of the vinyl.

15. Preheat the iron and press the onesie for a few seconds.

16. Apply the transfer tape to the onesie.

17. Cover with a muslin piece.

18. Press the image with medium heat iron for thirty seconds.

19. Remove the transfer tape from the onesie.

20. Your Cricut designed onesie is ready.

Making Leather Bracelet Using Cricut Machine

Supplies needed are as follows:

- Cricut machine
- Cricut Faux leather
- Cardstock
- Adhesive
- Snap closure
- Snap tools
- Cricut extra-strength cutting mat

Steps in making a leather bracelet:

1. (If your wrist is six inches, add half an inch for overlap.)
2. Cut out the measured wrist length from the faux leather.
3. Log in to the Cricut design space.
4. Start a new project.
5. If you have made design and saved it on your computer, upload the system to your design space by clicking on the Upload icon.
6. If you are yet to create a design, you can use the Insert Shapes icon's basic shapes to create your image.
7. Adjust the design to the length and width of your leather size.
8. Save it as a cut image.
9. Click Go.

10. Set your cutting dial to custom.

11. Select the faux leather setting.

12. Place your faux leather on the Cricut extra-strength cutting mat.

13. Feed the mat into the Cricut machine.

14. Ensure the cutting mat reaches the rollers.

15. Let the Cricut machine cut out the design on the faux leather.

16. Remove the faux leather from the mat.

17. Apply snap closure to the end of the designed leather.

Your Cricut designed and cut leather bracelet is ready.

Make Buntings and Other Party Decoration with Cricut Machine

Supplies needed for bunting:

- Fabric

- Fabric stabilizer

- Ribbon

- Iron-on glitter vinyl

- Fabric adhesive

- Inkjet printer

- Cricut machine

- Weeding tool

- Transfer Tape

- Needle

- Thread

- Fancy multicolored buttons

- Iron

- Grease-proof paper

Steps to creating your buntings on Cricut for a birthday party:

1. Log in to the Cricut design space.

2. Click on Create a New Project.

3. Use the Insert Shape icon to select the basic shape you want the bunting to be in. (I will explain using the star shape.)

4. Highlight and unlock the Padlock at the lower side of the shape.

5. Edit or resize the shape to your content.

6. Copy and paste the shape as much as required by your text.

7. Click on the Text icon.

8. Type in your text: "Happy Birthday."

9. Choose the font that you want the text to cut in.

10. Move to the preview screen.

11. Adjust the shapes to the size of your Fabric.

12. Apply the fabric to the cutting mat.

13. Push the cutting mat up against the rollers.

14. Load the mat into the machine.

15. Set the cutting dial to custom.

16. Select the fabric setting.

17. Click Go.

18. Cut out your shapes on the Fabric.

19. Cut out the shapes on the fabric stabilizer too.

20. Place the iron-on glitter vinyl shiny side down on the cutting mat.

21. Load the mat into the machine.

22. Push the cutting mat against the rollers.

23. Set the dial to the iron-on glitter vinyl setting.

24. Cut out your text with the Cricut machine.

25. Unload the mat.

26. Remove the iron-on vinyl.

27. Use the weeding tool to weed out the waste from the vinyl.

28. Apply transfer tape to your vinyl.

29. Cut each letter of the text separately.

30. Glue the fabric shape together with the fabric stabilizer.

31. Ensure there is no air bubble and that the edges do not overlap.

32. Turn down a point of the buntings to make it "hangable."

33. Sew a button each to the turned-down edge of the buntings.

34. Pre-press the bunting shape with a medium heat iron for a few seconds.

35. Apply each vinyl letter on each bunting.

36. Place a greaseproof paper on it.

37. Apply a medium-heat iron on it for thirty seconds.

38. Peel away the transfer tape.

39. Reapply the paper and press again with medium heat iron for a few seconds.

40. Tie a bow with the ribbon at one end.

41. Thread the ribbon through the buntings' turned-down part until all the buntings are linked together by the ribbon.

Your buntings are ready to be hanged.

To make any other type of buntings requires this same process; the only difference would be the text and shape.

How to Make Party Decorations Using a Cricut Machine

Supplies needed are as follows:

- Cricut machine
- Cricut cuttlebug
- Cutting mat
- Embossing folder
- String
- Inkjet printer
- Fabric

Steps to making party decorations banner:

1. Log in to the Cricut design space.

2. Create or upload your design to the design space.

3. If it's a text you want, click on the Text icon and input your text.

4. Change the text font to that of your desire.

5. Highlight the text and change its color.

6. Click on the Print option and change the file to a print file.

7. Highlight the text, ungroup it, and adjust the spacing.

8. Group the text back.

9. Flatten the image/text.

10. Click on the Cricut Go icon and print your design on the Fabric.

11. Place the designed Fabric into the cutting mat and cut the design.

12. Then you emboss the banner.

Labeling Things in the Pantry

Supplies needed are as follows:

- Cricut machine

- Sticker paper

- Inkjet printer

Steps to labeling things in the pantry:

1. Log in to the Cricut design space.

2. Click on the Text icon and input the Jam.

3. Select the font you want to use.

4. Highlight your text and change the color from the ones available on the color tray.

5. Click on the print option and change the file from a cut file to a print file.

6. Highlight the text, ungroup, and adjust the spacing.

7. Highlight the text and Group it.

8. Then design the shape of the label.

9. Highlight the text and then use the "Alignment" drop-down box.

10. Highlight the text and select Move to the Front.

11. Move the text over to the shape.

12. Select both and click on the Group.

13. Highlight the design and click on Attach.

14. Click on the Cricut Go button.

15. Place your sticker paper onto the cutting mat.

16. Load the mat into the machine.

17. Click the button on the machine to scan the registration and cut.

18. Weed the sticker after cutting.

The sticker for labeling jam is ready.

Repeat the process until all the things in the pantry are labeled.

CHAPTER 13:

Editing Cricut Project

With the most up to date form of Cricut Design Space, altering content in the program couldn't be simpler! The content editing alternatives enable clients to make the ideal content for their uncommon tasks. A few choices sprang up in the word processing board and realized what everyone does enables clients to benefit as much as possible from their content editing. We should investigate all the word processing board decisions and alter the messages in Cricut Design Space.

Changing the Font Type

Snap the "Text style" alternative to change the textual style type. The text styles separate into "Framework" textual styles and "Cricut Fonts." Cricut Fonts are ones that are accessible through Cricut Design Space.

Some are accessible for nothing, others are accessible with a Cricut Access Subscription, and others require an extra charge.

When you have discovered a textual style that you like, click on it to see the content in that specific textual style. If you are content with the decision, progress forward.

If not, keep looking until you've discovered the ideal text style. They are finding the best text style for my undertaking more often than not takes me some time!

The Font Style alternative enables clients to utilize their favored text style are customary, intense, italics, or composing style.

In any case, not these choices will show up for each textual type.

The style decisions will be different, as indicated by what is accessible for that text style.

Utilize the Font Size choice to make the content bigger or littler. If you don't have a clue about the definite number to re-size the textual style, remember that you can generally make the content bigger or littler utilizing the bolt on the base right of the content box, as well.

Changing the Space between Letters

Did you realize that you can change the space between letters in Cricut Design Space? It is a marvelous element that keeps clients from composing and space each letter separately. Utilize the Letter Space choice to make the space between every individual message more giant or littler.

Changing the Space between lines of content

This choice works when there is more than one line of content in the content box, as appeared in the photograph above. Use Line Space increment or decline the space between the lines of content. It works for lines inside a similar content box.

Changing the Text Alignment

With the Text Alignment choice, clients can adjust content to one side, right, or focal point of the content box. Remember, this does not change the message inside the whole task itself, just inside the content box.

Propelled Text Tools

The Advanced catch takes into consideration ungrouping the content. The "Ungroup to Letters" enables the client to ungroup the content into individual letters. The "Ungroup to Lines" allows the client to ungroup the content to separate lines.

This alternative possibly works if there is more than one line of content in the content box. If you are utilizing a multi-layer text style, then you may likewise have an "Ungroup to Layers" choice accessible. When lines or letters have been ungrouped, clients can alter and control those letters or strings autonomously.

I utilize the Advanced option commonly to ungroup lines of content. Intermittently, I will have designed something in a content box and conclude that I wish to move the reality of content someplace differently.

The "Ungroup to Lines" proves to be useful for this. I utilize the "Ungroup to Letters" when bending range.

Bend Text

The Curve Text Icon is a hotly anticipated expansion to the content editing board in Cricut Design Space. I've made a post and video to show how to utilize this unique new element. Peruse increasingly about it in Curving Text in Cricut Design Space.

How about we bend some content

Here we are going to include our stunning impact!

Select the primary line of content and snap on a bend, and type - 5.104; this will make the line bend down.

Then, we will choose the second line of content, yet this time, we are going to type 5.104. It will make the line bend up.

At long last, for the third line of content, we will rehash something very similar we did with the mainline. Snap-on bend and type - 5.104

Sort out the majority of the components

We should play with Linetype and Fill.

Typically, you would adhere to one Linetype; however, we will utilize the draw and cut and print alternatives with the end goal of this instructional exercise.

I chose drawing as a line type for the top line, and after that, I went with a light turquoise for shading.

For the subsequent line, I went with Cut as line type to enact the filling choice. Then I chose to print as fill and a turquoise shading.

For the last line, I needed to investigate designs! So, I chose slice as line type to initiate the fill alternative, and afterward, I changed the print type, for example.

You can choose numerous choices; however, I needed to stay with a turquoise design.

CHAPTER 14:

How To Create Personalized Pillows

Among my favorite characteristics of Cricut Design Space is your capability to use system fonts. Consequently, you may download fonts from the Web and use them in your regular crafting world! I like it. Whenever you have the liberty to use any font you would like, typography projects' alternatives explode!

There are many sites where you can download fonts at no cost, but my favorite is dafont.com. Dafont.com permits users to upload fonts they've designed. Be aware that most of the fonts have special instructions and asks that you use them for individual use only.

Want to make this pillow? It is ready-to-make

Materials needed:

Cricut Explore® or Maker machine

Cricut® 12" x 12" standard grip mat

Cricut weeder tool

Purple iron-on

Gold iron-on

20" x 20" pillow shape and protect

Easy press or iron

Press fabric or clean cotton fabric

1: Download your favorite

The fonts you will need to make this job are Mastic, Bream Catcher, and Authentic Hilton. Click the hyperlinks takes to www.dafont.com.

****Please be aware that Mastic and Authentic Hilton should uses for individual use only. ****

You have to download and install these fonts for the job to get the job done.

To install, start the downloaded font (tagged .ttf) and put it in it to your PC.

It works better if you download the fonts before launching Cricut Design Space. Otherwise, you will want to close the browser and reopen it after installing the fonts to refresh your font file automatically.

2: Produce design

Insert text on the canvas. After the font installs, these fonts will automatically become part of the system fonts. You can filter the fonts in the "design space" by clicking the system fonts in the top window. Once I have determined which words I need in each font, I begin placing them in a design. The very first step would be to weld the script fonts collectively. Choose the words and ungroup the letters.

Transfer the letters to each other before you are happy with how they look. Then pick each the letters and weld them together.

Organize all the words on your layout, pick all the terms, and weld them together so that the words will cut as one complete design.

3: Put iron-on

Weed excess iron-on round the picture.

4: Use iron-on on the pillow

Follow the Cricut ironing program's instructions to paste the cut phrase on the front of the pillow.

First, use our EasyPress or iron on the purple picture and then process the golden image.

Supplies you'll need:

Cricut Explore or maker machine

Cricut® tools, weeder

Cricut® iron-on lite in gray

Cricut® iron-on lite in cyan

Cricut® iron-on lite in maize

White canvas cloth

Red cotton cloth

Blue cotton cloth

Literary cotton cloth

Dark cotton cloth

Dark and white cotton cloth

Iron or EasyPress

Press fabric or clean cotton fabric

Scissors

Sewing machine and thread

1: Cut your pictures

Some essential tips for this job:

Make sure to click on the "mirror picture (for the iron-on)" button for each mat in the mat preview display position. Considering that every one of the mats includes iron-on, you'll have to click onto each carpet and select to mirror the picture.

The program determines where the cuts will happen on the mat. I needed to save my iron-on material for this job, so I moved the pictures around on the mat to make the leading area's best use. Additionally, this performs in the mat preview display.

Simply click on each picture and move them around until they are tucked right into each other. This ninja star would not have cut since the iron-on substance is 19" long, and the lead was set lower than that on the mat.

Assess each mat. I transferred pictures around on all of them.

2: Iron images onto canvas

Iron the pictures onto white canvas leaving approximately 5-6" of the distance between cutting and stitching images. It is possible to accelerate the process using our EasyPress as it's a larger surface compared to a conventional iron and much more consistent heating throughout the plate. For the layered images, begin with ironing the base layer set up. Eliminate the liner.

Twist the top picture over the base image and iron in place. You can find more directions about the best way best to use Cricut® iron-on here.

3: Cut fabric shapes

Use scissors to cut each picture. Make sure to leave at least 2-3" of space around the images for stitching seam, trimming, and cutting.

You do not need to be perfect! The attractiveness of these attractive cushions is their wonky shape that adds to their appeal.

4: Cut outsourcing

Set the cut canvas pictures to face down on the backing cloth (right sides together). Use scissors to cut the backing to coordinate with the front part.

5: Stitch fabric together

6: Switch pillows and materials

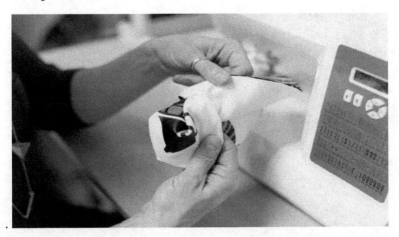

Turn the inside of the mat over and fill it with fiber filler.

7.Hand-stitched opening Sew the closed door by hand with needle and thread.

CHAPTER 15:

The Way To Make Personalized Totes and Decorations

Flower Garden Tote Bag

Flower Garden Tote Bag You can never have too many tote bags, whether you use them as reusable shopping bags, giant purses, or anything else.

Create this cute flower garden bag to carry wherever you need to, and keep nature right by your side all day!

Choose your favorite flowers, and the more variety you have, the more interesting the bag will be to look. Canvas bags are an excellent neutral base that will last you years, but you can use this idea with a different type of tote as well.

The white vinyl gives a silhouette effect, but you can use a different color or even make each flower.

You'll need a Cricut EasyPress or iron for the heat transfer vinyl.

Supplies needed

- Canvas tote bag

- White heat transfer vinyl

- Cricut EasyPress or iron

- Cutting mat

- Weeding tool or pick

Instructions

1. Open the Cricut design space and create a new project.

2. Select the "image" button in the lower-left corner and search for "flowers."

3. Choose your favorite flower and click "Insert."

4. Continue with various flowers, lining them up together to form a straight edge at the bottom.

5. Place your vinyl on the cutting mat.

6. Send the design to your Cricut.

7. Use weeding tools or remove the excess vinyl from the system.

8. Place the design along the bottom of the tote bag with the plastic side up.

9. Carefully iron on the course.

10. After cooling, roll to peel it off.

11. Carry around your new garden tote bag!

Dinosaur T-Shirt

Dinosaur T-Shirt Everyone loves dinosaurs, and kids can't have enough t-shirts. Use iron-on vinyl to create the perfect shirt for your fossil-loving child!

The sleeves' small designs add a little extra, bringing it up a level from your standard graphic t-shirt. Just as with the rest of these projects, you can use the same idea with different designs. Customize a shirt for any of your child's interests.

The Cricut EasyPress or iron will help you attach the vinyl designs to the t-shirt. You can use Cricut Explore One, Cricut Explore Air 2, or Cricut Maker for this project.

Supplies Needed

- T-shirt of your choice

- Green heat transfer vinyl

- Cricut EasyPress or iron

- Cutting mat

- Weeding tool or pick

Instructions

1. Open Cricut Design Space.

2. Select the "Image" button in the lower-left corner and search for "dinosaurs."

3. Choose your favorite dinosaur and click "Insert."

4. Select "Image" again and search for "fossils."

5. Choose your famous fossil and click "Insert."

6. Copy the fossil once so that you have two of them.

7. Place your vinyl on the cutting mat.

8. Send the design to your Cricut.

9. Use weeding tools or remove the excess vinyl from the system.

10. Place dinosaur in the center of the t-shirt, and a fossil on each sleeve, with the plastic side up.

11. Carefully iron on the design.

12. After cooling, roll to peel it off.

CHAPTER 16: **Personalized Home Décor**

Making mugs, plates, bottles, jars are the favorite project of a couple of crafters and people. It is an easy way to update home decorations without going through acquiring new items. All you have to do is add a simple decoration to the already used things, and then you'll find yourself with new things.

PERSONALIZED COFFEE MUG

Coffee mugs are easier to make than you think. However, you cannot wash your personalized coffee mugs with the washing machine, which will peel away the vinyl designs. Most of the washing machine equips with heat-sensitive settings that are not suitable for the mugs. The heat will melt the vinyl designs and thereby causing damage to them. Therefore, personalized coffee mugs are to be hand-washed; hence, if you are making one give away as a gift or to sell, you need to indicate that it should be washed with warm soapy water and the hand and not a machine.

Materials and tools needed

- Cricut Machine

- Scraping Tool and Weeding Tool

- Transfer Tape

- A coffee mug of your choice

- Permanent Vinyl

The steps include:

1. You have to log in to your Design Space on your computer.

2. Upload and customize your design. You have to select a design of your choice. There are plenty of plans available to you- you can get some for free while you have to pay for some if you have a subscription to Cricut Access, you will be able to access all designs. However, things to be on the lookout for when choosing a plan- are careful of dot-like tiny things. Small items observe to be very had to be stuck on the transfer tape, making it very easy to miss them. The dot on the top of 'i' is like the most significant nuisance when designing this punctuation-like period. It is effortless to miss out on such items. You can also create your designs by yourself as this is ideal, although you have to be creative and play around with your plans. Do not forget that the thicker or bigger your system, the easier it is to get it on the transfer tape. Once you have arrived at a particular course, you should upload it on your Design Space and then modify the dimensions.

3. Attach your designs so that they do not appear on different mats. It helps all of your systems or letters cut out to be together. You should then 'Make It.'

4. Have the vinyl prepared and cut the SVG (or the image you have designed by yourself). It requires making use of your Cricut machine to do the cutting. In addition to having a vinyl+ setting on the dial (which means setting it between vinyl and ironing transfer), the green felt pad (medium glue) could also use for Oracle 651. It discovers that sometimes it does not cut entirely, and this was traced to the regular vinyl setting, although having a dull blade will also prevent it from cutting entirely.

5. The design is bound to have a lot of negative spaces around it once itis cut. The unwanted vinyl detaches with utmost care and precision. You advise starting your trimming from the vinyl sheet, although the background vinyl should remove first. This process calls weeding- you have to remove unnecessary and extra vinyl that does not include all of them in your design. The inside of your plans and letters like O can take out by using the weeding tool. Your final product should have a look at what you so desire.

6. You should then go ahead to prepare your tape and the mug. A piece of the transfer tape is all that you need. However, you have to be sure that the cut piece of transfer tape is sufficient for your design. The mug should also prepare for use. You should make sure the mug is in a condition where dust and oils (your hand produces natural oil, and you should make sure your mug is free from those too). In a bid to achieve this, you should wipe it with a cotton ball soaked in alcohol. You should also brush your hand with this.

7. You should then get your transfer tape applied to your vinyl design (weeded image). Be sure to have your transfer tape sticking to your vinyl very well. It is usually stuck, especially when it is the first time; however, you can

press it down with your fingers to ensure it stays well, as this is usually effective. There might be air bubbles trapped under the transfer tape; hence the scraping tool can remove them. You should not forget to lift them to make sure that you have not skipped the annoying dots!

8. Be careful when applying the image on the mug, and be sure to do so firmly too. Hold down and rub on it as it is essential to have it sticking very well to the face. You can also make use of the scraper to be sure it is perfectly stuck on it. As there is no harm in being too confident, you can again rub those dots down or brandish them to confirm their stickiness. If you are sure of your eyesight, you can eyeball it to ensure that the transfer tape is kept straight.

9. Remove the transfer tape from the mug. It is one by peeling off with the utmost care. Once this does, you should have your unique personalized coffee mug.

10. However, the transfer tape is reusable; hence, you should not throw it away; instead, you should keep it for other projects, therefore saving money.

NOTE: When placing your design on your mug, it is essential to position it well. It would not be nice to have your plan set too high hence when people are drinking. They would have the system on their lips again. You should also decide on the side (left or right) you want to position it as you might wish to the system facing you while you drink or away from you. It is more of an individual choice, however.

CHAPTER 17:

Cricut Suggestions For Promoting Your Greeting Card Projects

If one of your great loves in life is arts and crafts, there is a new dream machine that will add a lot of spice to your Cricut projects! Cricut has just made your artistic endeavors that much easier to obtain. This revolutionary machine has just completed the daunting task of cutting obsolete with a straightforward device. Fear not; replaceable Cricut blades make this machine sharp and intact whenever you need it!

The original Cricut machine is an electronic cutter that can perform various creative projects with one button's touch!

Cricut crafts machines come with cartridges with many designs that you can choose from, ranging from innovative designs, letters, and numbers.

It is a stand-alone machine that you only a plugin for use; a computer is not necessary!

If you like to add a personal touch to your holiday and birthday bags.

Cricut crafts will do just that for you. You can design personalized cards and gift bags with font sizes that range from one inch to five and a half inches to make your project just perfect! Seasonal cartridges are also available along with personalized phrases to make your person of choice feel special.

If you have children that love animals, this would be an ideal creative craft choice to bring a smile to their faces.

AMAZING CRICUT CARD IDEAS FOR YOUR FAMILY

Why spend more money on greeting cards now that you possess a Cricut cutting machine?

Asides from Christmas and the New Year, the next holiday coming up on the calendar is Easter.

Suppose that one of the Cricut cartridges you have is the Cricut Doodlecharms cartridge. In that case, you can make an incredibly charming high-quality welcome card of the Easter Basket or an Easter Bunny filled with colored eggs. Or on the other hand, perhaps another of your Cricut cartridges is the Cricut Wild Card cartridge so that you can make a Filigree Easter Egg card. Another of my Cricut Card thoughts is on the off chance that you have the Cricut Stretch Your Imagination cartridge. You can make a card with a Bunny shading Easter eggs or a bunny in a basket.

As far as the entirety of the Cricut card ideas I could concoct for Easter, not every one of them has to have eggs or bunnies on them.

Then the next big card day is Mother's Day. Think of how your Mom will feel getting a handmade greeting card from her child. You will make her day. No matter what Cricut cartridges you have, you will be able to find something that will put a smile on her face, and of course, you will do all of this with your magnificent Cricut cutting machine.

The extraordinary thing about your Cricut cutting machine and all the Cricut cartridges that are accessible to you is that it gives you a vast number of Cricut card ideas.

You will see that your cards look so professional you will not wait to send them out or start selling them. I'm going to get busy making my handmade greeting cards on my very own Cricut cutting machine; how about you?

CHAPTER 18:

Project Ideas For Special Situations:

Geometric Lampshade Or Hanging Décor

While this pendant may look intricate, it is a comfortable design that can add a little modernism to your space. You can use it as a lampshade or add it to your décor for just a design detail. You can also consider adding a metallic version on the inside of the white pendant to add a little sparkle and interest to the project.

You'll need:

- White cardstock

- Metallic cardstock, if you prefer

- Ribbon or string

- Hot glue gun

Step 1

In Design Space, go into the library and enter the "Make It Now" unit. Find the project labeled "Geo Ball."

Step 2

Once the project loads, place your cardstock on your cutting mat and send it to score the fold lines.

Step 3

Once your paper scores, glue the metallic and white pieces of paper together. Begin folding the paper to create the geometric shape.

Place a line of glue along one edge and bring the project into its final form.

Step 4

If you are hanging your pendant, make sure to attach your ribbon or string to the bottom of the shape and hand it from your ceiling!

Takeout-Style Boxes

Yes, you could use the go-to plastic to-go containers, or you could whip up a few custom ones of your own. You can serve leftovers in these simple packages, or you can add all sorts of embellishments, like stickers and labels.

You'll need:

- Sticker paper for labels or stickers

- Cardstock

- Hot glue gun or glue dots

Step 1

If you add labels of stickers to your boxes, design them in Design Space with the image or text you prefer. Consider adding the title of the event and the date to the label, so guests know right away how long they have the leftovers for in their fridge. Create a variety of sizes so they will fit over the cardstock boxes you are about to create or other containers you might need to use.

Step 2

Once your stickers or labels create, send the file to print and cut.

Step 3

Search in the Design Space library the template for Chinese Take Out Boxes and load it into a new workspace. Choose a variety of sizes. Load your cardstock onto your cutting mats and send the file to cut.

Step 4

Fold your cut cardstock along the score lines. Apply glue along the edges to assemble the box and reinforce the seams.

Step 5

If you are adding stickers to your boxes, add them now. For other containers, keep the stickers nearby or apply them onto them as well. You are ready to send your guests away in style directly!

Latte Stencil

In the morning coffee game, sprinkle a little cinnamon or espresso powder on the foam. You can also modify it to increase cocoa beans' life instead of the whipped cream on hot chocolate.

You'll need:

- Cardstock or vellum

- Coffee in a mug and a dusting material

Step 1

Measure the top of your mugs or your favorite mug you use often. In Design Space, create a circle or shape that will rest over your mug's lip and add another small circle to the side of it to be the tab that you will hold while the stencil is in use.

Step 2

Write your message or create your image on your stencil. Make sure to center your image in shape. Send the file to cut on your vellum. Weed the small pieces in the center of your design and peel away the outside vellum or cardstock you do not need.

Step 3

When your latte is ready and still lovely and hot, place the stencil over your mug and tap your dusting flavor over top of the stencil. Gently lift the stencil away to reveal your barista design. If you used vellum, wash the stencil off and lay aside to dry for your coffee creation!

Felt Owls

You can use these as ornaments or hang around for some fun fall décor. You can also have your kids help you create these adorable pine cone owls.

You'll need:

- Various pinecones washed and air dried

- Felt in various colors like brown, black, white, yellow, and teal

- Hot glue gun

- Ribbon

Step 1

First, you will want to design the pieces of the owl face and wings in Design Space. The beginning makes two large circles attached. The eyes are two-layered circles, and the nose is a teardrop shape.

The wings are two-layered teardrops and can have small circle embellishments.

You can also create a stomach piece, which is a circle with little circles inside of it. "Eyebrows" in two wings or a small triangle are also suitable embellishments to design.

Step 2

Send your images to cut out of your felt. Tape down your felt pieces with masking tape or painter's tape if you want to make sure the fabric does not move around while cutting.

Step 3

Begin creating your pinecone owls by taking the pieces and start gluing them onto the pinecone. Alternate colors and styles to make a little village of owls.

Glue a small amount of glue to the top of the pinecones to be able to hang them, if you want, or leave them to sit flat on a surface.

Paper Flower Wreath

Decorate your door with a festive wreath. You can make it any colors or styles you want based on your décor and taste. When you select your colors, you also choose a color "pop," like the teal color in this example. Also, make sure to make different leaves out of green shades. Your wreath base can be anything like foam or twine. If you have a not attractive base, grab some coordinating fabric to wrap around the wreath or make enough flowers and leaves to cover the bottom completely. You can also add embellishments like beads, buttons, felt balls, and more to your project to take it up a notch.

You'll need:

- Wreath base
- Colored cardstock
- Hot glue gun
- Coordinated fabric, if desired

Step 1

In Design Space, find a variety of different flower and leaf projects. Aim for about three or four different flower designs that are different in size. Try to make as many as possible in different colors and sizes.

Follow the instructions for compiling the petals and creating the flowers. Pinch the leaves or fold the bottoms over to add dimension to the leaves. A good goal is to have about 30 different flowers and 15 other leaves to start.

Step 2

If you decided to wrap your wreath with fabric, add a little glue to one end of the material to the wreath and begin wrapping it around the wreath and securing the other future with hot glue when it is covered.

Step 3

Begin adding your flowers to your wreath with your hot glue gun. Make sure you are mixing shapes and colors on your wreath. Once all the flowers add to your wreath, fill in with the leaves. Add other embellishments if you want. When the glue is dry, get ready to hang your wreath!

CHAPTER 19:

Ideas for Halloween Decorations

Coffin Favor Box

Easy I Less Than 30 Minutes

Description:

This project cuts out a 3D treat box in the shape of a coffin out of cardstock.

Finished Size:

Approximately 3.6" x 2.6" (9.1 cm x 6.6 cm)

Materials to Cut:

Everyday Iron-On, White 12" x 24."

Patterned Cardstock, Black

Patterned Cardstock, Gold

Everything Else:

EasyPress

EasyPress Mat

Adhesive for Paper

Brads, Gold

Candy

Preparation:

If you wish to modify the task, select Customize, and then use the modified module tools to create adjustments already when you sliced.

Cut:

Mat1 - Put the metal white onto the pad.

Mat2 - Place black patterned cardstock onto the mat.

Mat3 - Place gold patterned cardstock onto the mat.

Assemble:

Using a Weeder technique to cut the iron-on negatives, so only your logo stays on the transparent linen

2. Using a Cricut EasyPress and Cricut EasyPress Mat with our heat exchange Method, below, to attach the iron-on layers to the top of the coffin (the piece with the sharp edges).

3. Fold along coffin score lines. Glue along the tabs to start making the cavern Materials.

Embellish with the gold crafting brads.

Glue the gold patterned cardstock to the inside of the top and bottom coffin pieces.

Fill with candy and enjoy it!

Gravestone Candle Wraps

Easy I Less Than 30 Minutes

Description:

Add a bit of spooky glow to your home.

Finished Size:

8" W x 3.6" H

Materials to Cut:

Cardstock, Black

Cardstock, Grey

Everything Else:

StandardGrip Machine Mat - 12" x 12"

Weeder

Craft glue or adhesive tape

Flameless pillar candles

Preparation:

This project makes wraps for three candles. Redimension the picture in the Modify section when you press Go.

Cut:

Cut photos from cardstock in Design space.

Assemble:

Use craft glue or a tape adhesive to adhere the layers together.

Wrap the graveyard border around the candle and secure with glue or tape Adhesive.

Mr. Pumpkin Head Spider

Easy I Less Than 30 Minutes

Description:

Guard your porch with this dapper spider pumpkin.

Finished Size:

Approximately 10" x 10" (25.4 cm x 25.4)

Materials to Cut:

Cardstock, White

Cardstock, Black

Cardstock, Dark Gray

Cardstock, Glitter Red

Everything Else:

LightGrip Machine Mat

Adhesive for Paper

Preparation:

If you wish to modify the task, then choose customizable, then use change module tools to make adjustments already when you sliced.

Cut:

To cut the photos from the cardstock, obey the instructions 'n Design Space.

Assemble:

In Design Space, add the cut cardstock in the very same sequence as it occurs in the settings option, beginning from the lower side and working up, using glue.

Adhere the bow-tie piece to the pumpkin.

Gothic Graveyard Scene

Easy I Less Than 30 Minutes

Description:

This project cuts cardstock for gothic gravestones.

Finished Size:

Approximately 3" x 1.5" (7.6 cm x 3.8 cm)

Materials to Cut:

Cardstock, Dark Gray

Cardstock, Gray

Cardstock, Light Gray

Cardstock Pale Gray

Distress Ink, Silver

Adhesive Foam Dots

Hot Glue Gun and Glue Sticks

Chunky Candlesticks, Gray, 3

Cut:

Follow the prompts in Design Space to cut the images from the cardstock.

Attach your device to score when requested

Assemble:

Use distress ink to accent the edges of the cardstock cutouts and create a more weathered look.

Assemble the pieces of the card, using adhesive and adhesive foam dots, then embellish.

Adhere the assembled gravestone pieces onto the base rectangles with hot glue, then glue the bases into the candlesticks.

Victorian Hearse and Coffin

Advanced | 2 — 3 Hours

The images used in this project are unique to Cricut Access subscribers.

Description:

Assemble this ornate Victorian-style hearse and coffin to bring a chilling accent to your Halloween display.

Finished Size:

6.5" x 3.25" x 25"

Materials to Cut:

Cardstock in gray

Cardstock in dark gray

Cardstock in black

Everything Else:

Cricut Explore machine

Design Space software

Cricut 12" x 12" StandardGrip mat

Black 1/4" brads (2)

Black embellishments (assorted)

Fancy black 1" buttons (4)

Black paper straws, pencils or

dowels

Hot glue gun or fast-drying glue

Distress ink (optional)

Preparation:

This project makes one hearse and coffin set,

The finished hearse is about 11" long and 10" tall; the wheelbase is about 6.5" across.

The finished coffin measures about 6.5" x 325" x 2.5" Our file is approximately 1:12 scale.

If you need to adjust the dimensions, click Customize to open the project canvas.

Make sure to select all pieces and resize them at the same time to make sure they will all still fit with each other.

Assemble:

Refer to the 3D assembly instructions for the Casket and Carriage. Assemble the gray hearse first, then attach the black pieces over the assembled carriage for easier assembly.

Embellish:

Embellish the carriage with black stick-on embellishments or rhinestones. Use black decorative buttons as hubcaps. Use grayscale washi tape and black glitter tape to decorate the coffin lid. Distress ink may also be used on the cardstock before assembly for a more weathered look.

Halloween Scene Glass Dome

Easy I Less Than 30 Minutes

This spooky scene is just what you need to push your Halloween decor over the top.

Description:

This project makes a 3D Halloween scene inside a glass cloche.

Finished Size:

Approximately 6 inches x 8 inches (15.2 cm x 20.3 cm)

Materials To Cut:

- Chipboard, 2mm
- Cardstock, White
- Cardstock, Gray
- Cardstock, Black
- Cardstock, Brown

Everything Else:

- StrongGrip Machine Mat
- LightGrip Machine Mat
- Knife Blade

- Masking Tape
- Adhesive for Paper
- Hot Glue Gun and Glue Sticks
- Glass Dome
- Wire
- Pebbles
- Styrofoam
- Paint, Brown
- Paintbrush
- Moss
- Ink Stamp Pad, Black

Preparation:

1. If you'd like to change the layout, click Modify, use Modify row tools to make adjustments before you slice.

2. For hardboard-Use, the Pad Review display to adjust textures or move parts to various pads, make changes to this design.

3. Make sure all of your pieces are within an 11" x 11" (27.9 cm x 27.9 cm) area, oriented to the top left corner of the mat.

4. The chipboard should be exposed and left aside for 24 hours for the best results to acclimatize to your environment. When your chipboard begins warping, place it under a heavy object.

5. Before slicing, if you coat the chipboard, cover both the paper's underside and the chipboard's surface even with sticky covering.

6. Push the sheet or picture with the brayer (or firm, even hand stress) and allow it to dry completely before slicing. For full cutting, multiple passes may be necessary.

Cut:

1. Follow the instructions for slicing pictures from the cardstock in Creative Spaces.

2. Mat 5 - Using sticky tape or painter tape to protect chipboard outlines to your pad.

3. Using the correct cut setup and the Knife Edge, follow the instructions in Design Space to cut photos from the chipboard.

TIP: if you've never used Knife Blade previously, please check the connection in the More support page down. When extracting your product from the device, second check to ensure that your design has sliced through and, if required, carry out another slice attempt before packing the mat.

Assemble:

1. Glue color cardstock over chipboard cutouts.

2. Glue mansion to center of styrofoam using hot glue.

3. Glue tree and cat to styrofoam in front of the mansion.

4. Add moss and pebbles around cutouts using hot glue.

5. Hot glue ghosts to wire and attach to the back of the mansion.

6. The cover scene with a glass dome.

CHAPTER 20:

Ideas For Christmas Decorations And Christmas Gifts

Adorable Snowman

Materials Needed:

1. Stitching cotton in snowflake white
2. Stitching cotton in scarf print
3. Felt in tan (This should be acceptable quality felt or the firm assortment.)
4. Felt in dark
5. Cricut Washable texture marker
6. Iron or warmth press and press fabric
7. Sewing machine
8. Needle and string
9. Batting
10. Loads (a few marbles)

11. Cricut Sewing Kit (Discretionary yet Very Helpful!)

Procedures:

1. This snowman is a piece of that pack, so the example is free. Simply search snowman, and you will discover the model.

2. Snap the image of the snowman, and you will carry to a screen with all that you have to make the venture. You will discover the materials required and directions.

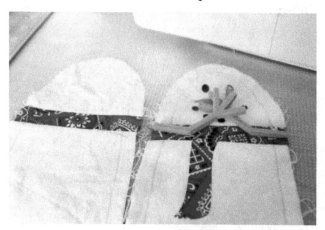

3. You can discover nitty gritty guidelines with pictures when you pull up the venture in configuration space.

4. Start by clicking "make it" in configuration space and pulling up your mats for cutting. Burden each tangle, sharp edge, and even the washable pen when incited to miss the entirety of the pieces expected to make this adorable snowman.

5. Configuration space will walk you through each tangle, and you will be left with the entirety of your pieces superbly slice and prepared to make your undertaking.

6. Notice that the washable texture pen makes lines on a portion of the pieces. It will stamp the zone, so you realize where to put your face and denote your crease lines.

7. When your pieces cut, you can start to sew them together. What's more, yes, that is a pin pad molded like a Cricut machine!

8. Sew the front and back of the snowman together according to the directions.

9. At that point, include your face and scarf piece to the front of the snowman with iron or warmth press.

10. You can pick to weave the face. Include the arms and pin the right sides of your two sorts out to get ready for sewing.

11. At that point, simply stuff your charming snowman and hand sew your opening shut to finish your undertaking.

Adorable Christmas Tea Towels

Christmas tea towels are a fast and straightforward starting project for the Cricut cutting machine. Just incorporate heat transfer vinyl and almost infinite design choices.

Instructions:

- I opened Cricut Design Space and began a new project. The Design Space Image Library has over 60,000 pictures, so it's simple to start designing your project in no time.

- Press the image you want to work with, and the software inserts it into a new project document. I chose these wonderful hand-lettered "Merry and Bright" and "Merry Christmas" designs for my towels and arranged them for vinyl heat transfer sheets.

- Explore Air's favorite features are dial settings (you don't have to worry about manually changing blade depth or remembering which center aligns with each material).

- With Cricut Explore Air, you just turn the knob to grab stuff you're working with, and the machine looks after the straightforward peasy.

- Set the "Iron-on" dial, and you're prepared to cut.

- Place a vinyl heat transfer sheet, load it into the device, and press the cut button.

- Use Cricut Weeder to remove the excess vinyl from the design.

- I put the vinyl on my folded tea towel, covered it with cloth, and ironed it in the package's instructions.

- Once the vinyl heat transfer firmly adheres, and the plastic support discards. I slipped a piece of cardstock under the towel top and used silver, gold, and champagne-colored fabric paint to add some shiny polka dots.

CHAPTER 21:

Troubleshooting

W hen technology gives us problems, we abandon it because we don't know what to do. Personally, calling someone for help is too much effort, and quite frankly, I am also proud of it. So I suffer from my pride and do things on my own. Luckily for people like me, some tips and tricks can try in these situations. Of course, many things can go wrong with your machine. It's electronic; of course, it will malfunction from time to time. Here are a few things that I have learned by dealing with these issues myself.

These are also the most common issues, and if you experience anything more than this, I'd advise contacting Cricut to get help with your problem. These issues aren't severe and can fix. That says, if you are ever unsure, don't be as proud and stubborn as me. Just call someone. I wish I had before I spent hours trying to figure these things out.

What to Do When

The Machine Doesn't Cut Through the Material

Check your blades to make sure that they are blunt. That is usually the reason why this happens.

Make sure that your material isn't too thick. Remember 2mm or less for Explore machines and 2.5mm for Cricut Maker.

You also might want to check your settings. It is easy to miss the Smart Set Dial setting where the materials are listed. Make sure that your dial sets to the material that you are trying to cut through. It also goes for Design Space. Make sure that the appropriate material selects from the Custom Materials list.

Another reason this can be is that your blade might have some build-up. To fix this, remove the blade housing and make sure that there is no build-up. If there is nothing there, remove the blade and inspect both closely. Remove any debris that might stucks to the edge or housing.

Your pressure might be too low. To fix this, simply go to your Manage Custom Materials page on your account menu in Design Space. Try increasing the pressure by two and do a test cut. If this doesn't work, increase the pressure 4-6 times, doing test cuts every time.

You can try cutting a different material. Remember to adjust the setting to accommodate the new material and cut. If it works, then the problem is with your material, not the machine.

If all of these options fail, you might want to call the customer care line.

The Blade Isn't Detected

In Design Space, you will see that it recommends a blade in the Load tools step. It is on the Preview screen. When I don't have the right tool, I just unload the mat, select the Edit Tools option in the project preview screen, and select a different device. It usually does the trick. Remember to use B-clamp.

If this doesn't work, try cutting a different shape with an additional tool. If it works, it means that the problem lies with the device and not the machine. It means that you can buy a different blade instead of a whole new Cricut machine, which is significantly cheaper than what you would have paid for a new Cricut.

There are other options, too, though. You can remove your blade housing and clean it off. There is a little reflective surface on the housing. If that blocks by debris, there is no chance your blade will detect. Make sure that you have it cleaned properly. I like to wipe mine down every day I do projects. I can't be bothered to struggle with it, so I just keep it clean from the get-go.

You also have to make sure that the tool sensor is clean. Be very gentle about this and use a microfiber cloth. Any form of dust build-up can cause issues, so best keep it squeaky clean all the time instead of struggling with it when you want to start projects.

The Machine Turns Off Unexpectedly

It usually happens when you cut metals or foil. The reason for this is the accumulation of static electricity. Dry environments can also cause this, so don't worry too much about this.

To solve this issue, you can spray some mist into the air to humidify it. Do not, under any circumstances, spray it directly onto the Cricut machine. When I go to a mainly dry area with my Cricut, I like to have a humidifier handy. It is instrumental, and it might be worth investing in if your machine continues to give you this problem.

Conclusion

Thank you for making it to the end. Whatever you might do with a Cricut is only limited by your imagination. This gadget can also be relatively straightforward to watch over. The designs can be chosen from the cartridge or custom-made, utilizing the Cricut design studio to have originality to elevated heights - but that the computer is vital for this function.

Cricut is the handicraft enthusiast's best buddy, or for anyone who'd love to design and create. It supplies over 250 distinct designs in many sizes. The plans could be more significant compared to an inch or larger around one inch. The different cutting angles offer precision decrease - all of this, together with templates that are attractive collectively with interlocking alphabets, provide considerably to select.

Now everybody can use a little additional money. Your first of many Cricut jobs will be to produce an assortment of about one0 to one2 cards. Be creative; you will find many ideas; it is possible to take into account. Contained inside this variety, you've got to obtain a couple of greeting cards (make sure you make cards for women, men, and also cards for children); make sure you include thank you, anniversary, get well, and a sympathy card. Some more tasks that you're in a place to make on your Cricut cutting machine will be to make sterile inside note cards for nearly any purpose.

You will have any card ideas such as blossoms that could be layered over the cover using a rhinestone center or just the expression hi adorned with a couple of unique shapes. You're ready to package them up in sets of 4-6 cards. With your Cricut cutting tool that makes a variety of tasks are in a little button. All types of thoughts will start flowing from your creative ideas. You can produce decorated boxes to place your cards.

Now you need to take your Cricut jobs with lots of your suggestions and take them into shops (florists, bakery, and salons, along with tiny gift shops) and talk to the proprietor. Have a look at that pricing available for every shop proprietor. Make sure you customize the price sheet with the name of this company that you're incredibly likely to furnish them. You'll discover looking like a very professional business person instead of merely a crafter expecting to provide your card ideas. Some owners may permit you to leave your cards from their shop on consignment and only have a percent when you market them. (I have done consignment earlier at a local florist and a luxurious nail salon. Also, did great what a great spot to display your Cricut cards compared to a means that is 95 percent of women that would be the very best shoppers. Besides the cards that I provided in these shops, I got special buys for baby showers and birth announcements). Just be sure that you leave your business cards at these shops.

Clients might wish to get you for specific orders. It's likewise possible to market online. An excellent location on the internet calls shop handmade; it's perfect since its prices. Or it's also possible to advertise your Cricut tasks at local craft displays. While creating your cards, remember Christmas alongside other big holidays in which people send cards such as Christmas Day, Easter, Mother's Day, Father's Day!

Another of many jobs is very likely to create together with your Cricut cutting machine to create a custom baby shower or marriage or maybe a wedding invitation. There are lots of thoughts about these sorts of cards. You will encounter a lot of Cricut cartridges that are made specifically for these jobs. A cartridge called a wedding to get all those fabulous wedding contours in the Cricut choice collection.

It is possible to envision and have a home accent cartridge with unique swirly flowers and shapes. It is also feasible to use for a wedding theme. In case you choose to proceed into the baby shower or birth announcement training course, you'll see great cartridges such as new arrival and soon to be printed a youngster's year.

Which path you require to be sure that you create several samples in several distinct fashions. I just had another one to find a superb job. See, I told you that your images would start to stream after starting with your Cricut cutting device. If you have any party centers for children's birthday parties locally, it's incredibly likely to supply customize and interrogate goodie bags and title tags. Show them samples of numerous topics that you've got (determined from the Cricut capsules that you have got). Maybe you will compose a catalog to leave there so customers will discover the choice you'd love to supply you.

Cricut is a well-known manufacturer of equipment drifting everywhere in the country. It is an exciting and one of a type of gadget utilized by most women and guys who would like to make exceptional and innovative tasks. At this moment, there are just three different versions of Cricut: the Cricut generate machine, luxury Cricut cutter, and of course, the base variant Cricut personal electronic cutter machine.

Before improving what Cricut can raise the society, let's have a peek through its base. Cricut using a massive firm called Provo craft, which was a tiny store. Approximately forty decades before, the Provo Craft Company started as a retail store in the small town of Provo, Utah. With their resourcefulness and creativity, the company eventually enlarged the following several years. They finally have a total of ten stores with an approximately 200,000-foot distribution center.

I hope you have learned something!

CRICUT ACCESSORIES, SOFTWARE, AND APP:

Maximize Your Cricut Machine Like A Pro &
Turn Your Skills Into A Business

Kimberly Maker Smith

TABLE OF CONTENTS

Introduction

The Cricut gear conveys with it a heap of excellent potential outcomes that incorporate Cricut projects. Individuals take a gander at the Cricut machine as a simple device for scrapbooking; however, if you take a gander at it more profoundly, you will see that it is prepared to do quite a lot more. One use of the Cricut gear that can assist you with procuring benefit is solicitations. The intro page design of the welcome cards is the place a Cricut machine can render its administrations. With the utilization of a software instrument, you can search for models that can fit the greeting's event. If your address is for a child shower, you can search for a model that shows an infant shower image, thus some more.

Right now, the economy ordinarily doesn't go your direction, and you have to amplify whatever means you have. I ensure anybody that if you place into a circumstance, such is reality and passing, every one of your faculties will shiver like "Spiderman's bug - sense. "You will take a gander at things from a progressively genuine edge, and your cerebrum will work. In the scrapbooking realm, the Cricut has related to only making scrapbooks, and that's it. Be that as it may, if you grow your vision and take a gander at this remarkable instrument from a business point of view, you will see the potential that this device can have. As an issue of reality, there are many income-producing Cricut projects that you can take part in.

Another utilization of the Cricut hardware is on making Cricut schedules. Each schedule has a year on it, and you can utilize the Cricut machine to cut designs that help show the state of mind related to a particular month. If it is Halloween, you can search for a model with Jack - o - lights and creepy apparitions thus some more. Welcome cards are the place Cricut machines can likewise utilize for. If you are searching for an extraordinary design for any gift voucher, the utilization of software tools, for example, the Cricut design studio and the Cricut hardware, can help. There are hundreds and many pre-stacked designs that you can look over, and the extraordinary things about this software instrument are that they permit the client to alter the plans that work in them. Those are a portion of the remarkable Cricut projects that you can take part in. Keep in mind, think past the crate. That is the top way that you can create more and advantages yourself.

Individuals feel that the Cricut machine is the one instrument that is answerable for conceptualizing the designs we find in scrapbooks. The designs originate from the brain of the client and are made unmistakable by the Cricut cutting machine. What's more, different tools help make designs, such as cartridges and software tools. The most outstanding software instrument out there is the Cricut Design Studio. With this software, you can alter your designs and even change existing models that are pre-stacked.

Life is acceptable to be sure! Individuals likewise feel that using a Cricut cutting machine is just restricted to the universe of scrapbooking. Very few individuals know about this, yet there the Cricut machine, alongside the cartridges and the software tools, utilize many things. There are a ton of Cricut projects that you can use the Cricut cutting machine for, and just your psyche can restrain what you can do.

Welcome cards are extraordinary Cricut projects for anybody to take part in. With the designs you can get from the Cricut cartridge and the software tools you have set up, your design covers that resist the capricious. The issue that the vast majority experience when they attempt to buy welcoming cards in shopping centers is that they can't discover the design of the map they are searching for. It can cause pressure and a great deal of dissatisfaction on the purchaser's part. You are such a significant amount of happier, making your welcome cards.

Cricut schedules are additionally another good thought for a Cricut cutting machine. A program loads up with a year. You can get inventive and search for designs in your software or cartridge that can mirror the month inside your schedule. So if we are in December, you can search for models that match the state of mind and December's climate. Search for snowmen, reindeers, and Christmas trees. I promise you that you have all the designs you will ever require within your software or cartridge.

Keep in mind and just your creative account can restrain what you do. These Cricut projects utilize either for individual fulfillment or income-producing purposes. Be innovative with your Cricut machine. No one can tell what wild and insane ideas can fly into your head.

CHAPTER 1:

Cricut Accessories

So, you have a Cricut cutting machine in which now you are entirely hooked on cutting, attracting, as well as making all the important things!

There are so many incredibly awesome devices that support your machine that isn't purely required; however, they sure are enjoyable!! Right here is the need to have Cricut accessories that you can't (do not wish to) do without!

I enjoy my Cricut Manufacturer, and also it has remarkably transformed the method I stitch.

There are numerous unique things that it can do, and also I am discovering brand-new pointers as well as tricks for using it day-to-day. I have created a list of all the fun devices that I like and utilize with my Cricut.

Infusible Ink

Infusible ink is an enjoyable new Cricut classification. It is the Circuits' take on sublimation.

Wavy Blade

The wavy blade is fantastic for usage with material and felt.The jagged edge is one of the newest blades for the Cricut Maker as well as cannot make use of with the Explore line of machines.

Brightpad

The BrightPad is impressive for so many factors. It is terrific for weeding vinyl, yet you can do a lot more with it! I use it for paper stitching. It is beautiful for tracing as well as adjusting patterns. It is seriously among my preferred tools in the craft room.

Xl Scraper

This enormous scrape is a should have. The small scraper is excellent, and all; however, really, it is hard to hold and also doesn't cover many locations. This scraper is best for a little larger vinyl project, and also it is friendly and robust, which assists get all the bubbles out. It functions excellent with transfer tape as well as adhesive vinyl also.

Easy Press

I will certainly be sincere before I had the EasyPress; I prevented iron-on or heat transfer vinyl like the torment. It never stayed and always left me very irritated. This maker is fantastic for affixing iron on. It functions great, it warms up quickly, and also it is easy to use. A consistent temperature level is crucial for sticking iron-on and keeps a steady temperature while again using stress. I certainly recommend this if you do any kind of iron-on. It also functions terrific with Warm N Bond for appliqués and including Deco Foil; make sure to let the aluminum foil cool before peeling because the glue demands to cool a bit to transfer the aluminum foil. See my reduced stitch napkins for a fun EasyPress tutorial. Currently, you can likewise get the EasyPress 2, which comes in several dimensions.

The huge perk of the 2 is that it bears in mind the last temperature level you set, so if you use the very same temp each time, you won't need to click with a bunch of times to get to that same temperature. They both work equally terrific. However, EasyPress 2 has a couple of extra rewards that make it unique. The weblink will undoubtedly take you to all the alternatives on the Cricut website, so whether you are shopping on a budget plan or searching for the perfect size with a few additional rewards, you can locate journalism that is right for you!

Pen Set

I love these pens! The colors are so beautiful, and they are excellent for all of your Cricut attracting projects. I such as to claim I have scribbling skills by viewing my Cricut do the scribbling for me! Make use of these to resolve your envelopes or sign your cards with gorgeous script handwriting. There are seriously so many fun choices! Do not utilize them on material because only textile markers work well on material! (See my fake cross stitch gift tags to see just how I use these markers).

Craft and Machine Tote

If you don't have a table or counter area for your equipment after that, you should have a great place to store it. Grab a tote to keep every one of your Cricut devices as well as your equipment. The material is lovely as well as it merely yells for some customization with iron-on! Right? It finds in numerous colors, so you can order whichever one fits your fancy!

Weeder

This simple weeder is fantastic if you do not do too much amount of weeding. It is a basic weeder with a lengthy side that permits you to get under the vinyl and easily remove it. If you do even more weeding or more elaborate designs abilities, this one and also see the weeding collection listed below.

Weeding Tool Set

If you do a great deal of weeding, this is a great device set for you. There are several terrific weeding tools that you will undoubtedly want to have a look at. One has a long straight point that is excellent for minimal weeding, pierces the vinyl, and pulls it directly with this device. There's also a weeder with the conventional curve; however, it contours once again just at the factor. It is fantastic for a pulling movement when weeding. This tool functions excellent for a more significant area of weeding. Obtain under the vinyl and afterward maintain hold of it with the pointed end as you pull away. This collection additionally consists of two sets of tweezers as well as the typical weeder revealed above.

All Function Mat Set

Cricut has four various shades of mats today. The pink carpet (not noted or imagined) creates for cutting textiles. Heaven mat is the light grip mat that you will utilize with paper and other lightweight materials like crepe paper. This mat has much less adhesive and allows you to reduce materials that formerly would have stuck to a typical mat. The trick for utilizing heaven mat is to turn the floor covering over and peel off the floor, covering far from the paper instead of peeling off the paper away from the floor covering. The environment-friendly mat is your standard floor covering that functions well with vinyl, iron-on, and I likewise utilize it for really felt. The purple mat is the strong mat that you will use for thicker products like timber veneer and various other heavy-duty materials. The added ling floor coverings are great for making multiples or larger designs. This package is a great deal and also an excellent way to stockpile on floor coverings.

CHAPTER 2:

Cricut Tools and How to Use Them

The Cricut Welder Tools

The welder tools, which resemble a dental pick, are utilized to expel negative space vinyl from a project. A welder is a MUST in case you're working with plastic by any means. Attempting to dispose of that overabundance of vinyl is unimaginable without it. Particularly with materials like the sparkle iron-on. Cricut has two weeding tools: the standard welder and the snared welder, which is a piece of the weeding tool set. However, bunches of individuals like that snared welder—attempt both and see which works better for you!

Attempt to utilize types of cement-like paste dabs. Rather than lifting them with my fingers, use the welder, and it keeps fingers sans sticky.

Options: you can utilize an ordinary dental pick, an art blade, or an enormous stick. I, by a wide margin, lean toward a weeding tool over any of those alternatives!

The Cricut Scraper and XL Scraper

Cricut has two scrubber tools—the standard scrubber and the XL scrubber. Both are great, yet utilizing XL scrubber is more effective because it does likewise work yet quicker. The edge of the scrubber is dainty, enabling it to get under materials effectively.

The scrubber tool is a lifeline when you have to clean your tangle after cutting something with a ton of negative bits. It works best with paper, yet different materials scrape up too. It frequently puts web over my thigh/knee and scratches the remaining piece legitimately into the junk can. If the knot is adaptable over the knee, it strikes well without pulling up any of the knot's glue. Additionally, we will, in general, utilize this with the Cricut logo looking down. The scrubber is additionally utilized as a bone envelope when collapsing on scoring lines to get a new edge. Indeed, haven't hauled out of old bone organizer in months since the scrubber works similarly. Also, use it as a shining tool when utilizing Cricut's exchange tape—it works like a fantasy for that. Likewise, it can twist lace, rather than a scissors sharp edge (The littler scrubber is useful for this).

Many individuals scratch their mats with a charge card or other comparative unbending surface. In any case, Cricut's scrubber and XL scrubber carry out the responsibility SO WELL that it very well may suggest lifting one. They're not unreasonably costly, and they'll spare you a massive amount of time.

The Cricut Spatula

The spatula is an absolute necessity to have on the off chance that you work with paper. Pulling the form off a Cricut tangle can regularly mean tears or twists in case you're not cautious. The spatula is so slight, so it slips effectively under paper projects, enabling you to dial them down the tangle painstakingly. Here's are the best tips and deceives for expelling materials from your Cricut tangle.

Before the utilization of a scrubber, utilize this to scratch scraps off the tangle.

Some individuals locate that a charge card or even a metal kitchen spatula is an excellent option compared to the Cricut spatula. Outline likewise has its very own spatula that has, to a greater extent, a wedge shape that a few clients like.

The Cricut Tweezers

Tweezers are a very famous tool in the Cricut toolbox. There are a few styles and edges, so you can genuinely pick what works best for you.

•Fine Tweezers (some portion of the Weeding Toolset)

•Reverse Tweezers (some part of the Basic Toolset)

Fine Tweezers

The fine tweezers are my most loved of the bundle. They also work to some other pair of tweezers you may possess and are incredible for grabbing little pieces to work with.

Invert Tweezers/ Reverse Tweezers

If you are doing projects with a ton of embellishments or little pieces, the invert tweezers are a decent alternative. They discover to be somewhat unbalanced from the outset—they are in reverse from how typical tweezers work. You crush them, and they open, rather than pressing them shut. It is splendid. It implies you can lift something up and, after that, let go of the weight, and the tweezers hang on tight to whatever it is. It'll spare you from dropping little pieces over and over, and your hand doesn't seize up as quickly since you're not crushing tight the entire time.

Snare/ Hook Tweezers

The snare tweezers are like the fine tweezers, yet they have a little snare on end. You may think this improves them at snatching littler pieces, yet it improves them at getting more significant bits because there is more territory of your tweezers on your part.

Broad Tip Tweezers

The broad tip tweezers are incredibly incredible for grabbing cut fabric pieces off your FabricGrip tangle. The more extensive surface region helps shield sensitive strings from falling apart, and they additionally protect you from contacting your knot. Since the oils in your grasp can separate the cement, they aren't fundamental for everyday Cricut creating; however, if you do a ton of fabric cutting, they prove useful. Any old tweezers will likely accomplish most making, except if you're searching for the turnaround tweezers' usefulness or expansive tip tweezers.

The Cricut Scissors, Shears, and Snips

Cricut makes a few pairs of marked scissors, shears, and clips. Scissors are certainly a personal inclination—you needn't bother with Cricut marked scissors to do any of your Cricut makings.

Essential Scissors

Cricut has a little pair of fundamental scissors that accompany the Basic Toolset and the Essential Toolset. It's decent that these toolsets attend a pair of scissors simultaneously; honestly, never use them. They are tiny and awkward to utilize. Continuously default to an alternate pair of scissors.

5" Fabric Scissors

With the arrival of the Maker, Cricut added fabric slicing tools to their collection. Their little 5" fabric scissors are like the essential scissors. They are ultra-sharp for slicing through thick materials. I don't have a pair. However, they are tiny—I'd much rather work with a giant pair of scissors. The 5" fabric scissors are sold as an independent item and as a piece of the Scissor Combo Pack.

Thread Snips

Cricut likewise has a pair of string cuts. They're substantially similar to some other couple of thread clips; however, they resemble them more than any different amounts. So they're usually the first ones to be grabbed when sewing. The clips are sold as an independent item and as a piece of the Sewing Kit.

The Cricut Scoring Tool

You need to do any projects that include score lines (like collapsing cards into equal parts or doing 3D projects like boxes). The scoring tool will get it going.

If you have a Cricut Maker, in any case, the Scoring Wheel is best.

Likewise, using this as a scoring tool not with the Cricut is expected to crease some paper into equal parts for a non-Cricut project. And utilized the scoring mechanism in addition to the acrylic ruler, and it worked splendidly.

The Cricut Trimmer

Cricut additionally has a trimmer in the Essential Toolset, which cuts materials rapidly into the size you need. It continuously utilizes, yet now acrylic ruler is, for the most part, utilized rotational cutter and self-recuperating mat. It's only simpler to use since those tools are always out.

The Cricut True Control Knife

At the point when Cricut discharged their marked art blade, it was incredulous. It does not sell on requiring another specialty blade—it believes in working fine and dandy. However, once you begin utilizing it, it discovers that Cricut honestly solved a couple of issues. Cricut True Control Knife can be used to cut a wide range of materials. As cardstock, vinyl, acetic acid derivation, fabric, and the sky is the limit from there.

Initially, it has a decent vibe when I'm holding it. The blade's body is thicker than some other specialty blade utilizes, and it feels great to hold. The hold is delicate, however firm and has a sense of safety in hand. The other art blade had a more formidable grasp, which exhausted my writing more.

The cutting edge itself is likewise secure. On the off chance that issues with another (immediately supplanted) make blade where the cutting edge came free, and haven't keep running over this with the True Control Knife.

The True Control Knife mold such that when it's topped, it doesn't move off the table—which you know is astounding on the off chance that you've at any point evaded a specialty blade that tumbles off your desk.

CHAPTER 3:

Cricut Materials

Numerous individuals guess a Cricut processing gadget is just for cutting paper or vinyl; anyway, it can accomplish such a great deal more noteworthy than that! More than 100 certain substances that a Cricut Explore PC can cut and the new Cricut Maker have a sharp revolving edge and a profound blade cutting edge that can decrease significantly! So, in case you're addressing what various materials a Cricut machine can cut, look at this amazingly great rundown underneath!

I likewise have a real data to the additional items and parts that every single Cricut tenderfoot wishes (and which ones are just "pleasant to-haves" that you can binge spend on the off chance you need). Furthermore, in case you're in any case wavering or still have inquiries concerning the Maker, look at my post responding to all the essential questions regarding the Maker! A Cricut Explore processing gadget can decrease exceedingly an incredible arrangement for anything as long as it is 2.0mm thick or slender.

Cardstock and Paper

The Cricut is stupendous at cutting paper and cardstock. However, it doesn't just cut scrapbook paper! Look at all the selective sorts of paper a Cricut work area can cut:

• Cement Cardstock

• Cardstock

- Oat Box

- Development Paper

- Duplicate Paper

- Level Cardboard

- Rushed Cardstock

- Rushed Paper

- Foil Emblazoned Paper

- Foil Publication Board

- Cooler Paper

- Sparkle Cardstock

- Sparkle Paper

- Kraft Board

- Kraft Paper

- Metallic Cardstock

- Metallic Paper

- Metallic Publication Board

- Scratchpad Paper

- Paper Basic food item Sacks

- Material Paper

- Paper Board

- Pearl Cardstock

- Pearl Paper

- Photos

- Photograph Encircling Mat

- Post Its

- Publication Board

- Rice Paper

- Scrapbook Paper

- Gleam Paper

- Strong Center Cardstock

- Watercolor Paper

- Wax Paper

- White Center Cardstock

Vinyl

Another magnificent texture that the Cricut PC can cut is vinyl. Vinyl is great for making signs, decals, stencils, illustrations, and so forth. In case you're keen on endeavoring out vinyl with your machine, here's an essential instructional exercise on the most proficient method to lessen vinyl with a Cricut.

• Glue Vinyl

• Blackboard Vinyl

• Dry Delete Vinyl

• Sparkle Vinyl

• Reflexive Vinyl

• Holographic Vinyl

• Matte Vinyl

• Metallic Vinyl

• Outside Vinyl

• Printable Vinyl

• Stencil Vinyl

Iron-On

Iron-on vinyl, also perceived as warmth move vinyl, is one of my favored materials to cut with my Cricut! You can utilize iron-on vinyl to enhance shirts, tote packs, or any unique material thing.

• Ran Iron-On

• Foil Iron-On

- Sparkle Iron-On

- Shiny Iron-On

- Holographic Shimmer Iron-On

- Matte Iron-On

- Metallic Iron-On

- Neon Iron-On

- Printable Iron-On

Textures and Materials

The Cricut works admirably at lessening textures. However, you should sincerely like to include a stabilizer like Heat and Bond before you start cutting. These textures and materials cut with a Cricut Explore machine, yet there is much more than you can decrease with the rotating cutting edge on a Cricut Maker machine.

- Burlap

- Canvas

- Cotton Texture

- Denim

- Duck Material

- Artificial Cowhide

- Artificial Softened cowhide

- Felt

- Wool

- Cowhide

- Material

- Metallic Cowhide

- Oil Material

- Polyester

- Printable Texture

- Silk

- Fleece Felt

Different Materials

Other than texture, paper, and vinyl, many other solid point substances a Cricut can cut too. Here are a lot of energizing thoughts!

- Cement Foil

- Cement Wood

- Aluminum Sheets

- Aluminum Foil

- Balsa Wood

- Birch Wood

- Plug Board

- Ridged Paper

- Art Froth

- Channel Tape

- Embossable Foil

- Foil Acetic acid derivation

- Sparkle Froth

- Magnet Sheets

- Metallic Vellum

- Paint Chips

- Plastic Bundling

- Printable Magnet Sheets

- Printable Sticker Paper

- Psychologist Plastic

- Soft drink can

- Stencil Material

- Tissue Paper

- Impermanent Tattoo Paper

- Straightforwardness Film

- Vellum

- Washi Sheets

- Washi Tape

- Window Sticker

- Wood Facade

- Wrapping Paper

Cricut Maker

If you have the Maker, you can diminish considerably more noteworthy things! The Cricut Maker has 10x the cutting power of the Explore machines; in addition to it has a rotating edge and a sharp blade edge that empowers it to cut many more materials. The Cricut Maker can slice materials up to 2.4mm thick, in addition to over 125+ sorts of texture, including:

- Chiffon

- Cashmere

- Wool

- Jersey

- Jute

- Sews

- Moleskin

- Muslin

- Seersucker

- Terry Fabric

- Tulle

- Tweed

- Velvet

Contingent upon the Cricut model that you have, the materials that can diminish may likewise vary. So underneath, the full rundown of substances can cut with the guide of the Cricut Maker, and Cricut Explore has a record.

Supplies Expected

Did you get another Cricut Explore or Cricut Maker diminishing machine, or wanting to get one, and thinking about what else you need? I received many inquiries about my Cricut craftsman's gifts and the producer's Facebook, and I chose a failure! So, let me advise you precisely what Cricut adornments I think are going to be absolute necessities and decent to-haves so you can get making with your PC right away!

To begin with, you don't need every one of the things. Your Cricut will accompany a ton of fundamental things. Here's a rundown of what your Cricut attends:

What Cricut frill do you truly need?

Getting Another Cricut and thinking about what extras you need to begin? I demonstrate to you the special must-have Cricut extras and supplies you have to start making marvelous things immediately!

Did you get another Cricut Explore or Cricut Maker cutting machine, or intending to get one, and thinking what else you need? I get such a significant number of inquiries concerning my Cricut Crafters and Makers Facebook group members that I decided it used to be the ideal opportunity for a rundown! Let me let you know precisely what Cricut extras I think will be unquestionable requirements and pleasant to-haves so you can get making with your processing gadget right away!

To start with, you unquestionably don't need every one of the things. Your Cricut will accompany a ton of the extraordinarily essential things. Here's a rundown of what your Cricut attends:

Cricut explore incorporated into box adornments and supplies:

• German Carbide Premium Fine-Point Sharp edge and Lodging

• Adornment connector (for a scoring stylus or Cricut pen) — presently not secured with the Cricut Explore One

• Material example (for the primary undertaking)

• USB wire and power connector

Cricut Maker incorporated into box frill and supplies:

• German Carbide Premium Fine-Point Sharp edge and Lodging

• Rotating Cutting edge and Lodging

• 12" x 12" Light Grip Cutting Mat

• Adornment connector (for a scoring stylus or Cricut pen)

• USB string and vitality connector

Past what comes in the container, all I had when I initially began with my Cricut Explore Air 2 used to be some cardstock. In any case, there are all kinds of practical problems, and that is the problem we want to integrate!

So, what Cricut embellishments are absolute necessities?

Must have frill: Cricut Devices (Particularly weeding device and scrubber apparatus)

What to get: Some specific hardware is helpful, chiefly a weeding gadget and a scrubber.

For what reason to get it: On the off chance that you lessen vinyl, you're almost really going to need a weeding instrument to get every one of the bits of vinyl you do now not want to move to your endeavor evacuated. What's more, a scrubber not good or bad gainful when cutting paper, as it requires a significant period to get those little bits of paper up off your tangle.

Where to get it: You can get only the Cricut weeding instrument here and the Cricut scrubber apparatus here; anyway, it's a superior arrangement to get a Cricut Essential Device Set straight here on Amazon. You'll furthermore discover these gears supplied at the significant specialty stores.

Must have extra: Cricut Profound cut cutting edge (Maker and Explore) or Cricut Blade Sharp edge (Maker As it were)

What to get: The Profound Cut Cutting edge (Explore and Maker) and the Blade Sharp edge (Maker just) let you cut thicker materials. Neither of these will accompany your Cricut until you purchased a select group that ensured it.

For what reason to get it: On the off chance that you want to lessen thicker materials, you'll need one or every one of these cutting edges, depending on your machine. It will open up many more open doors for cutting! A few of the free undertakings on my blog name for one of these sharp edges include the Riddle and the Cricut Device Seat.

Where to get it: You can get the Profound Cut Sharp edge and Lodging here (indeed, you need both) and the Blade Edge and Lodging directly here on Amazon. You'll likewise find them supplied at the first specialty stores.

Must have extra: Cricut scoring stylus/scoring device

What to get: One of the fine extras I expect another Cricut proprietor needs is either a scoring stylus (for Cricut Explore proprietors) or a scoring apparatus (for Cricut Maker proprietors). Note that Cricut Maker proprietors can likewise utilize the scoring stylus on the off chance they wish; anyway, the scoring gadget will give you a more profound score. I use scoring stylus and device always, and a significant number of my papercraft activities utilize it.

For what reason to get it: With a scoring instrument, you can make a more extensive scope of papercrafts. The majority of the papercrafts of my weblog have some sort of scoring included. It's a simple instrument that makes an essential qualification for paper crafting.

Note that you needn't bother with this embellishment on the off chance that you don't have an organization to do paper crafting.

Where to get it: You can get the scoring stylus here and a scoring gadget here on Amazon! You'll likewise discover them loaded at the significant art stores.

Must have adornment: Aluminum foil ball

Why did you get it: A stack of aluminum foil can keep your fine cutting edges sharp and clean? Maybe you are advised not to buy a replacement blade for a long time (I haven't bought it yet). It has been an elective advantage for more than a year).

Where to get it: Your close by supermarket will have a few! Be that as it may, I'll surmise you as of now have some out in your kitchen!

CHAPTER 4:

Cricut Joy

Cricut Joy has a mini size that allows you to store it in any corner of your house and even transport it from one place to another in a simple way.

You can both cut and draw as with the rest of the plotters but with a maximum width of 11 cm. The big difference with the others is that it has only one car. Both the blade and the marker place in the same place; you have to exchange the accessory as you want to cut or draw.

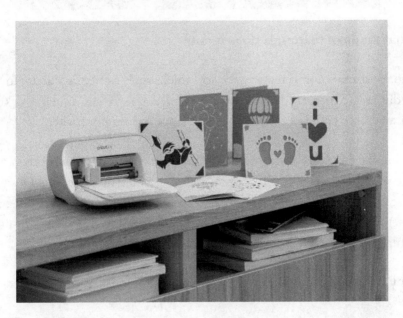

Another significant novelty is that it incorporates a new unique card mat. You can cut folded cards, the machine will cut only the top layer, and you can put cards with effects underneath.

Well, yes, what we were all wishing for has finally arrived, to be able to cut without a mat. It can cut 10 cm wide and 1 meter long but can repeat cuts on vinyl up to 6 meters long.

What kinds of materials does it cut?

The most common ones are not too thick, such as textile vinyl, vinyl, cardboard, paper, and sticky paper. If we try to cut much thicker materials, we could break the machine since it does not make.

It doesn't have any buttons; you have to connect via Bluetooth. You can use it correctly from your mobile or tablet through the Design Space app. If you want to work with the pc, it will have to have Bluetooth; otherwise, it will not work for you. It's the easiest-to-use cutting plotter, perfect for doing last minute and small projects.

Why buy the Cricut Joy?

Many people already have another larger cutting plotter and end up buying the Cricut Joy because it is the most practical on the market. You save time, it doesn't make any noise, and you can take it anywhere with you.

In conclusion, it is the perfect cutting plotter for people who have none or complement the great ones.

What does it include when you buy it?

- The Cricut Joy machine
- Blade + blade holder
- 0.4mm black marker
- Normal grip mat 11.4 x 6.5 cm
- Welcome book
- Power adapter
- Free trial for Cricut Access (for new subscribers only)
- 50 free projects
- Sample materials for a first test

Cricut Joy Key Features

CUTTING AREA

As you can see in the photos, it is so small that it fits in the palm to be easily transportable and comfortable to place anywhere. Its maximum cutting width is 11.4 cm, but it can cut up to 1.20 meters at a time using Cricut Smart Cut materials that do not require a drag blanket.

You can also cut up to 6 meters by repeating the same design, allowing minimal material to waste thanks to the complete and revolutionary range of textile vinyl and adhesives that quickly load into the machine.

CUTTING MATERIALS

Cricut joy can cut conventional materials such as label and textile vinyl, cardstock, paper, thin acetates, thin synthetic leathers, and not very thick or dense materials.

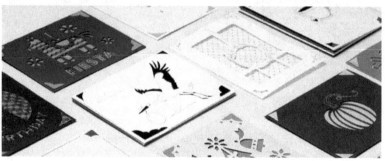

Cricut markets its Smart Cut materials, with which you can cut without a mat since they have a rigid conveyor or liner that prevents damage to the machine. Although not recommended by Cricut, you also have the option of creating your smart materials by cutting them with a guillotine to a width of 14 cm. Although the cut must be perfect and clean, or you can damage the machine.

It is interesting in textile vinyl that has a plastic carrier. In the signage, having the paper liner, you can get to pass in the cut if you do not adjust the material correctly.

ACCESSORIES

The purchase of the Cricut Joy includes the blade and the specific holder, a black marker with 0.4 mm line thickness, and the conventional drag mat with a cutting area of 11.4 x 16.5 cm. The blades and markers are specific to Joy, so you will not use those of other machines. You can also purchase the long cutting mats, the standard adhesive, and the low adhesion one, which has a cutting area of 11.4 x 12 inches. You can also buy a special card mat.

CONNECTIVITY AND SOFTWARE

Cricut Joy does not have USB ports; you can only connect to it via Bluetooth. The software is the Cricut Design Space that already has a desktop version, so you don't need to have an Internet connection to use your Joy. The best thing is that you can use the plotter from your phone or tablet using the free app available in your electronic device's application store.

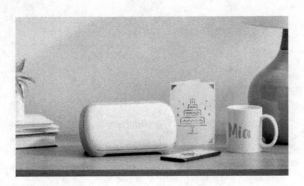

What objects can I customize with the Cricut Joy Mini Cutting Plotter?

The Cricut Joy Mini Cutting Plotter is an impressive toy suitable for developing any crafts hobby and entrepreneurs who need to enrich their creations with unique details.

Create adhesive stickers for helmets, skateboards, flashlights, wooden signs, methacrylate panels, and, of course, also embellish corporate cards, greeting cards, or invitations.

A powerful machine has the same precision and speed as its bigger sisters Cricut Maker and Cricut Explore Air 2, and always ready to be transported. Ideal for adding personality to your day to day and create original things that make the people you love feel special.

With the Cricut Joy, you can create identification stickers to organize your kitchen sections or dress your children around the school by stamping countless objects without neglecting that it is a handy business tool thanks to its incredible versatility.

CUSTOMIZE GLASS BOTTLES, CUPS, OR JARS WITH CRICUT JOY

Now, for the excellent news, we have seen its main functions and put it into use. We start by customizing a metal bottle; you'll see how simple it is.

Upload your image, trace it according to its complexity, and save it as a cut image. We are going to mount two types of vinyl, so we will upload and draw two pictures:

- Insert them in your workspace. Change the color of the layer below to make it stand out, and align them.

- Resize to fit in the area of the crawling mat.
- With your joy selected above, hit 'does it.'
- Select the 'On Mat' material loading option. You will see that the two cuts appear separately.
- Choose the one you want to cut first and select a material from the list. Remember that you can create your materials and edit them by clicking on settings.
- We are going to select premium vinyl for the sign vinyl.
- Cut the vinyl using a guillotine or scissors and place it on the drag blanket.
- Ensure the blade is in place and load the cutting mat; it automatically inserts as you bring it closer to the rollers.
- Presses GO, and it will start cutting.
- After cutting press DOWNLOAD
- Now remove the material from the mat, place the other one, and load it into the plotter.
- Press GOES, and it will cut the second vinyl.
- Unloading and taking off from the drag blanket.
- Now you must discard the excess of the two types of vinyl. Help yourself with peeling tools.
- Cut a piece of the vinyl protractor, peel off a part, and glue it over the top design with a putty knife.
- Slowly lift the protractor, and you will see that the design sticks.
- Lay it on the bottom vinyl, use the putty knife to fix it properly.
- Pick up the protractor, and you have the two designs together.
- Carefully place them on the bottle, centered.
- Press firmly and remove the protractor.
- Eliminate possible air bubbles so that it does not come off.

You already have the personalized bottle ready!

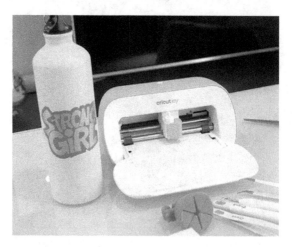

CREATIVE CUSTOM CARDS WITH CRICUT JOY

We have previously commented that there is a special mat to make creative cards, so we better show you how it works by making one for Mother's Day. We will also combine the use of the marker and the blade:

- Using the shapes panel, create an 11.4 x 15.9 cm rectangle; this will help us position the entire design.
- Create 2 cm diagonal lines and place them in the central corners. It will help us to insert a special card.
- Upload your image, trace it, save it as a cut image, and insert it into the workspace.
- Resize and position the image.
- Now click upon the 'path' drop-down and select 'draw.'
- We will add a text and a heart for you to cut. Position everything in the right place and turn off the rectangle layer
- Select all the layers and hit 'attach,' then click 'do it.'
- Select the card mat this time.
- The press continues and selects the material. We have chosen a medium card stock to cut ordinary cardstock.
- Cut a 22.8 x 15.9 card stock and fold it in half.
- Open the inside of the card mat and insert the folded card.
- Remove the protective plastic and secure the card so that it does not move during cutting.
- Now you must load the pen into the Joy. Open the tab, remove the blade, and drop the cell until it stops. Close the account and load the mat.
- In design, space press goes, and it will immediately start drawing. In a complex drawing like this, it can take a few minutes.
- When finished, change the pen to the cutting blade, and the software hits IR.

- It will start cutting. When finished, unload the mat and remove the card carefully as it is quite stuck.
- We will insert inside a card that we have previously cut with a metallic effect taking advantage of the corners' cuts.

You can create spectacular greeting and invitation cards with your Cricut Joy Mini Cutting Plotter!

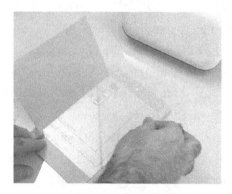

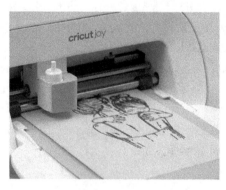

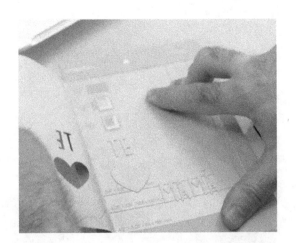

CHAPTER 5:

The Best Cricut Machine to Purchase

The Cricut Expression Cutting Machine

The Provo Craft Cricut Expression Cutting Machine is a massive hit among crafters. It has received plenty of antiques and awards testimonials from many resources. Suppose you are a scrapbooker, teacher, activities director, or anyone else who wants to earn papercraft tasks. In that case, you will need to find out more about the benefits and pitfalls of the Cricut Expression.

The Cricut Expression will lessen newspaper, cardstock vinyl, and vellum to letters, shapes, phrases, and other economical designs. Now you have the option of using a 12"x12" cutting mat to secure more compact systems as well as the 12"x24" cutting mat to get larger ones. On the opposite end of the spectrum, it's likely to decrease pieces as few as.25" that lets you eat all these small pieces of paper you've been saving. Several lightweight cartridges high in thousands of layouts are available to extend your Expression's flexibility.

Cricut Expression versus the First Cricut

You Might Have heard about the Expression's Creator, the Cricut, also referred to as the 'small insect.' The Cricut Expression uses the same capsules and knife blades because of the first Cricut, allowing more flexibility. As a result of the compact dimensions, the first Cricut is only good at cutting edge designs roughly half of the sizes of these you're in a position to create using all of the Expression. The multiplier also has plenty of attributes not on the very first Cricut, the capacity to alter languages and elements of measurements, cut in portrait or landscape view, use hundreds of cuts for thicker fabrics, or even create mirror images using another attribute. The LCD screen is another new feature that permits you to see what you cut until you cut.

The Cricut Expression includes a few Disadvantages inside the very first Cricut. The Expression is more extensive and demands additional space on your desk or desk. If you would like to visit crops or friends' homes to concentrate on tasks, the plateau is much thicker and much more embarrassing to move. The expression could be costly. On the reverse side, it empowers much more flexibility in your designs. The capability to reduce bigger things is useful for generating signage or banner and is quite valuable to folks who have to decorate bulletin boards or other significant distances.

#Cricut Expression. Cutting Edge Technology

Generally, the Cricut Expression Cutting Machine is an exciting new alternative for crafters. It is especially useful for people with arthritis in their palms or whose palms are a little trembling. Most crafters may discover it won't take very long to represent the first cost of the Expression at the amount of cash and time they save in not buying or reducing their designs. The price has dropped considerably from the hefty first retail price tag of $499. If you shop carefully, you can now find the Expression for under $300. There is no pc or higher-tech understanding necessary to use this catchy machine. You can plug it into any wall socket and also intend to start your work. You will want to replace the knife cutting mat, and you may opt to purchase additional cartridges to broaden your layout skills. It's not a bad idea to buy the optional instrument kit, but perhaps, to create the paper a lot easier to lift from the central mat. Besides that, the Expression is almost carefree. The moment you've got a Cricut Expression Cutting Machine, then it will get such an essential part of your crafting, which means you could wonder how you ever got along without it.

Best Strategies For Choosing the Ideal Cricut Personal Electronic Cutter

The Collection of Cricut Personal Digital Cutter machines create to automate several fiddly crafting tasks. In case you haven't ever heard of them before, then continue reading if you want to understand how to select your home crafts to a different degree.

In the event you know of them, you may be asking yourself how to determine which of these cutting machines will probably be acceptable for you. In the process, you're likely to observe the benefits and pitfalls of each device to aid you in producing an educated decision.

The Four variations we're going to be Studying would function as standard Cricut Personal Electronic Cutter, the Cricut Create," that the Cricut Expression, and the Cricut Cake.

The Easiest version to test at first is the Cricut Cake. It differs from other people, as it creates with one aim in mind. That is, to create expert looking decorations.

It might cut shapes from bread, fondant, gum paste, and additional raw materials. It is incredibly similar to that Cricut Expression method; however, the functional components alter to make them suitable for meals. It means that parts that need cleaning can easily remove. If you are looking to create edible ornaments, then this is the sole option from the range. This variant frees from roughly $270.

The Extra three Cricut Personal Digital Cutter models are appropriate for printing. They cut out of the same substances, such as vinyl, paper, card, and vellum. Which version you select will be contingent upon your budget and requirements.

#Budget

The Regular Cricut Personal Digital Cutter is the lowest price from the Scope, costing at least roughly $100.

Cricut Generate, Arriving at $160 and upwards.

The variety variant's surface is The Cricut Expression, which will place you back about $225.

Prerequisites

All Models are harmonious with the Entire choice of Cricut Cartridges. It typically means you've got a nearly endless source of cutting edge designs, as you can always purchase capsules. So there are two significant aspects on you should push your pick. These can be the measurements of machine and cuts, in addition to the variety of cutting edge options.

Sophisticated Cricut Suggestions for Your Craft Project

Cricut Private Cutters are all carrying Handcrafts into a different new level. Individuals throughout the country are astounded at the astounding and innovative Cricut ideas this system can result in a project record. You can create practically anything astonishing and one of some kind utilizing the Cricut cartridges.

How can one Cricut machine function? It's relatively straightforward. Put into a Cricut cartridge into the device, select what color card stock you want to use for your design, and cut away. Each capsule includes distinct themed designs from seasonal plans to favorite animation characters. You can select from the cut methods outside their use for decorations, picture frames, picture frames, picture frames, picture frames, customized greeting cards, wall hangings, calendars, and far more.

Among the Awesome Cricut ideas, you're in a position to make because the craft is the Cricut calendar. Each month may generate in a different webpage, and you may decorate those pages utilizing a variety of designs. Couldn't it be fantastic to create your February page working together with all the Love Struck Season Cartridge? The Easter Cartridge will provide you with infinite designs for the April webpage calendar. Your May calendar can draw up in the Mother's Day Cartridge. How interesting can it be to design your July page with trimmings created from the Independence Day Season Cartridge? December May Be outfitted with the Joys of the Season Cartridge Together with Snow Friends Cartridge. You can pick to your heart's content.

Another Amazing thought You're Going to Be Able to make potentially is the scrapbook. This well-loved craft occupation is why Cricut the Cutting machine invents in the initial site. With The Cricut trimming platform, it is possible to personalize your children's decorations, for example, Mother-daughter or daddy and kid keepsake. Cricut generated capsules that every little kid would delight in creating, such as the Once Upon a Princess Cartridge or even The Disney Tinker Bell and Friends Cartridge. Your little hero will surely adore the Batman design from the Batman: The Brave and the Bold or Robotz cartridges. Cricut supplies you with humungous systems to pick from to this Scrapbooking ideas.

The Cricut Designs are not merely laid out ideas but also fonts and alphabets from the Sesame Street Font Cartridge and the AShlyn's Alphabet Cartridge. Use these exciting tools after producing your personalized present like a wall-hanging picture frame of experiencing a picture of a memorable event of the recipient of your gift. Embellish your walls dangling with sheer cutouts made by this Cricut cutter.

Your Cricut ideas are infinite by Way of this excellent machine and the Cricut capsules to coincide with any occasion and occupation which it's possible to take into account. Developing a Cricut project with the full family is a great way to spend time together, and creating those magnificent things can be an excellent experience for all to attain.

Cricut Manual for Beginners and Advanced Users

The way to use the Cricut? Fundamentally You insert the capsule, then place the crucial rubberized overlay onto the keyboard and flip the unit on, then put a sheet of 6-inch paper to the mat that communicates the device (make sure you line up this up with the tiny arrow on the mat)

Press the "load paper" button, then feed on the mat/paper into the device, then press the principal (s) one to get everything you'd love to cut and press the "cut" button.

If you're a total newcomer, you ought to receive a scrapbook album with protective sheets (they are relatively cheap, you don't have to get the expensive ones). A fantastic color is usually best, for example, dark, royal blue. Additionally, they've patterned/designed ones.

* You ought to get any newspaper (12x12, 8x8, 6x6, etc...) Not too expensive ($2-4 packs)

You should Locate some adhesives to stick Photos to paper (don't utilize glue sticks, which means they are inclined to lift the form and mess it up) ($.99-3.99)

* Get your hands on vases (such as Example, decoration, stickers, brads, etc.) (Ranges from $.99-4.99)

Every one of these is just the actual product. Don't permit shoppers to choose the best of you. It occurs to the majority of folks scrapbookers. We see something cute that we like, although not use it, do not desire it. Assess for earnings. Use coupons at the event you're in a position to. Check stores like the.99 penny shops that sell rolling up sheets to get a low price and precisely the same item since the adhesive you would find in Michaels for $4-7. Walmart also has a Component of scrapbooking items more affordable than local craft stores (Michaels, JoAnns, Hobby Lobby, etc.)

Evaluate eBay too. There are lots of Inexpensive priced items to buy.

Just how To/What to Execute exactly:

1. Opt for the paper which you would like to use.

2. The photo which you will need to incorporate to report. (Be sure the excess sections of a picture cut --to find a more superior look, use your paper trimmer.

3. Using your rolling adhesive (or"dots"), run it through the corners of the image (don't need many just corners &middle).

4. Place an appearance in the paper in which you would like to.

5. Place any embellishment that you may have to decorate it. (This element allows you to be as creative as you want to become.)

6. Journal all those friendly/fun to remember from whatever happens or jumped in that film. 7. If you've got anything like brochures, ticket stubs, or whatever, then place them. Make pages look nicer too.

CHAPTER 6:

Add-ons and How to Use Them

Mat

Get more mats! There are four different mats currently available for the Cricut machines. Preferably, you should get all of them, but the choice is up to you—the Pink mats specifically design for fabric. The blue mats are for light-duty materials like foils, the yellow ones are for the likes of thick cardstock, and the purple mats are for heavy-duty projects that make use of leather or wood. You can't have enough of these things, and buying them when you purchase your Cricut machine will ensure that you can practice every design you want without worrying about ruining your only mat. Be sure to check which mats come with your device, though!

Cartridge

Cartridges are expensive, they genuinely are, but they are easy and fun to use. There are many different ways to use just one cartridge, even though the designs are limited. Now, if you are getting the Cricut access package, this might not be worth it, but for those of us who don't want to pay for a subscription service yet and want to cut things, this could be an excellent option to try out. You can also import images, of course, with the Cricut design space on the most current machines, and these machines also work with Cricut cartridges. For crafters who don't want to design their cuts, this is ideal. You can also use both together, and there are benefits to this, too. To use the cartridge, you just put it into the machine, go to Design Space, and then follow the steps. Once they're linked up, you can essentially choose the cartridge you want to work on, and you're ready to go. This system's advantage is that you can get many ink cartridges, each with a unique design. Once you link them together, you can easily mix and match them.

For newbies, these especially great as you learn how to get better at designing. They are a bit bare-bones, but they're worth it. The cartridges are a little more expensive than the Design Space and Cricut access alternatives. They're about $20 each unless you're lucky enough to find them on clearance, but here's the thing – you could get hundreds of designs out of that small investment, and if you're not yet sure how to use your Cricut machine, these are great for you to work with. The Cricut machine is like any other machine, and it can have problems. You may need to do a hard reset if you can't resolve the issue any other way. When troubleshooting, it's critical to follow the manufacturer's instructions. To do otherwise can damage your machine and void your warranty. For that reason, I am giving you specific instructions from the manufacturer's website.

You want to make sure that you follow these steps correctly and use the specific instructions for your model.

Sharpies

Sharpies - you will not be sorry that you have them. You will have multiple colors and save a few dollars in the process.

CHAPTER 7:

Practical Examples

Vinyl Projects

The vinyl's versatility as a base for designing craft projects demands a section of projects solely dedicated to it. Following the instructions below and feel free to further customize your designs with various colors and patterns.

Trick or Treat Bag

Step 1

Click on the "Images" icon and type in "Halloween" in the search bar and then click on "Insert Images" at the bottom of the screen. The image selected is shown in the picture below.

Step 2

You can edit either or both the image as needed by clicking on appropriate tools on the "Edit Bar."

Step 3

Select the entire design and click the "Group" icon. Then click "Save" to save the project.

Personalized Mugs (Iron-On Vinyl)

Step 1

Click on the "Images" icon on the "Design Panel" and type in "America" in the search bar. Click on the desired image and then click on the "Insert Images" button at the bottom of the screen.

Step 2

Click on the "Templates" icon on the "Designs Panel" on the left of the screen and type in "mug" in the templates search bar and select the mug icon.

Step 3

You can update the size of the template by clicking the "size" icon and selecting "custom" to change the "type" and "size" of the template to decorate non-standard size cups.

Step 4

You can further edit your design by clicking on the "Shapes" icon adding hearts, stars, or other desired shapes to your system.

Step 5

Click "Save" in the upper right corner of the screen, and then specify the desired name for the item, such as "Mug Decoration," and then click "Save."

Step 6

Design can be printed and cut.

Step 7

Using the "Cricut Easy Press Mini" and "Easy Press Mat," the iron-on layers can quickly transfer to your mug. Please wait for a few minutes before peeling off the design while it is still warm. (Since the system is delicate, use the spatula tool or your fingers to rub the letters down the mug before starting to peel the design)

Personalized Coaster Tiles

Step 1

Let's use our image for this project. Search the web to find a monogram image that you would like and store it on your computer.

Now, click on the "Upload" icon from the "Designer Panel" on the left of the screen.

Step 2

A screen with "Upload Image" and "Upload Pattern" will be displayed. Click on the "Upload Image" button.

Click "Browse" or simply drag and drop the image onto the screen.

Select the image type "Simple" and save the picture as a "Print Then Cut image."

Step 3

Choose the uploaded image by clicking on the "Insert Images" and edit the image as needed.

You can personalize the monogram by adding Text to the design by clicking on the "Text" icon and typing in "Your Name" or any other phrase.

Step 4

For the image below, the font "American Uncial Corn Regular" in Regular and color (green) select.

Select the Text and the image and click on "Group" then copy-paste your design for as many times as needed and save the project.

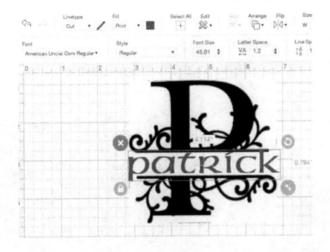

Step 5

You can resize the design as needed to match your coaster's size, although the recommended size is 4 x 4 inches for most common tile coasters. The system is ready to be printed and cut. Simply click on the "Make It" button and follow the screen prompts for using an inkjet printer to print the design on your printable iron-on vinyl and subsequently cut the design.

Step 6

Wait for a few minutes before peeling off the system while it is still warm.

Vinyl Chalkboard

Step 1

Click on the "Projects" icon and type in "vinyl chalkboard" in the search bar.

Step 2

Use transfer tape to coat vinyl cutting strips on the blackboard. Lastly, use a chalk pen to write messages.

Vinyl Herringbone Bracelet

Step 1

Click on the "Images" icon on the "Design Panel" and type in "#M33278" in the search bar.

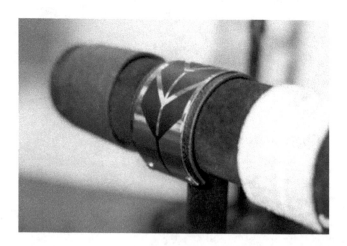

Cloud Vinyl Wallpaper

Step 1

Click on the "Images" icon on the "Design Panel" and type in "#M4C5D3" in the search bar. Select the image and click the "Insert Image" button at the bottom of the screen.

Step 2

Using a weeder tool, remove the negative space pieces of the design. Use transfer tape to apply vinyl cutouts to the wall in a wallpaper-like pattern.

Printable Vinyl Easter Eggs

Step 1

Click on the "Projects" icon and type in "vinyl Easter eggs" in the search bar.

Step 2

I am using the dye to paint the hard-boiled eggs. Then, use transfer tape to cut the thinly sliced eggs into thin slices.

CHAPTER 8:

How to Make Money with Cricut Machine

J ust as the Cricut machine can use in a million and one way (figuratively speaking), the ways to generate money from it is also numerous.

Some of the ways to generate money from the Cricut machine highlight below:

Make and Sell Leather Bracelets

Bracelets are fashionable items, especially leather bracelet. The Cricut machine can easily cut real or faux leather giving you less work to do. You decide to cut, make, and sell leather bracelets, considering the materials needed are just snaps, your Cricut machine, leather, and probably card stock.

If you are interested in selling this craft, you can also create room for preordering, where a buyer can order for a particular design to make by the designer.

Sell Iron-On Vinyl

It is another money-making opportunity that the Cricut machine provides. You make a design with the iron-on vinyl and sell out to people. The iron-on vinyl can be in the form of text or design. It can also make for each season or celebration, be it Valentine, Halloween, Christmas, or Easter. Buyers may also order for what they want.

Sell Stickers

This idea targets kids. You can make money by designing educative and entertaining stickers for toddlers and other age groups. Stickers of the alphabet or map of a locale can make. Stickers also use in decorating places like the wardrobe or closets.

Make and Sell Party Decorations and Buntings

There is always a celebration in our day-to-day lives as human beings. It can be a milestone celebration or merely a fun-seeking escapade. Party decorations made with the Cricut machine can sell on these occasions.

Other Ideas to Explore

The following are other income generating ideas with the Cricut machine:

1. Window decals—everyone has a peculiar image, an object we are practically obsessed with. Getting a vinyl window decal of one's favorite image will go a long way in giving your decor a boost. Making and selling window decal is relatively easy and profitable.
2. Make and sell canvas wall art—customized wall art would generate quick and easy money. Get inspirational sayings or design and make them into wall arts for sale.
3. Design and sell onesies or bodysuit are generally cute clothes that can be better with fantastic artwork. Onesies for babies can make with much other Text apart from "Daddy loves you" or "Momma's baby." Other mushy word art can use in designing onesies for kids.
4. Become a Cricut affiliate—this entails pay to make tutorials video by the Cricut company. These videos are

uploaded to the internet for the netizen to make use of. To become a Cricut affiliate, you need to have a strong internet presence. You must also have a substantial amount of followers on his or her social media accounts.

5. Post tutorial videos on your vlog—this has nothing to do with being an affiliate; instead, you create a blog for videos and upload tutorial videos and get paid through the generated traffic.

6. Use of social media—you can make any of the craft you find comfortable and post pictures of it online, announcing to those on your list that it is for sale. It works better because whoever is buying gets to see the picture of whatever he is getting before ordering for it. Personalized crafts should also include in your order of business.

7. Design and sell T-shirts—T-shirt is a clothing piece that is always in vogue. Most significantly, for college students, a designed tee would be a great fashion item. Creating a designed T-shirt would generate income.

8. Design and sell hoodies—hoodies are great wears for cold seasons. A designed one would roll better with the youth. The design can preorder too.

9. Design and sell leather neckpiece—a leather pendant can be designed for a necklace and sold out to interested buyers. An all-leather neckpiece can also be made and sold.

   a. Design and sell banners—banners can make for celebration, festive periods, camping, parties, religious activities, or sporting activities. All these can be made and sold.

10. Design and sell window clings—window clings with the seasons' design can be made and sold. Other methods or images can also use for creating window clings.

a. Design and sell stencils—stencils can be created and sold for those that want to hand-paint a post or sign. It will also generate a considerable amount.

b. Design and sell safari animal stickers—stickers of safari animals are attractive items. They can be and sold to animal lovers. The sticker is easy to make and will also be a source of income generation.

c. Design and sell labeling stickers—labeling stickers can be made for labeling things in the house.

d. Design and sell labeling vinyl—labeling adhesive vinyl can be made for labeling things in the house.

e. Design and cut appliqués—fancy fabrics can be made into appliqués to design or decorate a place or object.

f. Design and sell Christmas ornaments—Christmas is when people celebrate and decorate their workplace, abode, and religious settings, among others.

g. Design and sell wall decals—different designs of wall decals can be made and sold for a low and affordable price.

h. Design and sell doormats—beautiful doormat can be made with the machine and sold to customers. It can design with either Text or images. Customized doormats can also sell.

i. Design and sell kitchen towels—towels used in the kitchen can be designed and sold at affordable prices. The towels can create with Text or images of delicacies.

CHAPTER 9:

Cricut Software

Design Space

Design Space is for any Explore machine with a high-speed, broadband Internet connection connected to a computer or an iOS device. This more advanced software allows full creative control for users with Cricut machines.

Craft Room

Some machines, such as the Explore and Explore Air, cannot use the Craft Room, but many other models can. Craft Room users also have access to a free digital cartridge, which offers images that all Cricut machines can cut.

Moving on to Creating Your Project Template

On the home page, select "New Project," followed by a page with a blank canvas that looks like the grid on your Cricut mats. The words "empty canvas" is a nightmare in itself to any artist, so please bear with me since we will fill that bad boy up in a second. But first, let's go through the menu options.

New, Templates, Projects, Images, Text, Shapes, and Upload. You will see these things on your left-hand side when you have the canvas open on the screen.

New

New means that you will start a new project and click the tab to redirect you to a blank canvas. Be sure to save all changes on your current project before you go to the original canvas. Otherwise, you will lose all of the progress you have already made on that design.

Templates

Clicking on Templates will allow you to set a template to help you visualize and work with sizing. It is convenient for someone who is not familiar with Cricut Design Space and doesn't know what sizes to set. If you are cutting out wearable items on fabric, you can change the template's size to fit whoever will be wearing it. I'm sure you can agree that this feature is especially beneficial for the seamstresses out there.

Projects

Meanwhile, projects will lead you to the ready-to-make projects so that you can start cutting right away. Some of the projects are not customizable, but others are when you open the template, which is pretty cool.

Many of these are not free either, which irks me to a new extent. You can choose the "Free for Cricut (whatever machine you have)," and the projects that will turn up won't have to pay for.

Images

Images are where you can search for thousands of photos to use for the craft. Those images with the green flag with the "A" on them are the ones that come only with Cricut Access, so be aware if you do not have it. It is sort of like a Pinterest image search engine with a lot of pictures in its database.

Text

The Text goes without saying. When you select this option, you can type whatever you want and scale it onto your canvas. You may choose any font saved on your computer too; that's why collecting those has never been more useful! There is also an option called "multi-layered font," which gives your Text a shadow layer. It can create very cool effects, so make sure you try that option out. Furthermore, remember that when you pay to do a job, the font you are using might require a license to operate.

Shapes

Shapes lets you add necessary forms to your canvas, which you can tweak to fit your own needs. The conditions include circle, square, rectangle, triangle, et cetera.

Upload

When you click the Upload tab, you can upload your images and transform them into cuttable pieces. Along with the Text, is the only reason why I still use Design Space? It is fantastic to be able to use this feature.

Cricut Basic

Its program or software designs to help the new user quickly start creating new crafts and DIY projects. This system will allow you with image selection to cutting with the least amount of time spent in the design stages. You can locate your image, pre-set projector font, and immediately print, cut, score, and align with tools found within the program. You can use this program on the iOS 7.1.2 or systems and iPad and several iPhones from the Mini to the 5th generation iPod touch. Since it is also a cloud-based service, you can start with one device and then complete it from another device.

Sure, Cuts a Lot

It is another third-party software with a funny name, which gives you the ability to control your designs without some of the limitations of using cartridges used within the Cricut Design Studio. You will need to install a software update to use this program to download it for free. It allows for the use of TrueType and Open Type font formats and simple drawing and editing tools. You can import any file format and then convert it to the one that you need. There is an option for blackouts and shadow.

Cricut Design Studio

This program allows you to connect with your software and provides you with much more functionality as far as shapes and fonts are concerned. There are various options for tools that offer you resources for designing more creative images. You will be able to flip, rotate, weld, or slant the images and fonts. However, you will still be limited in the amounts or types of fonts you can use based on the cartridges' ones. There is a higher level of software features that allow for customization.

Cricut Sync

It is a program designed for updating the Cricut Expression 2 and the Imagine machine and the Gypsy device. You just connect your system to the computer and run the synced program to install updates on the features that come with your machine. It also uses troubleshoot any issues that could arise from the hardware.

Play Around and Practice

You can combine your shapes and images, add some text, and create patterns. The possibilities are endless. The best practice is to familiarize yourself with the software before attempting to cut expensive materials. Start small and cheap - printer paper will be an ideal choice - and cut away. See what works well for you and stick with it. There are many options concerning the Cricut Design Space. The only way to learn all of this is to experiment and click on every tab you see and try different combinations of options when playing around on the software.

Make the Cut

It is a third-party program that works with the Cricut design software. It offers a straightforward look at the design features that Cricut has. This system can convert a raster image into a vector so that you can cut it. There is also a great way to do lattice tools. It uses many file formats and TrueType fonts. There are advanced tools for editing and an interface that is easy to learn and use. This system works with Craft ROBO, Gazelle, Silhouette, Wish blade, and others. It allows you to import any files from TTF, OTF, PDF, GSD, etc., and convert them to JPG, SVG, PDF, etc. It is flexible and user-friendly.

CHAPTER 10:

How to Make Stickers

Not exclusively will I show you how to make your stickers without any preparation, yet I will likewise give you six unique sorts of formats that will assist you with building and make the most staggering stickers on the planet.

Cricut Maker and Explore with three distinctive sticker sheets

How about we make these stickers together!

Before we go into a bit by bit instructional exercise, I need to give you a little see of the things I will cover for you in this article (I don't need you to get lost).

Print at that point cut: the alternative in Cricut Design Space permits you to cut your stickers.

Diagram of your machine determinations and size cutoff points.

Bit by bit instructional exercise How to Make Stickers inside Cricut Design Space.

Instances of how to utilize the Free Templates I gave you to Make Stickers.

I am sure that If you follow this instructional exercise to the tee, you will be engaged to make stickers whenever, for any event.

It is safe to say that you prepare?

How about we Daydream Into Reality?

Tip: If you see there's something that doesn't exactly appear to be identical in the product screen captures (trust me, I am striving to transform them), if it's not too much trouble, look at my Stay fully informed regarding Cricut Design Space article, so you recognize what changes you have to remember.

What is Print at that point cut, and how can it identify with stickers?

Print at that point Cut is the alternative in Cricut Design Space that permits you to print your plans and cut them with your machine afterward. There are two different ways to advise your machine to print at that point, Cut. The first is by changing the Fill to Print and choosing your shading or example. The subsequent one is by straightening the layers with the Flatten apparatus situated toward the layers board's finish. For best practices and zero disappointments, don't stress this during your plan procedure; it will just worry you.

Include your shapes, content, pictures, and toward the end, level the entire thing. (I will give you this in the bit by bit instructional exercise)

Note: Although I spread a few subjects of Print at that point, Cut on this article; remember that this device is a too hearty one.

There are two things you need consistently to ensure when making stickers with your Cricut.

The first is size. You can just print at that point Cut plans that are up to 9.25 x 6.75in. So check the size before you send your undertaking to cut, or you will get an admonition saying the picture is excessively enormous.

The other thing that you have to consider is your machine's confinements:

If you have Cricut Maker, you can use colored paper (not very occupant) and polished white materials.

You have to utilize white paper with matte completions on the off chance that you have an Explore machine.

The most effective method to creator stickers with your Cricut (Maker/Explore)

Bit by bit Tutorial/Make Stickers with your Cricut

Since you know your machine necessities, it's the ideal opportunity for you to figure out how to make stickers.

Materials

Cricut Maker/Explore

Sticker Paper

Printer

Fine Point Blade

Light Grip Mat (blue)

Outline sticker paper versus Cricut Printable sticker paper

If you have the Cricut Sticker paper, take a stab at sparing the Print and take it to Staples or Office Depot to print it. On the other hand, if there are too many problems, please switch to another one. Time is cash!

Making a Methodology

Since you can utilize content, pictures, shapes, and nearly anything in Design Space to make stickers, you may get overpowered and don't where to begin.

In this way, for you to have extraordinary involvement in making stickers, I've built up a "frustration proof" strategy.

These are the means we will follow:

1. Make a format (By including shapes)
2. Include Color or Patterns
3. Include content and Images
4. Check the estimate and Flatten
5. Cut your stickers

When you follow this request, you can focus and spotlight on one stage at that point, and that, my companion, is ground-breaking!

Note: Save your task as you go. It's very tedious, and Cricut doesn't have back up alternatives.

Stage 1 - Create a Sticker Sheet Layout

Cricut Design Space Screenshot: Add a square shape to make a rule for your sticker sheet

Include a 9.25 x 6.75in square shape to use as a guide

To include the government, click on the shapes button situated on the left of the canvas and select the appropriate choice. At that point (while choosing the square), go to the alter menu on the canvas and snap the little square in the center to open extents. (We will utilize this term all through this instructional exercise)

At that point on W (width) type in 6.75 and, on H (stature) type in 9.25. After resizing the square, change the line type shading for white, so it's simpler for you to have a superior thought of your plan.

Note: Check out my how-to alter shapes If you feel a mistake for changing the extents, and so forth.

Case of the entirety of the shapes you can use for your stickers

In the wake of making your guide, including the shapes you need for your stickers. Cricut has nine distinct alternatives for you to look over. For this instructional exercise, I utilized squares, hearts, circles, and triangles.

What we have to do now is to fill our guide with various shapes. Remember to open extents so you can make a wide range of square shapes.

Cricut Design Space Screenshot: adjust stickers, so they are all together

Tip 1: Use the adjust alternative to keep your shapes and the various forms you're adding to your sticker design sorted out. Select the components you need to adapt and rely upon to adjust them to multiple choices.

As a rule, you will utilize Center and Distribute on a level plane or vertically. Along these lines, give it an attempt! You will commit a few errors while you become accustomed to it, yet once you get its hang, you won't return.

Tip 2: Create various figures for your stickers. Look at the accompanying picture for a bit by bit process.

Cricut Design Space Screenshot: bit by bit on the best way to add various components to the Cricut sheet

Stage 1: Add a square shape and triangle (you should turn the triangle, so it's topsy turvy)

Stage 2: Place the triangle toward the finish of the square shape. They should cover (only an indent).

Stage 3: Select the two shapes and weld to make another component for our stickers. (Weld situates at the base of the Layers board)

Stage 4: Rotate to accommodate your sticker design

Keep including shapes in various sizes and let your creative mind fly! Your stickers will be so charming toward the end.

At the point when your design finishes, you need to erase or shroud your guide. Kindly remember to do this. Something else, your stickers won't cut after you level.

Presently, select the entirety of the shapes and change the line type shading for white; this will permit you to have an all the more away from what you will do straightaway.

Stage 2 - Add Colors and Patterns

It's an excellent opportunity to add shading to your stickers!

As I referenced above, don't stress over line type or Print at that point Cut. To add shading to your sticker, you can pick a firm foundation or a Pattern.

Add a Solid Color to your Stickers

Select the component you need to add shading to and change the shading box beside the line typesetting, situated at the canvas territory's top board.

If you click on cutting edge, you will have the option to see a more extensive range of hues, and you can likewise utilize a code to locate a particular shading.

Cricut Design Space Screenshot: add hues to your stickers

CHAPTER 11:

Let's Make Your Design Dreams Come True

S o we have covered what your machine can do and what you can use it with. Now we need to let you know how to use the app to your advantage. The significant part about the machine is the app. The app has many benefits and helps you with your projects, so the best thing here is to know how to use the app.

Open you're Cricut Design Space, and when you open it, and you want to create a new project, you will see a blue square that says create a new project. Once this is done, you will find that you can design. It will be white and blank. If you click on the image option at the bottom of your screen, that will lead you to a new screen.

There is a box at the top for searching, and you can type in what you want to make. For example, if you're going to make a holiday card, type in the holiday card. Remember that there are many search options, so try different words to try and see new pictures. The images may be different on the screen than what you see in other places because they change often. This company is excellent about continually evolving to give you everything you need as far as awesome ideas in their project center that they are offering you.

Some of them are costly, but most are free. Keep in mind that some are for cutting and others are for printing.

It's relatively easy to tell. You just have to look for the price at the bottom of the picture, or if there is a little printer, then it means it's printable. Remember that when you start.

If you think you will use your machine a lot, you may consider subscribing to the Cricut Access Standard because it gives you more options. Once you choose your project, click the button that says insert. You will find it at the bottom of the screen. Now that you've done this, your project will be in the workspace.

Once your project is in the workspace, you can make any changes to it that you want for your first project. We would recommend not making any significant changes because you're not used to the app yet, but as you practice, you'll learn more about creating different changes and adding your flair to your projects.

In this case, it might be tiny for a card, so you might need to make it bigger, and some of them only come with an envelope to make with it, or others require you to do more things to go with it. As such, these are things that you're going to have to think about. If you want to make the size bigger, then, of course, you're going to make it bigger and expand it.

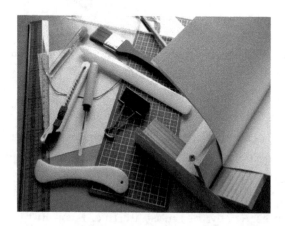

Once you have the required size and are ready to start cutting, click the "Make" button.

It's going to be a green circle at the lower right part of your screen. Once you do this, you'll be in the area where your product shows on the cutting mat. Click the arrow on the right and scroll through to see each mat you can or will use. It's a good idea to look through them so that you can get your paper or vinyl-ready in the order that they cut. Then scroll back to the beginning and click on the continuing circle. It's going to be a green circle.

From here, you can tell how the first mat will cut, so you'll be able to get this ready. The design space will guide you through this, so follow the instructions once they pop up. Each time you start, it's going to ask you to connect with a nearby device. It is a standard step, so don't worry. Depending on the project you choose, it could use the scoring stylus or other materials or items, so this is something to keep in mind. If you are using the stylus, make sure that it's all the way in, and it should click when it's down. Then you will need to close the latch and have it been ready.

Keep following the prompts, and it will tell you when to unload and load. Then you can watch the machine cut your design. Once you've removed it from the mat, you can fold it on the score lines, and your project will do. You can use the project in any way you like, but starting with something simple will help you get used to spacing and saving materials and time.

Ready to make projects are in the app as well, and all you have to do to pick one and be able to use it to your advantage is to pick one and go with it. You choose one, and then you send it to your machine and tell it to cut. Once you have this assembled, you'll have a project that looks professional and glamorous in just a few minutes.

When you see the opening screen of Cricut Design Space, you will see ready to do projects at the bottom, and then you can click on the collection by clicking the word projects. You can narrow the search by a category or using the menu that the projects have. It locates along the top toolbar on the top of the screen. There are hundreds of things for you to choose from, and when you've signed in, you can favorite the designs as well and find it much better and more comfortable by clicking the button that says 'My ready to do projects.' It will be in the drop-down menu.

You can customize it and make it. If you select to make it, you will automatically forward it to the cut screen in your design space. All of the design elements will already be sized and colored, as shown in the picture, and all you have to do is continue.

If you're working with iron-on materials, you also need to click the mirror button on each cut mat because it won't automatically see them and do it for you. When you're here, you can edit any part of the system just as you would your projects, and this way, the premade designs can be a great jumping-off point for your unique creations. Once you're satisfied with the edits in the customization, hit the green make it button to send the design to cut. Each ready to make project includes instructions for cutting specific materials for each particular project. From there, you would follow the instructions that pop up on the screen.

If you have the canvas screen, this refers to the screen you will be designing on. As such, click on the new project button. Then it will open up your canvas. Now we can begin your project. There is also a zooming in and out button to see the little more challenging details on your bottom left corner. On the left side of your screen, you will find the main controls for you to use.

The new button starts a new project for you.

The template button is one part that will help your project work on different items. You can change the size of the template here and the color as well.

Projects will open the different projects in the CDS.

CHAPTER 12:

Cricut for Business

Mindset

Okay, I know you want to have like, just quit your job. Only gain financial freedom, enough time to spend with your family and your friends or make just enough to go traveling or you want to build, well, I don't know if I could help you create a $1 billion business. Still, there are a lot of million-dollar trades that get made online all the time. You can even start selling your products as a side-hustle while you're still working. And then, if you are successful, you may be able to turn it into your full-time job. So whatever it is, set that intention and knows that just if you work hard enough, you don't give up; I bet you can do that. And this is the best business opportunity to do that right now in history. Yeah, I'll let you work hard, but Cricut is mainly fun, so don't forget to have a lot of fun with it.

So I'm going to tell you all the roadblocks that stop most sellers and then how you guys can get past it.

Just exponential growth and that's what will happen to you. But you need to take care of yourself.

Every single bit of that process is what was required for that tree to grow.

You have to be able to get inside the mind of your potential customer. Remember, especially online, the two things you got is your product and you're listing. Online, remember the only thing you got is your listing. They can't touch, feel, taste your product, none of that. It's all just those photos in those descriptions and, sooner or later, reviews. So you got to put all your effort and time into those when you get started.

You're Cricut Business through the digital world

In today's day and age, if you are not advertising on the Internet, you are losing a significant amount of business. It doesn't matter if you are going to be a Cricut savvy or not. It would help if you found your way to be online anyway.

By taking advantage of the Internet, you allow your business to grow in ways that it could not if you were to advertise with conventional methods.

As with any new business, do you need to do some research?

Let me tell you that you are in advantage compared to the other online beginners because you know which direction you are taking; you want to work with your Cricut!

It is much easier to manage a store or anything online related to your interests; it cannot deny.

Attention, I am, are not saying that it is not possible to do it inside a niche that you do not know or that does not represent your direct passion, for example, if you can't work woods with your Cricut. You are more passionate about creating intangible files; indeed, it will be a bit more complicated because you must use the materials and react to the design.

It is because if you know about the topic covered in your niche, you will be able to more easily recognize the elements of value to offer to your potential customers. The more specific and specialized you are, the more you win over your competitors.

You will be able to identify the best products to market using qualitative and high-level descriptions. And don't think you are limited because you are using your Cricut. It is not a professional tool because with it and coordinating with some local professionals like a carpenter r a tailor, .you can create many tangible and intangible items that result in being very professional and good looking.

You will be able to answer even the most technical and complex questions your customers will ask you, and it will be much easier to identify all the elements to be used to get a better grip on the public.

Brainstorming

So, go with this practical step by step essential guide to start your business and not quit until you made it.

Phase 1

1. Think and write down your plan of action. There is no path for those who don't have a clue where they are going to.

The first things you need to determine are:

-What kind of product you're going to sell,

-What type of customers you're going to reach,

-How you are going to find them.

For example, you want to sell customized woods for little coffee shops or small farms. You don't want to take the risk, so it is better to test your local area to see how it goes.

2. Search about your competitors

What your competitor's top-selling products are?

How much they charge for their products

What channels (online or offline, or both) your competitors are using for marketing

Find out where your competitors are lacking

You need to take your time and do marketing research about your competitor's success and its products.

Phase 2

Cost of Materials –

1. Make sure the cost of material is actually at a bare minimum,

-also consider all the activities involved, which includes manufacturing, purchasing, and delivery

-the quality of the material and the final product must be high enough to satisfy the customer need

There are going to be some unused scraps and material when buying in bulk.

Phase 3

Who do you sell to? What should you sell? Where can you sell it?

I know that you are excited to start selling your products, but it is essential to take responsible steps before starting.

Many of your business decisions will depend on the target audience, so you must first determine the target audience.

For example, if your Business Idea is to create Menu Boards, your possible Target Audience can be restaurants or coffee shops in your city

Phase 4

<u>Testing your Business</u>

You don't want to create a product that no one wants to buy; otherwise, your time, money, and resources will be wasted entirely.

If you want to succeed in your business, you need to take responsible steps, and you can test the market to see if people will want to buy what you plan to sell. So, give some try by producing a few prototypes to offer your unique products to potential buyers and see how they react.

<u>Marketing your Cricut Business</u>

The more you know about your target audience, the more you know where to put the market. By breaking down the different groups, we can sell to and understanding where to find them in local and internet-based sales, you can determine the best way to put your precious time and energy. If you decide to be a local seller, it's best to choose between one of these two segments.

Focus on one of those above, spend your energy in one that, and results will come soon.

If you decide to provide custom works, please do not try to become a dashboard simultaneously, after establishing an initial foothold and obtaining considerable sales.

Business to Business

The opportunities are fewer, and client expectations are higher. So, for this reason, I recommend starting an easy path.

Another thing to consider is accounting; if you a top creative but lacking, you need to take very carefully in your Business strategy. Unfortunately, one of the top reasons most businesses fail is managing finances and their inferior accounting methods. You might consider investing part of your money in buying accounting software that can help you with that. There are a few affordable tools that you can find online to keep track of your expenses.

CHAPTER 13:

SnapMat and Cricut de Mobile

S o Cricut Design Space on the mobile app is very similar to working with it online. Some differences are easy to adjust. For instance, the placement of the panels is all different for obvious reasons. The mobile app also has a fun feature called SnapMat. I want to go over that now.

SnapMat

SnapMat is a tool that allows you to use your phone or iPad to take a picture of a Cricut mat that you have already set up for cutting. Here is an example of a mat that I used in SnapMat:

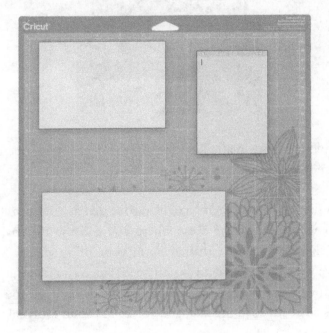

To use SnapMat, you first build your project in Cricut Design Space on your iOS. Once you reach the point that you are ready to "Make It," one of the options pressing "Make It" will give before pressing the "Continue" to cut your image is "Snapmat" on the bottom, left-hand side. By insisting that a screen like this will pop up:

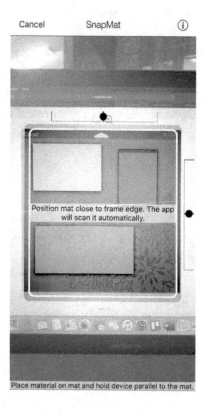

My picture has a mat added for visual effects. Your open screen won't have the mat there yet.

Cricut Design Space will then recognize your mat as you scan it. When it does, it will populate the areas where you laid the materials down with the shapes on your virtual mats in your print screen. You can then move your figures around as you need. Since you're using the mat you're cutting with, and the material already loads on it, all you have to do then is correctly load the mat, and you're in Cricut Heaven!

Creating in iOS

I'm going to go ahead and show you the few differences there are between the web-based version and the iOS version. The Android version is also very similar. We'll stick with the iOS version for illustrating purposes.

When you enter the Canvas, you'll notice it looks almost exactly like the web-based version. The most significant difference is the size and shape and that the panels are all along the bottom.

The first thing I'm going to point out is the Menu at the bottom. You've got everything on there. Your panels will pop up depending on what you push. I include screenshots of each piece for your convenience.

You can see the Design Panel below the "Insert Fonts" box. It is where your "Insert Images" button is as well.

You'll notice that you also have the same options as you have in Cricut Design Space as far as filtering fonts goes as well. You can choose between "Cricut" fonts, "System" fonts (and I was pleasantly surprised by how many fonts I had on my iPhone), and "All" font.

You also have the "Filter" option on the upper-right-hand side. It's by search fonts. This time, though, it looks like an oil filter instead of saying "Filter."

I have a picture of for you is the "Insert Images" pane. It's similar to the web-based Cricut Design Space's "Insert Images" as well. This area also has the oil-filter shape to represent the "Filter" option.

"You'll remember that you can choose between "Categories" and "Cartridges" before you search to help narrow down your results. You can see that in the screenshot below.

When you categorize something, you might stick it with other things in that category, but it's just filed there for safekeeping. The same is true for "Categories" here. When you pick sorts, you're, in essence, selecting a file folder full of similar, individual items.

"Cartridges." Think about when you go shopping online, and you place everything in your cart. When you click "Purchase," you're purchasing everything in your cart. A "Cartridge" is a "cart" full of similar images.

But you're not buying them individually. You're purchasing the full cart at one time.

The Panel is "Upload Image." The great thing about uploading an image to Cricut Design Space on your iOS is that you not only have the option to upload a current file, but you can also take a new idea to upload using your camera!

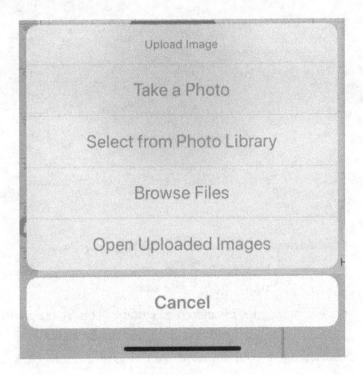

Over in the menu bar is "Actions." It includes all the actions that are on your Layers Panel as well as "Advanced."

If you push the menu over to the left a little, you'll see that it continues beyond "Actions" to "Edit."

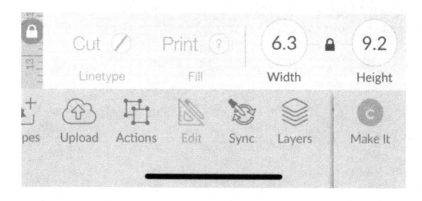

Edit harbors a whole array of exciting treasures. These include:

- Linetype/Cut/Print
- Adjust the width and height of the image or text
- Aligning Horitonztally
- Aligning Vertically
- Changing the H and V positions (This is the North to South and East to West positions on the canvas)
- Arranging your items (Move Forward/Send to Back/etc.)

- And Distribute (Distribute will take stacked up items and spread them out evenly over a given space)

The tool on the menu bar is the "Color Sync." You already know what that does. It allows you to drag your pieces around and drop them with other items to color the same color.

You see, "Layers." It functions the same way as "Layers" in the web-based version of Cricut Design Space.

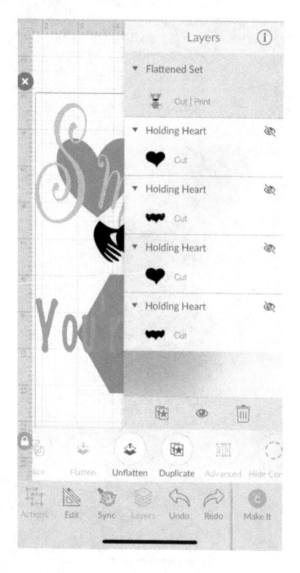

Then, you'll see the handy "Undo/Redo" buttons.

The "Camera." And, no. You don't have that on your computer. The neat thing is that it allows you to use the background as the object you plan to project onto.

Say, you're going to put an image on a mug. You can turn on your camera, pull your face in front of where you're working, and use it for a background. It lets you more fully visualize your project as you customize your color choices and other details.

Lastly, after your project is all made how you want it, you click "Make It" in the bottom, left-hand corner. And I think we've already taken it from there.

Make sure you hit the save icon in the top, left-hand corner beside your icon. When you click that, it will bring up two options: "Save to the Cloud" and "Save to Phone." If you're working offline, you'll have to save it to your phone, but be careful with that. Phone and iPad storage fills up quickly!

One of the main functions of Cricut Design Space is that it is located on the cloud, making the project accessible between devices. If you save something on your phone, it won't be available on your computer.

Create Offline!

You can create offline with the Cricut Design Space iOS app! You just have to be sure to download your images and fonts that you want to use offline while you're online.

Download Images

To download an image, open "Insert Images." When you tap on the image, a circled checkmark appears in the bottom right-hand corner that says insert. On the other corner, though (bottom right), is the option to "Download Selected."

When you're ready to use your downloaded images, go into "Insert Images." Open up your "Filters." Select "On this Phone" and "All Ownerships." Then you can select and insert your image as usual.

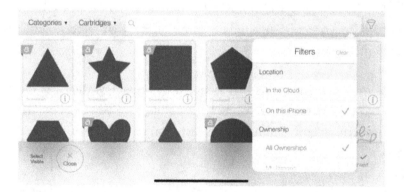

Downloaded images will only be available for a total of seven days unless you go back online onto Cricut Design Space and renew the permissions again.

Download Fonts

Select "Text." When the text box pops up, you'll notice that it has the word "Select" in the top, left-hand corner of the box. Click it.

It will populate with a long line of circles down the left side—one for every font.

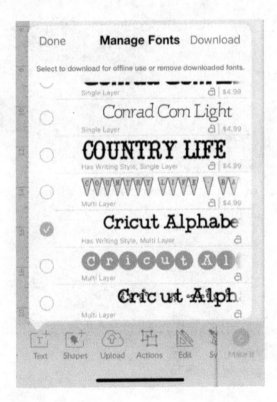

Click the circle for the fonts you want to download. If you don't own it and it has a charge to it, you'll have to purchase it before downloading it.

Download Ready-to-Make Projects

You can download the groups of images that go together to create the ready-to-make photos onto your iOS device, but you cannot save the pictures and instructions with it.

First, navigate from "Canvas" to your "Homepage." You do this by clicking the button in the upper, right-hand corner of the screen. It will look like a sliding bar.

When you click on it, it will expand to show "Home," "Canvas," and "Make." Click "Home."

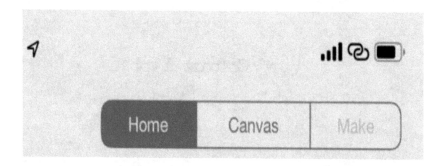

Choose a project. Click "Customize." It will open onto your Canvas. Click "Save As" and then choose to have it saved to your device.

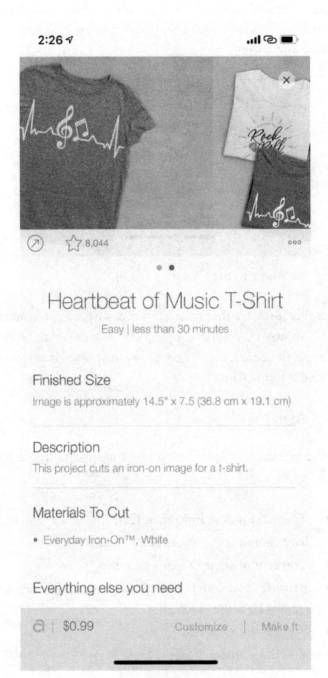

Removing Downloaded Images

Go into the "Images" screen and bring up your downloaded images. Tap any that you want to delete. Tap "Remove Selected" in the bottom, left-hand corner.

"Reloading" a Project to the Cloud

As I said earlier, projects that save to your phone are not committed to the cloud. If, however, you have a project you were working on online and want it on the cloud, that's easy to do. Just open it up, click "Save As," and save it to the Cloud.

Option Not Available

When you're working offline, you do not have access to the following features and tools:

- You cannot do a Print then Cut.
- You cannot use Custom Materials.
- You cannot set up a new machine.
- Because you can't download a cartridge anyway, you cannot view the cartridges.
- You cannot view categories.
- You can't upload images.

CHAPTER 14:

Design Space Software Secrets

C onfiguration space programming is technology. It is the result of the soul, not the product of the deductive examiner. There are no calculations, strategies, examples, procedures, or pseudographs that can be programmed well.

Programming is an inventive work of art driven by a dream. The dream is taken advantage of by concentrated ingenuity, center, thought, and long periods of readiness.

It prompts snapshots of understanding, trailed by a long period of reasoning, coding, and thinking some more.

It is the place incredible structure originates from.

Profound Knowledge

The crude materials of configuration may be documentation, a perfect workbench, studio, easels, paints, ability, and information. The performer must know the scale. The painter needs tones.

Stone carvers need keen insight to find negative space. An essayist must have a feeling of style.

For the most elevated fixings, a craftsman needs to examine every one of the works that preceded, both great and awful.

A decent design space software ponders how things work in their field.

It is, so the fashioner isn't tottered by obliviousness or dirtied by assumptions. A comprehensive introduction to the art places things conversely more plainly.

Hard Practice

Learning alone, however, doesn't convert into aptitude. We expand on the establishment with a long period of training.

It doesn't make a difference if the training occurs at the easel, composing work area, or workbench. For forever, creatives have drawn from the experts' artistic creations and composed awful tune after terrible tune until they got to the great ones.

Creators practice that the art turns out to be natural; it resembles contact composing on the console. In the end, when the dream strikes, we make without the slightest hesitation.

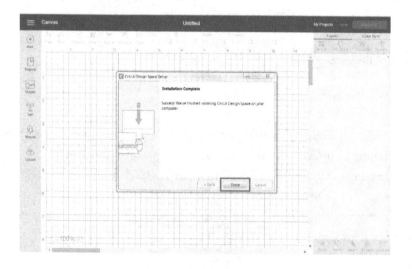

A decent artist can tune in to a tune and figure out its structure. A decent coder can see a UI and, in a split second picture, the fundamental code's structure. Some of the time, the psychological picture is superior to the first.

A decent coder can take a gander they haven't seen previously and begin discussing how it functions. Watchwords rise out of letters. Thoughts spring from images and blank areas. Dreams of registers and arrangements show up alongside mental illustrations of boxes, lines, and bolts.

Code is the plan similarly composing is. When the words are on paper, the author shouldn't engage with the production forms.

For the coder, the "distributing staff" is the compiler and loader. This product transforms plans into something of administration.

At any point, the principal program I composed, as straightforward as it might have been, showed me this. Coding was mysterious in that I could outline something on paper, lift it, and go. Maybe I could draw a motor, and it would only work. Or then again, not do; however, I could redraw it. There was no lengthy procedure of making each part and manufacturing out of metal or collecting the sleek chaos before testing. I just incorporated my structure.

This high artistry isn't generally so high. It's what ought not to out of the ordinary of everybody who brings home the bacon programming for general society. It's a gifted calling that asks for motivation and makes progress toward increasingly elevated polished methodology.

Without a doubt, you can hack code together as you can rapidly complete paint by numbers. It resembles these sites I see with heaps of short, without content posts spewing oxymoronic "tried and true way of thinking."

They're frequently composed of individuals who read 500-word computerized showcasing to put similarly wobbly "content offers" behind email dividers. It resembles noting a paper promotion on the most proficient method to profit in the classifieds, burning through

$9.99 to discover it's to run advertisements about how to benefit in the classifieds.

Without a doubt, you can utilize Grady-Booch's strategy and power many developers into an inflexible and religious deft arrangement. They'll limp on always and make increasingly more code that does less and less. The swell and bugs will develop into a moderate, deadened, self-serving mess, all gratitude to a misinformed supervisory crew determined to make easy money either by IPO or securing by a more prominent organization. Everybody will forsake the code for the startup in a ceaseless semiannual walk to obscurity.

All that those indigent clients see are bugs and confounding interfaces that moderate with each discharge.

Learning of the User

Configuration spaces programming, similar to all structures, must focus on the client. They are the explanation behind the product in any case. Something worth being thankful for about present-day ways to deal with programming improvement is acknowledging this reality in any event in their unique pronouncements.

They request that the client includes. They should be fused into the procedure, sharing thoughts regarding what works, what doesn't, and why.

Regardless of whether the Design spaces programming incorporates the client, it's insufficient because it's uncommon that a client comprehends information structures. Counseling clients is great. Accepting they can enable the creator to consider the system; however, a software engineer must personally know. the client's experience. Fashioners need to do the client's activity for some time and sympathize with the client's agony.

This procedure just the most recent days it takes as long as it must for the software engineer to observe answers for the client's issues instinctually. I've realized fashioners to ride in an emergency vehicle every night for two or three months. The framework to help emergency vehicle drivers that they made was excellent. There is no swap for comprehension.

Calm

In the wake of structure information, rehearsing hard, and figuring out how to see the world through the client's eyes, it's an excellent opportunity to get tranquil. Stop. Think. Sketch. Pause. Hold up some more, and in the end, the thoughts will begin streaming.

Once in a while, it takes some time. Once in a while, the musings you had during the exploration part of the improvement spring to life rapidly; however, typically not. When it begins, however, it floods. Keep a note pad, a heap of paper, or an application close by. Whatever you use, hold writing down the out of this world.

Language is a baffling thing—verbal contemplation. Contemplative words can improve considerably. It is the procedure before the plan. A story is continuously helpful.

Presently begin coding. Aggregate soon, and accumulate regularly. Think. Assemble. Coders fool themselves with cases to envision every one of odds and ends and afterward simply compose. You should code. The code is the plan!

Where to begin is as much motivation as the general arrangement of assault. Rely upon the dream for that also. Regularly the spot to start is the place the information enters the framework. Or, on the other hand, it may be the part of the frame that catches your eye the most. On different occasions, it's ideal for assaulting the most overwhelming details. Like mythical beasts, they should transform into windmills.

Anyway, you begin, code like a breeze. Toss stuff out and code once more. Fred Brooks said you couldn't generally compose a prerequisite report because such vast numbers of the necessities implant in the plan itself. You can't characterize the interfaces first; however, you should end with great interfaces.

None of this is conceivable except if you get tranquil and let the breeze blow in thoughts. Tune in for the dream. If you pause, accepting you have the learning, practice, and love for your clients, the plan will come. It's as specific and characteristic as a supported seed growing.

When it at last comes, begin. The code will rise and develop in layers. The code will hurl. Alter, order, test, rehash. You'll have splendid thoughts and not know where they originated from. It's everything from the dream. Who knows where the breeze blows?

Adaptability

A few people make all the more successfully on a fixed calendar. John Cheever went to a cellar office for eight hours consistently. Others of us need to make the most of current opportunities, regardless of great importance.

Tune in to your very own innovativeness, and realize what works best for you. Ken Thompson's hours pivot on a more prominent than 24-hour plan. Dennis Ritchie would appear for lunch, go through the evening at Murray Hill, return home, sit in front of the TV, and work until the early morning.

Imagination and configuration are natural in each one of us. Simply perused all the more broadly, and you'll see that I'm not saying anything new. Authors, painters, and arrangers have taken in this. Our cosmetics are simply youthful and getting more youthful always.

The average software engineer is still in their twenties. Youth, particularly those that focus on innovation, frequently neglect to investigate the humanities' best pieces.

For what reason do we neglect to hang tight for the dream? For what reason does it take a negligible seven years for the product world to relapse once again into supposing it can timetable plan?

I speculate it is a should be in charge. During a time of two-day shipping, we hope to make an interest. This need seeps into all parts of life. We are the moment society, and we should have everything quick, what's more, it.

GETTING STARTED IN THE NEW CRICUT DESIGN SPACE

First, you must remove the old program from your computer by accessing your control panel. Then you will go to Cricut and download the new software. Follow the on-screen instructions after downloading.

After downloading the new software, start exploring! There are changes, and some things are the same. Here are some of my observations:

NEW CRICUT DESIGN SPACE HOME SCREEN

First of all, the home screen is a bit different and easy to navigate.

Choose a new project or click on one of your saved projects.

CRICUT DESIGN SPACE CANVAS OPTIONS

When you're on another task or Canvas, you have practically indistinguishable choices from far as embedding's pictures.

Pictures are for Cricut pictures and tasks.

Snap-on TEXT to add content to your undertaking

Snap-on SHAPES to embed different premade shape alternatives

You can likewise UPLOAD your very own pictures.

When you embed any of these things, you can tap on the limit bolts to turn, resize, and open the measurements.

Conclusion

Thank you for making it to the end. If you are reading this article, it means you are ready to start doing a project. You are now capable of generating money through crafting; just a few more words to guide you on how to make money through Cricut.

First, set out to be different. Simply act naturally. Carry your idiosyncrasy and inventiveness to the table. Please keep it simple and narrow. Do not intend to be the Walmart of the specialty world; mean to be a specialist, and the best there is in your general vicinity of slyness. So, pause for a moment and choose what you will know for.

Be consistent. Work on your Cricut business reliably. In an ideal world, you should work consistently. Some of you may simply need to sell as a diversion and can take a shot at it once every week. Whatever your calendar is, do it as reliably as could reasonably be expected. You're never going to go anyplace if you overlook your business for quite a long time or month's one after another. Be reliable with estimating and quality as well. Your clients should realize what's in store for you. They will recommend you to others again and again if they know they can rely on you.

Be Tenacious. Tenacity consistently wins. There will be days clients will tick you off. There will be days that nothing works well.

You're busting your butt and getting no place quick. So, work with persistence and tranquility.

Set your eyes on the bigger goals. Once you have the expense of provisions, you'll be more ready to value your things to sell. Remember the time it took you to make the thing except if you like working for nothing. A dependable general guideline is your selling cost will be between two to multiple times your expense of provisions. Try not to stress over individuals snickering at you that it's excessive. You're unique, you've limited your field, and you're a specialist and the best at what you do. Besides, you're utilizing quality items (more on that soon).

Gain some new useful knowledge every day. Don't fear gaining from the individuals who have gone before you. You don't need to make sense of everything all alone. In any event, toward the beginning of your Cricut business, you'll be accomplishing more advertising than making. Make it an objective to gain some new useful knowledge consistently that relates to your business. And lastly, do quality control. Sell quality items. Quality successes over amount each day of the week

The Cricut is an incredible machine for individuals into adoration making, and for or individuals who need to cut many things with various kinds of materials. A Cricut is a cutting machine, and fantasy worked out as expected for some crafters. Below are some advantages of having a Cricut machine.

Something that sets the Cricut Maker separated from other cutting machines is that it has a few exchangeable edges. Need to do some sewing, sewing, paper, create foam, balsa wood, felt, foil, burlap, cardstock, grain box, creased cardboard, basic food item sack, or a bazillion (alright, slight embellishment) different undertakings? This machine can deal with to such an extent!

You even get 50 free ventures alongside your Cricut Maker. It incorporates sewing designs, iron-on, vinyl decals, and that's just the beginning. Do a great deal of sewing? Or then again, perhaps you wish you could do a ton of sewing? It is the machine for you. It removes the hard (and dull) portions of sewing ventures so you can get down to the pleasant part quicker.

Need to utilize your example? Or then again, what about including your textual styles? You can do that as well. Simply transfer it to the Cricut Maker! This machine makes making a lot more available to everybody. Have you been sidelined by a disease or injury? The device assumes control over a portion of the assignments that have been made increasingly troublesome and can take you back to the leisure activity you love.

The capacity to exchange edges gives this cutting machine long-ago utilization – which means you can redesign by purchasing new advantages rather than a different device. The Cricut Maker has a versatile apparatus framework that permits it to cut with more force than past machines.

Happy Cricut!

CPSIA information can be obtained
at www.ICGtesting.com
Printed in the USA
LVHW052327211220
674785LV00001B/39